CATALINA FLYING BOAT CAPTAIN

Dedicated to all those who served with Royal Air Force Coastal Command during the Second World War

Squadron Leader Bruce Cunynghame Daymond DSO DFC in 1946. (Bruce Daymond)

The captain of a flying boat is by virtue of necessity and training capable of undertaking the work of any member of the crew. He is as good a navigator as the observer and is capable of taking over the navigation and has to do so on long trips. He is an air gunner and capable of taking over any turret. He is a badly trained wireless operator, but capable of transmitting messages and has a full knowledge of procedure. He is capable of doing the flight engineer's work and is responsible for mooring-up. Also he is the only member of the crew with a knowledge of seamanship, towing and taxiing on sea. No other member of the crew has these qualifications.

Duties of a Flying Boat Captain by Air Officer Commanding, West Africa, November 1942

Anti-submarine operations. This type of work is the most monotonous and unspectacular of any flying carried out by the RAF. Crews may fly for hundreds of hours over the sea without sighting a single U-boat. But at last this chance will come and then the Captain has only a minute or so in which to carry out the attack (less than that more often than not). But however boring the work may be, its vital importance to the successful prosecution of the war cannot be over-emphasised. Accurate anti-submarine bombing is by far the most difficult task that is given to any in the RAF to perform.

RAF Intelligence summary, 1943

CATALINA FLYING BOAT CAPTAIN

A PILOT'S WAR FROM THE ATLANTIC TO THE INDIAN OCEAN

SQUADRON LEADER BRUCE DAYMOND DSO DFC,
and DENIS SAUNDERS

AIR WORLD

AIR WORLD

CATALINA FLYING BOAT CAPTAIN
A Pilot's War from the Atlantic to the Indian Ocean

This Edition in Great Britain in 2026 by
Air World
An imprint of
Pen & Sword Books Ltd
Yorkshire – Philadelphia

Print ISBN 978 1 03618 331 8
ePUB ISBN 978 1 03618 333 2
ePDF ISBN 978 1 03618 334 9

A CIP catalogue record for this book is available from the British Library.

Typeset by SJmagic DESIGN SERVICES, India.
Printed and bound in the UK by CPI Group (UK) Ltd.

The Publisher's authorised representative in the EU for product safety is Authorised Rep Compliance Ltd., Ground Floor, 71 Lower Baggot Street, Dublin D02 P593, Ireland. www.arccompliance.com

For a complete list of Pen & Sword titles please contact

PEN & SWORD BOOKS LIMITED
George House, Units 12 & 13, Beevor Street, Off Pontefract Road,
Barnsley, South Yorkshire, S71 1HN, England
E-mail: enquiries@pen-and-sword.co.uk
Website: www.pen-and-sword.co.uk

or

PEN AND SWORD BOOKS
1950 Lawrence Rd, Havertown, PA 19083, USA
E-mail: uspen-and-sword@casematepublishers.com
Website: www.penandswordbooks.com

FSC www.fsc.org
MIX
Paper | Supporting responsible forestry
FSC® C013604

Contents

Foreword

This book is the wartime autobiography of Bruce Daymond DSO DFC, who as a 21-year-old joined the Royal Australian Air Force (RAAF) in January 1941. He learned to fly through the Empire Air Training Scheme in Australia and Canada, after which he flew Catalina flying boats on operations with the Royal Air Force (RAF) in Europe, East and South Africa, and East Asia. From the day he joined the RAAF, Bruce recorded his experiences and thoughts in a diary until he returned to Australia in April 1945 after war service. Recording such details as Bruce did about military operations was prohibited during the war and could have resulted in severe disciplinary action had it been discovered. Fortunately for us, it never was, and his story was worth the telling and definitely worth the reading.

In consultation with Bruce, his handwritten diary was transcribed by Denis Saunders, the junior writer of this book, and printed in fifteen bound and numbered books as a permanent war service record. In his introduction to the printed volume, Denis provided a brief explanation for how he came to undertake the task. That task was also the incentive for this book, which partially completes an informal agreement from 1940 between Bruce and three or four of his fellow Sydney University graduates, all soon to be on active war service, to record their experiences for inclusion in a book for possible publication post-war. Bruce was nothing short of diligent in keeping his part of the agreement; however, the other supposed contributors were not, and the original project idea lapsed. Instead, after Bruce's death in 2008, Denis condensed the diary into an edited autobiography of those years, which became this book.

Foreword

Even when specifically asked, many Second World War veterans were disinclined to discuss their wartime experiences with their families or even close friends, and as the years passed those experiences became less vivid, of seemingly lesser significance, and were therefore likely to be lost to posterity. Denis, having been told only smatterings of his father Eric's wartime exploits as a flying boat pilot, had his curiosity aroused by Eric's response to a request from a French historian for some information about wartime RAF flying boat operations off the East African coast. That request led to Denis learning about the diary that had been kept throughout the war by his father's close friend and fellow Catalina flying boat captain Bruce Daymond. Bruce photocopied pages from his diary that provided the information sought by the historian and Denis discovered that the entries in the diary were detailed, candid, compelling, in many places quite personal and, importantly to Denis, also provided a missing insight into his father's wartime experiences. Denis thought the entire record deserved a much wider reader audience, and he thus persuaded Bruce in 2005 to allow the diary to be printed. Copies were subsequently given to the Australian War Memorial, the Canadian War Museum, and the RAF Museum.

Bruce's diary revealed that he was receptive, focussed, and diligent in his preparation for and conduct of flying operations from his initial training. For example, of his own accord he undertook additional training in the Link Trainer (a synthetic instrument training device) to correct problems with his instrument flying. This continued through to the operational command decisions he made as a flying boat captain that resulted in his award of the Distinguished Service Order (DSO), an award that was usually granted to more senior officers. That he progressed from aircraftman 2 (AC2 – trainee aircrew) to squadron leader in only five years is indicative of his skill, his leadership, and his command capability, which can be readily identified in the experiences he detailed in his diary and that are recorded in this book.

His operational flying experience was entirely on the Catalina and included frequent flights of longer than twenty hours, almost entirely over the sea and often at night, on operations such as: convoy anti-submarine escort; clandestine operations in enemy-controlled waters; frequent flights in tropical cyclonic weather that in one incident, in a violent downdraft, caused a nearly unrecoverable descent into an angry sea; and flying an obsolescent although reliable aircraft type, mostly using dead reckoning navigation (there were no electronic navigation aids), out of sight of land over a mostly featureless sea.

To mitigate the daily risks on operations, even in such dire times and even in remote places, there seemed to have been unexpectedly ample opportunities for socialising and tourism and Bruce rarely allowed such opportunities to go begging or failed to describe them in some detail in his diary the next day. He spent time on leave in the UK, India, Kashmir, Ceylon (Sri Lanka), and also visited the Taj Mahal, and he recounted his experiences in interesting tourist-traveller-type detail.

Whilst reading this book, one regret the reader may experience for Bruce is the unfulfilled long-distance relationship with the love of his life up to that time. However, although it is unrecorded in this book, he nevertheless had a happy married life after his return to Australia and was the father to a stepson, a son, and a daughter.

On his return to Australia in 1945, for reasons explained in the book, Bruce declined a commission in the permanent air force and initially joined the family business before he became a stockbroker. However, he also served for a short time in the RAAF Reserve. Fittingly, his final RAAF flight was in a Catalina out of Rathmines Base on Lake Macquarie, New South Wales, with his long-time friend and squadron-mate Eric Saunders, who was the aircraft captain on Bruce's first operational flight on the Catalina, flying from the UK to Africa.

I greatly enjoyed reading the printed version of Bruce's complete diary as I was able to associate some of Bruce's early flying experience with my own experience during basic flying training in the RAAF, and my operational experience flying Caribou aircraft in Papua New Guinea, using mostly dead reckoning navigation over inhospitable terrain. I was also fortunate to fly the Tiger Moth occasionally after I left the RAAF. Similar to Denis, the diary also gave me a better insight into my father's flying experience in North Africa during the Second World War. I readily accepted Denis's request to review an early draft of this book, and I hope I have done it justice with this foreword. As a parting comment, unlike Denis, I only know Bruce through his diary; however, I have no doubt that had we met, we would have been friends.

Michael Greentree
Wing Commander (Retired), RAAF

Acknowledgements

I am grateful to my father, Wing Commander (RAAF Retired) Eric Saunders MBE, who despite being asked many times, talked little of his war service. When Bruce Daymond sent my father a copy of the thirty plus pages from his diary relating to the time they flew together on detachment at Pamanzi in the Comoro Islands, he passed them to me with the comment, 'You have asked about my war service, this explains a little about what I got up to.' That provided me with the impetus to ask Bruce to have his diary typed in full.

Because Bruce and my father had been friends ever since they served together in 1942/43, I had known Bruce all my life until he died in 2008. However, it was not until the late 1990s, when I persuaded him that his handwritten diary should be available to a wider audience, that I was privileged to become his friend. As I worked closely with him, I got to know a lovely, ordinary man, who because of the Second World War did extraordinary things in extraordinary times. This book is a testimony to his service, and the people he served with and met along the way. But for the war, he probably would have continued his studies in economics at Oxford University, and may well have become an academic. Who knows? I am grateful to Bruce for his friendship and for trusting me with his detailed account of his life during the Second World War.

I owe an enormous debt of gratitude to Vee, my wife of more than fifty-six years. She has been my partner, supporter, and the base on which we have built our married life and family, and my successful career as a research scientist with CSIRO's Division of Wildlife Research and successor divisions. However, in working on Bruce's diary, I owe a heartfelt apology to Vee. We had nearly thirty wonderful years in Perth, from our marriage in late 1968 until our daughters left home to commence their independent living. In 1997, CSIRO transferred us to Canberra, for me to take on a role as assistant chief (research) in my division. After being a research scientist almost full time in Western Australia, I became an administrator, doing research vicariously through others. It was an extremely stressful time for me. However, neither Vee nor I realised how hard the move would be for her. I had my job, stressful though it was, and my network of colleagues, but for a partner moving to another place, with no paid employment or no children at school, it was extremely difficult and depressing to find her feet and develop supportive friends. Five years after moving to Canberra I resigned from CSIRO. Like many people, I found the transition from full-time work to retirement difficult and, at a time when Vee most needed me, I used my collaboration with Bruce over his diary as therapy, and in doing so, neglected supporting Vee. For that I am very sorry.

My late colleague and friend Professor Richard (Dick) Braithwaite, author of *Fighting Monsters: An Intimate History of the Sandakan Tragedy*, during many discussions we had as his book evolved, impressed on me the importance of documenting the role of individuals caught in momentous and challenging times.

My friend Rick Dawson PSM used his technical wizardry to take many of Bruce and my father's old, scratched, more than eighty-year-old, historically important photographs, and 'cleaned' them so they revealed most of their original detail.

I am also grateful for the generosity of the people who read earlier drafts of Bruce's story and provided encouraging, candid, and critical comments to correct many of my mistakes and to make the narrative more readable. Diana Cooper, an old friend whose father, like Bruce Daymond, was a graduate of the Empire Air Training Scheme and kept a diary of his war service, read three iterations of the manuscript as I took it from over 140,000 words to the published version of about 52,000. Bruce's son Ian Daymond read an earlier draft. Mike Greentree, an old friend, is a retired RAAF wing commander and de Havilland Canada Caribou and C-130 Hercules captain. His father was also an Empire Air Training Scheme graduate. Mike read the original diary and compared it with an earlier version of the manuscript to ensure I incorporated the necessary detail to present Bruce's story accurately. He also wrote the foreword. Robbie Henderson AM, an old friend, has a strong interest in documenting the contributions of our parents' generation to the Second World War and its aftermath. Dr Louise Moran, an old friend, has an interest in social history. Professor Peter Stanley, one of Australia's pre-eminent military historians, provided invaluable advice and support throughout the writing and publication processes. John Templeton, a former journalist, has a private pilot's licence and an interest in military aviation.

The Western Australian Museum has a beautifully restored PBY-5A on display at the Aviation Heritage Museum, Bull Creek, Western Australia. I am grateful to the director of the Western Australian Museum, who gave me permission to take many photographs of the interior of the aircraft, some of which are used in this book.

I am also grateful to Mike and Sue Lawrie, Ken Murray's son-in-law and daughter, who provided information on Ken's overlapping service with Bruce Daymond in 209 Squadron, and to David Legg of The Catalina Society for his detailed information on the history of some of 209 Squadron's Catalinas, and Nina Hadaway of the Royal Air Force Museum, who arranged access to the 209 Squadron Operation Record Book for the period 1 March – 31 July 1942.

John Grehan, Lisa Hooson, Amy Jordan, Martin Mace, and Louis Archard, editorial staff at Pen & Sword Books, were extremely helpful and supportive in publishing Bruce's story.

With Bruce's death in May 2008, his daughter Debbie Higginson became the keeper of his legacy. I am grateful to Debbie for her enthusiastic support throughout the process of getting Bruce's story published for a much wider audience to appreciate.

Introduction

Bruce Daymond maintained a detailed, personal, daily diary from 6 January 1941, when he joined the Royal Australian Air Force aged 21 in Sydney, until he completed his repatriation from India on 16 April 1945. In his 330,000+ word diary he described his entry into the air force, training as a pilot and navigator, and anti-submarine, air-sea rescue, and special duties operations in Catalina flying boats with Royal Air Force Coastal Command squadrons in UK, East and South Africa, India, and Burma. For his outstanding service he was awarded the Distinguished Service Order and the Distinguished Flying Cross.

This important record of Bruce's war service remained unread until early this century when I worked with Bruce to type up and produce fifteen printed, bound, and numbered copies, illustrated with photographs from both his and my father's photograph albums. We donated copies to the Australian War Memorial, Canberra, the Canadian War Museum, Ottawa, the RAF Museum, London, and members of his and my families.

I have taken Bruce's original diary and condensed and rewritten it to produce this autobiography of his extraordinary war service. Despite the fact that Bruce died in 2008 and could not have commented on this book, he is the senior author, as the majority of the words and all the descriptions of events are his.

Denis Saunders, PhD AM
Weetangera, ACT, Australia

Chapter 1

Initial and elementary flying training and transit to Canada

(6 January – 14 June 1941)

I was born in Sydney in July 1919 and grew up in Haberfield, Vaucluse, and then Mosman, on the edge of Sydney Harbour. In 1935, I completed school at Scots College and went on to read economics at Sydney University. On completing my university degree, I joined the accounts department at Qantas Empire Airways in Sydney. When I joined the air force, Qantas generously added to my air force pay to make it equal to that which I received when working for them. This arrangement continued until my air force pay equalled what I would have earned at Qantas.

I planned to go to England and continue my studies in economics at Oxford University. However, like millions of others, my plans were thwarted in 1939 by the start of the Second World War. As soon as possible after the declaration of war, I applied for service in the Royal Australian Air Force (RAAF).

Because of the war, the Australian armed forces were expanding rapidly. This involved enormous administrative and logistical challenges. As a result, I spent several months between enlisting and being inducted into the air force in the RAAF Reserve, during which I undertook evening lectures and weekend activities to prepare for air force service. During this time, I was handed a white feather by a woman who believed that I was shirking military service.

On 18 December 1940, I received instructions to report to No. 2 Recruiting Centre at Woolloomooloo, Sydney, at 8.30 am on

Monday, 6 January 1941 for enlistment as aircrew, with the rank of aircraftman 2, in readiness to proceed to No. 2 Initial Training School (ITS), Bradfield Park, Sydney. The instructions informed me that I was enlisting for the duration of the war and up to twelve months thereafter, with a high probability of my service being overseas.

I, together with thousands of others, was about to undertake training under the Empire Air Training Scheme (EATS). In order to understand my war service, an account of the EATS is necessary. In preparing for war, the British authorities realised they did not have sufficient aircrew to enlarge the Royal Air Force (RAF) to provide for home defence and offensive operations. In addition, the RAF would need a steady intake of trained aircrew to provide for losses of personnel due to operations and accidents. In the lead-up to the outbreak of war, the British government discussed establishing the EATS with the governments of Australia, Canada, and New Zealand. The four governments signed an agreement under which Australia, Canada, and New Zealand agreed to recruit and train quotas of pilots, navigators,[1] wireless operators, and air gunners for service with the RAF. Each of these jurisdictions, through their respective air forces [RAAF, Royal Canadian Air Force (RCAF), and Royal New Zealand Air Force (RNZAF)], followed the same training protocols. After enlistment, Australians attended an ITS, where they were instructed in air force drills and other subjects necessary for their service, and their aptitude for aircrew was assessed. Students were assigned to the four aircrew categories and went from ITS to specialist training schools. Those selected for pilot training were sent to an Australian Elementary Flying Training School (EFTS) for basic training. On completing elementary training, successful students were classified for service training as pilots of multi-engine or single-engine aircraft and assigned to Service Flying Training Schools (SFTS). Many went to Canada, with smaller numbers remaining in Australia. Those graduating from an SFTS received their wings and were sent to Britain, where they spent their war flying as RAAF personnel under

RAF command. The first EATS course commenced on 29 April 1940, with successful graduates of the scheme reaching RAF squadrons in late 1941. To ensure a steady stream of aircrew, every few weeks a new course commenced training.[2]

In the intake when I reported as instructed to Woolloomooloo were a number of men I knew, either from school, university, or from lectures we had attended in the RAAF Reserve, as well as a couple of coves I met through friends. We were sworn in and taken by bus to Bradfield Park, arriving at No. 2 ITS in the evening. We constituted No. 10 Course, i.e., the tenth course at Bradfield Park since the commencement of the EATS.

Bradfield Park occupied a large area. It was a pretty spot with big, tree-covered hills rising from the Lane Cove River. My hut was No. 36 and, like the others, was 80 feet[3] long with twenty-four beds. Our hut was the most southern hut and looked down from the top of the hill to Fullers Bridge and the Lane Cove River. The mess huts held about twenty-five tables, with six lads per table.

The next eight weeks were busy, during which we were inoculated against tetanus and typhoid, issued with our clothing and toiletries, and lectured and drilled on the range of subjects we needed to know for our future service. Lectures covered administration, law, response to exposure to gas, maths, medical, Morse code, armaments, and engines. We conducted drills, route marches, rifle shooting, and were subjected to regular tests. Being a keen swimmer, I was a member of the Bradfield Park swimming team.

The days were long, starting at 5.30 am and finishing at 9.30 pm. We were allowed out on short leave. I was able to get home to Mosman and sleep there occasionally, as well as catch up with friends to go to the beach, play tennis, go to the cinema, and attend the occasional party.

We were required to keep our huts, including windows, clean and to clear all grass and weeds from under the huts, and from 18 inches around the outside of the hut. We did so much of this area

RAAF swimming team, initial training school, Bradfield Park, January–February 1941. Bruce Daymond is fourth from the left in the middle row. (Bruce Daymond)

beautification that we all felt that after the war, we would be able to apply for jobs as cleaners, gardeners: in fact, anything except flying.

If I had been asked why I joined the air force, I would have listed three reasons. First, I always wanted to fly. Second, the air force was believed to be the offensive weapon of the war and therefore it was the duty of all those with the required physical and mental capability to enlist in that service. Third, I was fed up with office work and was looking for adventure.

Jim Unsworth was the first of my friends killed during the war. He died in a flying accident near Brisbane on 31 January 1941 while flying with 23 Squadron at RAAF Amberley. He was 23.

On completion of the course at ITS, we were given our report cards and assigned to aircrew categories. My report card noted: 'Efficient and Determined.' I was seventh, with a score of 912 marks out of 1,000, and was posted for pilot training at No. 5 Elementary Flying Training School, Narromine, New South Wales. I was accompanied there by Rex Marre, Gordon Lee, Robert McGuinness, and Jack Thompson.[4]

We arrived at Narromine[5] on 5 March as No. 10 Course. To mark us as trainee pilots, we were issued with a small, white piece of linen for our forage caps. On our first afternoon we were lectured by the education officer and the commanding officer (CO) and were then assigned to flying instructors, who each had four students. Sergeant McMullen was my instructor.

Our training was on the de Havilland DH-82 Tiger Moth, a single-engine biplane with a tandem cockpit. It was a good training aircraft as its stall and spin characteristics were benign, making it easy for a beginner to handle. Narromine's fifty to sixty Tiger Moths were a

Line-up of Tiger Moths at No. 5 Elementary Flying Training School, Narromine, New South Wales, March–April 1941. The chief flying instructor's aircraft is in the foreground. It lacks a number on the front of the aircraft. (Bruce Daymond)

mixture of RAF aircraft that were partially camouflaged and carried RAF serial numbers (e.g. R4886)[6] and RAAF aircraft that were bright yellow with RAAF serial numbers (e.g. A17-24).

For two months it was up early, breakfast (tea and toast, buttered if one was early to breakfast), flying training, lectures on all aspects of service flying (armaments, rigging, engines, and airmanship), administration, parade drill, physical training, sport, and range practice. We were taught circuits and bumps,[7] stalls, spins, and side slips.[8] We were taught how to fly on instruments. The aircraft were fitted with a canvas hood that could cover the student's cockpit so the student could not see out and had to rely on instruments. We did cross-country flights and elementary aerobatics. In the evenings, after a day's flying, we had sessions with our instructors. These were informative as they helped clear up queries and loose ends.

When we were not flying we were supposed to attend hangar lectures. This was a misnomer as we were expected to wander around the hangar and ask the fitters and riggers questions. We did this for

Bruce Daymond in the cockpit of a Tiger Moth at No. 5 Elementary Flying Training School, Narromine, New South Wales, 1941. (Bruce Daymond)

the first few days, but soon started bludging by either wandering into one of the lecture rooms or hiding somewhere. I found that the front cockpit of one of the Tiger Moths parked in the hangar was ideal, as with the cockpit flaps up I was hidden and could read at leisure. Official activities were interspersed with periods of leave. On short leave we engaged in local outings, including visiting Trangie, a neighbouring town. Weekend leave enabled us to visit Sydney and home.

Flying can be exhilarating. I remember one morning early in my training when everything was perfect. The rising sun, the green interspersed with ploughed fields and orchards, and the winding of the Macquarie River all combined to form a beautiful picture. At times I found myself admiring the view instead of listening to my instructor.

We were under constant assessment, with notes placed in our flying log books by our instructors. For example, after I had amassed flying time of eight and a quarter hours, Sergeant McMullen wrote that my take-offs were quite good. These assessments were also used to weed out those who were not going to qualify as pilots. Hervey Longmuir[9] was the first to be scrubbed, early in the course.

Sixteen days into my training, I went solo. Going solo is believed to be the greatest day in an airman's flying life. First, I went for a half-hour check flight in A17-24 with Sergeant McMullen and then up in A17-88 with Flight Lieutenant Barker for the solo test. I did one circuit with him, after which he said I could go solo. His last words just before I took off were: 'If she bounces, do another circuit.' I did a fairly good take-off, and when flying along just couldn't resist letting forth three lusty 'Whackos!' I kept the speed constant on the glide in and made a good approach down to about 5 feet. Then I jerked the control stick and she bounced. I opened the throttle and did another circuit, this time doing an excellent landing. After I had picked Barker up and taxied the aircraft back, he evidently waited for me to switch the engine off. I didn't realise this, as in the test with the chap before me, Barker switched off. On asking him if he was waiting for me to switch off, he replied, 'Oh no, I'm waiting for the petrol to run out!' However, I was so happy the sarcasm slid right off me.

At the end of the fourth week, No. 9 Course completed their training and we became the senior course. We commenced training on the Link Trainer, a flight simulator. They were marvellous state-of-the-art equipment. They cost more than an average aircraft, had a full Sperry instrument panel with instruments for beam flying,[10]

Bruce Daymond in flying gear beside Tiger Moth R4886 with R4888 in the background at No. 5 Elementary Flying Training School, Narromine, New South Wales, March–April 1941. The canvas blind flying hood can be seen behind the rear cockpit. (Bruce Daymond)

Left to right: Leading Aircraftman Thorpe Hornby, Sergeant Heads (instructor), Leading Aircraftman Tom Blackley, and Leading Aircraftman Bruce Daymond beside a Tiger Moth at No. 5 Elementary Flying Training School, Narromine, New South Wales, April 1941. (Bruce Daymond)

and produced a paper trace of the flight. We spent about five hours on them.

Accidents were not uncommon. Gordon Lee dug the tip of the left wing of R4886 into the ground on landing, smashed the undercarriage, buried the nose, and smashed the propeller. Fortunately, Gordon[11] suffered no injury beyond a bruise under the nose.

A nasty thing happened near the end of the course. Des Persse was caught low flying by the chief flying instructor, tried before the CO, and sentenced to twenty-one days at Holsworthy Military Prison. The nasty part about it was that Des said he was only doing a recovery from forced landings. Alan Ada was guarding him during the trial and told Jack Davenport and me that Des didn't stand a chance as the CO had told him he didn't believe a word of it. The penalty seemed particularly severe as Jack Watson from the course before us, who shot up[12] houses on his solo cross-country and tore his wing on a wireless mast, was only given fifteen days in Holsworthy, while his two dog-fighting pals were only given ten days confinement at Narromine. It seemed like a gross injustice. Des served his sentence at Holsworthy and was discharged from the RAAF on 9 July 1941.

During our last week at Narromine we had a series of examinations: airmanship, theory of flight, engines, armaments, Morse, rigging, and navigation. The last test was my flying test in A17-221 with Squadron Leader Allshorn, the chief flying instructor. At the end of the test, he said, 'I was very, very pleased with your flying this morning Daymond. It shows concentration and hard work.' My pass of 85% for flying turned out to be Above Average. There were only three students rated Above Average. They were Jack Davenport[13] (88%) and Rae Frost[14] (83%). Ray Hornby[15] got A+ (79%).

At the conclusion of my elementary flying training, I was equal fourth with 86.88%. My ranking achieved 'Recommend for Bombers', which is what I wanted, as did Jack Davenport and Alan Ada, both of whom had become good friends of mine.

The people of Narromine and the surrounding districts were very hospitable and we students made the most of our leisure time. On short-term leave we visited several hotels for a few beers and ate at a café run by Greeks who served the best food in town. We played tennis at the local club, swam in the river, and went to local dances. We also were invited to BBQs at peoples' homes and went to the cinema. On weekend leaves Jack Davenport, Alan Ada, and I drove to Sydney in Alan's car to catch up with family and friends.

Students of No. 10 Course, No. 5 Elementary Flying Training School, Narromine, New South Wales. Bruce Daymond is seventh from the right in the centre rank. (Bruce Daymond)

We left Narromine for Sydney on 30 April. None of us had any idea of how the odds were stacked against us surviving the war. I found out long after the war, when archival records were available, that sixty-eight men, with an average age of 24.5, entered Narromine EFTS on my course, with fifty of us graduating. However, only twenty-eight graduating students survived the war. Of the twenty-two who died, sixteen were killed on operations and six in flying accidents (see Appendix).

For nearly three weeks after leaving Narromine, I was nominally based at No. 2 Embarkation Depot at Bradfield Park, waiting transport to Canada. 'Nominally', as we were able to tend to our own

On board RMS *Aorangi*, 20 May 1941, before leaving Sydney Harbour. Bruce Daymond is at top left of the photograph, Alan Ada is to Bruce's immediate left and slightly lower, with Ian Dunn beside him, Jack Davenport is at the lower left, and Bill Clark is the fourth from the right at the top of the photograph, partially hidden by the man to his left. The white linen strips in their forage caps denote aircrew in training. (Bruce Daymond)

Visiting Whakarewarewa hot springs near Rotorua, New Zealand, 25 May 1941. From left to right are: unidentified, unidentified, Alan Ada, Bruce Daymond, unidentified, Susan the guide, unidentified, Jack Davenport. (Bruce Daymond)

activities, in my case, catching up with friends, sorting out my legal and financial affairs, sailing, swimming, partying, and sleeping at home. I bought a good second-hand Pupille miniature camera from Kodak for £13. It had 1/300 of a second speed and an f3.5 lens, as well as a range-finder and a couple of filters.

We sailed for Canada on RMS *Aorangi* on 21 May 1941. As we passed under Sydney Harbour Bridge at dawn, a crowd, gathered in the gloom on the southern shore at Miller's Point, called out numerous 'Coo-ees.' Then some girl gave vent to a heartfelt and plaintive, 'Goodbye Charlie. I love you. Come back soon!' This was unnerving and made me realise that we had really begun our trip into an unknown future. Over fifty years later, I could still hear that girl's plaintive cry.

Apart from being organised into watches, undergoing physical training first thing in the morning, and getting together with some of the civilian passengers, including some lovely women, we had little to do until we reached Auckland. While in Auckland we did some pubbing, clubbing, and sightseeing, including an interesting day-trip to Rotorua. We left Auckland on 26 May having taken 200–300 New Zealanders on board. Some were officers and sergeant pilots, but most were leading aircraftmen like ourselves.

We arrived in Vancouver on 13 June and immediately entrained at the Canadian Pacific Railway station. Our contingent consisted of thirty-six student pilots destined for training on multi-engined aircraft, and sixty-four on single-engined aircraft. Each group was put in separate carriages, as were the navigators and gunners. So started a scenically spectacular trip across Canada. At Calgary the student pilots destined for multi-engined training got off. Those for single-engined training went on to Ottawa, navigators to Toronto, and gunners to Winnipeg. Practically all the Narromine crew went on to Ottawa, with only eight of us getting off at Calgary. It was hard saying goodbye to those leaving us.

Line-up of Australian (in dark uniforms) and New Zealand airman before an hour's leave from their Canadian Pacific train to see the sights of Banff, Canada, 14 June 1941. (Bruce Daymond)

Chapter 2

Pilot and navigator training, Canada and transit to England

(15 June – 1 January 1942)

We arrived at No. 7 Service Flying Training School,[1] Macleod, Alberta, on 15 June to begin No. 31 Course. We got a warm welcome from Wing Commander James, the CO. The chief ground instructor, Squadron Leader Bawlf, won us with his opening remark: 'Good morning, gentlemen, welcome to Fort Macleod.' He told us that on completion of the course, one third of us would be commissioned, another 17% would become sergeant pilots recommended for promotion to pilot officer a few months later, and the other 50% would be sergeant pilots more or less permanently. At the end of the course the brightest would be sent to Charlottetown, Prince Edward Island, for a general reconnaissance course to be trained as navigators. On completion of the course, students would be pilot-navigators, destined for flying boats in Coastal Command or Lockheed Hudsons in Canada.

We got stuck into training immediately. We were divided into two groups. One group flew while the other had lectures. The day was divided into two sessions, so each group flew and had lectures each day, alternating between morning and afternoon. My instructor, Flying Officer Weimer, was an American.

We trained on Avro Ansons, an obsolete, twin-engined monoplane. It was a terribly safe old bus, with a retractable undercarriage that had to be cranked up and down by hand. We also had sessions in the Link Trainer.

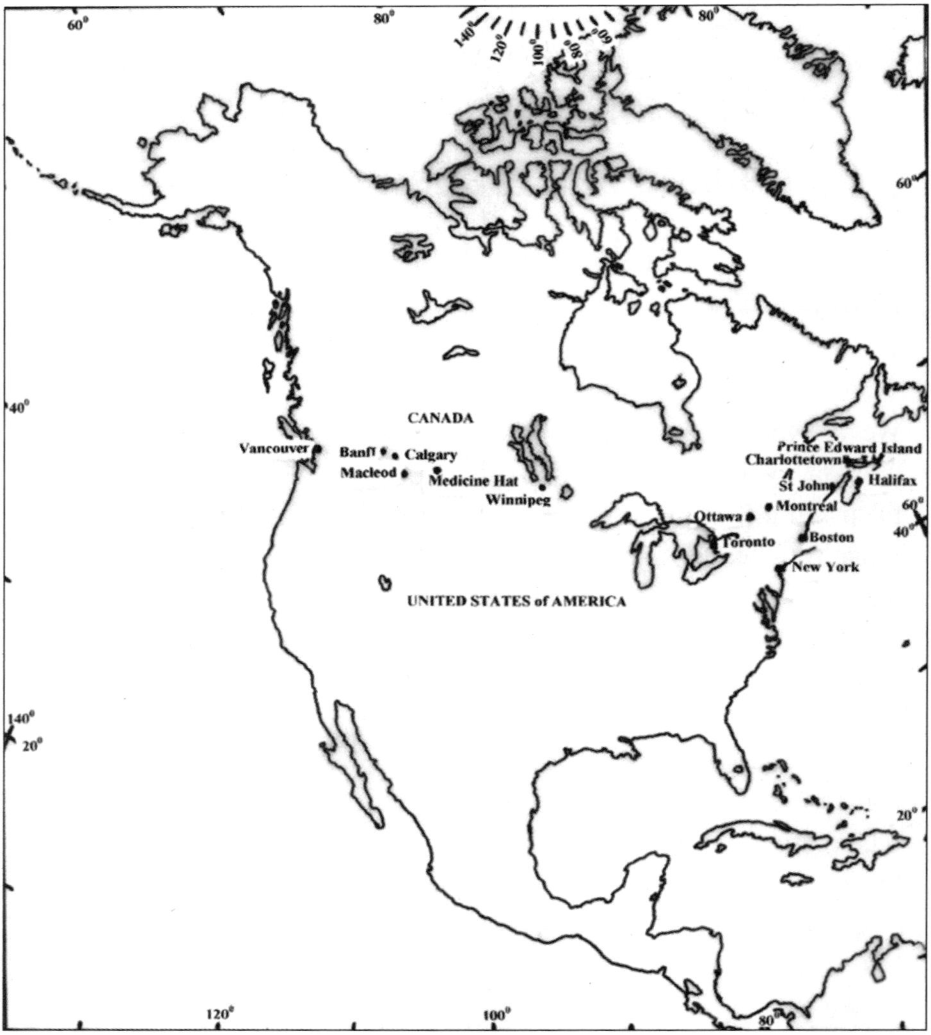

Map of North America showing locations named in the text.

There were a number of accidents on our course. John Weatherlake[2] was taking off when his Anson skidded sideways off the runway. The undercart gave in and she settled like a lame duck. The damage was estimated at $18,000. I saw Jim Thomson ground-looping on landing. The aircraft was pretty well buggered: a $35,000 damage effort. Fortunately, neither John nor Jim was hurt. During a night

Left to right: Bill Clark, Bruce Daymond, Ian Dunn, and Alan Ada hamming it up on 31 August 1941. In Canada there were big notice boards near all the air training schools. In Australia the air training programme was called the Empire Air Training Scheme, but it was the British Commonwealth Air Training Plan in Canada. (Bruce Daymond)

flying exercise, Tom Blackley[3] made his landing too fast, ran off the runway, and hit a dirt heap. Fortunately, he wasn't hurt.

After two hours and fifty minutes' flight under instruction, I went solo in Anson No. 6303. Flying Officer Maclean, officer commanding my flight, sent me off and fortunately did not expect me to crank up the undercarriage. That gave me more time to settle down. My landing was too high and she came down hard. When I finally had time, during the last cross-wind leg of the circuit, I let out a 'Whacko,' just as I did when I first went solo in the Tiger Moth. However, it was not quite as happy a yell as the first.

By early July, a number of our colleagues had failed the course and were sent elsewhere. These included: Jimmy Thomson,[4] Jim Kearns,[5] John Martin,[6] Charlie Lark,[7] and Bob McGuinness.[8]

The friendliness of the locals was exemplified by Jack Colwell, to whom we had been introduced early in our time at Macleod. He took us sight-seeing and entertained us at his home. He had a piano and Bill Clark and Ian Dunn,[9] who were fine pianists and singers, entertained us on a number of occasions.

In mid-July we began cross-country and night flying. The latter gave me the biggest thrill I had had since going solo at Narromine. I had one hour forty minutes dual[10] before going solo in No. 6348 at 2.45 am for seventy minutes. The last circuit on my first night solo was at dawn. It was a magnificent sight as the eastern sky glowed pink.

In late July I had a phone call from the family. In those days, phone calls were expensive and overseas calls had to be booked. The call connections were Macleod–Lethbridge–Calgary–Vancouver–San Francisco–Sydney. The call was to celebrate my 22nd birthday, and a wonderful thrill it was. Mum was quite broken up and I felt miserable for hours. To hear their voices again and realise that they were so far away and that I wouldn't see them for a long time, perhaps never, was not a happy thought.

In mid-August I went on an instruments flight in No. 6454 with Flying Officer Weimer. He took me for a final run before the instrument test with Flying Officer Maclean. After we completed my run-through, he showed Gordon Gatenby[11] and me precautionary forced landings. I asked him if he would show us some low flying and he did. We roared a couple of feet over Mud Lake at 140 miles per hour. He flew straight at a rise in the ground and then at the last second climbed over it. Next, he paid attention to a haystack, from which a couple of fellows were waving. Weimer flew at it and one fellow jumped to save some horses from bolting, then thought he'd better save himself first. We shot them up two or three times. We flew over crowds of horses and they bolted like blazes. It was damned good sport.

Bruce Daymond in front of an Avro Anson at Macleod, Alberta, July 1941. (Bruce Daymond)

By the end of the course I had logged 77 hours and 20 minutes on Ansons for a total of about 135 hours. At the end of the course, I came ninth out of the Australians and was commissioned as a pilot officer, as was Jack Davenport, but Alan Ada was not.

Our new status as officers permitted us to be transferred to the railway station in staff cars while the non-commissioned officers (NCOs) travelled in trucks. This class distinction continued as officers were accommodated in first class and NCOs in second class carriages.

Control tower and hangars at No. 7 Service Flying Training School, Macleod, August 1941. (Bruce Daymond)

Right: Flying Officer Weimer, Bruce Daymond's instructor, in the cockpit of an Avro Anson, No. 7 Service Flying Training School, Macleod, August 1941. (Bruce Daymond)

Below: Bruce Daymond and Alan Ada with a member of the Royal Canadian Mounted Police in front of Banff police station, 30 June 1941. (Bruce Daymond)

Left to right: Bill Clark, Alan Ada, Bob (Speed) Gordon, Bruce Daymond, Ian Dunn, and Jack Davenport outside the Prince of Wales Hotel, Waterton Lakes, Alberta, 27 July 1941. (Bruce Daymond)

Bruce Daymond saluting after receiving his wings from Wing Commander Mair at the wings parade, No. 31 Course, No. 7 Service Flying Training School, Macleod, 30 August 1941. (Bruce Daymond)

A group of Sydney lads at No. 7 Service Flying Training School, Macleod, 30 August 1941. Bill Campbell and Len Glenwright (first and third from the right in the back row) went with Bruce Daymond (fourth from the right in the back row) to Charlottetown to the RAF General Reconnaissance School. (Bruce Daymond)

Graduates of No. 31 Course, No. 7 Service Flying Training School, Macleod, 30 August 1941. Bruce Daymond is third from the right in the back row. RAAF graduates are in the dark uniforms, Cyril (Jimmy) Talalla, a Sinhalese from Malaya, is second from the right in the second row. He survived the war as an RAF flight lieutenant with a DFC and Bar. (Bruce Daymond)

Left to right: Alan Ada, Jack Davenport, and Bruce Daymond in front of an Avro Anson after the wings parade, No. 7 Service Flying Training School, Macleod, 30 August 1941. (Bruce Daymond)

As our train departed Macleod, an Anson came over and shot up the train. It just cleared the roof in one run over our carriage. The trip to Halifax took over a week and we took in the sights and partied across the country.

Halifax was a terribly dirty, dingy place. The town was populated by a large number of men in uniform from all services. It made us realise that we were at last getting somewhere near the war. We were billeted in the RCAF No. 1 'Y' Embarkation Depot. Shortly after we arrived, I was separated from Jack Davenport and Alan Ada, my closest friends since we joined the air force, as they went to the UK. Six officers (Bill Campbell, Len Glenwright, Ron Canning, Bill Clark, Peter Weaver, and me) and four sergeants (Tom Blackley, Bill Wheeler, Bill Wheeldon, and Peter Wright) had been selected to go to RAF No. 31 General Reconnaissance School[12] at Charlottetown.

At Macleod station on 1 September 1941, about to catch the train to Halifax on conclusion of the Service Flying Training School Course. Left to right: unidentified, Ian Dunn, unidentified, unidentified, unidentified, Alan Ada, Mrs Bawlf (wife of the chief flying instructor), Jack Davenport, Jean Bawlf, Bruce Daymond, and Bob Gordon kneeling in front. The white armbands on the arms of Bruce and Jack indicate that they had been commissioned on completion of the course. A silo of the Alberta Pacific Grain Co. Ltd is in the left background. (Bruce Daymond)

It was then clear that we were destined for flying boats in Coastal Command.[13]

We travelled by train from Halifax to the coast, by ferry from Cape Tormentine to Port Borden on Prince Edward Island (PEI), and then by train to Charlottetown, the capital of PEI. Our accommodation was better than we were used to. Bill Clark and I shared a big room in a newly constructed two-storey barracks. Rain, rain, and more rain was a feature of the place. At times we were walking to lectures in puddles up to our ankles. PEI was famous for its red soil. After rain, it made a frightful mess. The local community was hospitable. We were welcome at the golf club and free to use their clubs any time we wanted.

We were issued with publications and instruments, including a bubble sextant, a watch, and a planisphere, and given a briefing on the subjects we were to cover. The normal course was twelve weeks, but we were being pushed through in nine weeks.

Lectures covered all aspects of air navigation and communications, including signalling with the Aldis Lamp,[14] dead reckoning,[15] the Dalton Computer,[16] deviation in compasses, compass swinging,[17] aircraft crew drill, astro-navigation and the importance of the constellations, coding, reconnaissance, distant recorder compass, use of the sextant, ship recognition, visual signals, and meteorology. We spent a lot of time in the air. All of our navigation was done in Ansons: however, we did no piloting as we spent all our air time training to be navigators.

One day I received an envelope from Qantas containing the staff newsletter. Apart from the fact that I was mentioned a couple of times, once for arrival in Canada and again on receiving my wings and commission, it demonstrated how widely we had dispersed after joining the air force. John Wright was attached to a Coastal Command squadron having done a general reconnaissance course, Rod Archer[18] had become engaged to a Canadian girl and gone to England, Geoff Patterson visited Victoria Falls in Africa, Ern Hallet[19] and Keith Gremby were on active service in Egypt, and John Doepel[20] had begun his air force training.

It started snowing in late October, and by the afternoon of the first day about 4 inches had fallen. I had not seen snow for years, but many of my fellow students had never seen snow. As a result, there were many snowball fights.

In early November, we took our final examinations on the ground and in the air. Then, on 9 November, we had our last flight at General Reconnaissance School. By 12 November we had completed all of our exams.

After completing our general reconnaissance course, Bill Clark and I decided to spend our leave in New York. We found all those we came in contact with to be helpful, with all sorts of advice on how to navigate the subway, where to eat, where to have a good time, and

Charlottetown barracks, showing the mud in the foreground (unfortunately not in colour as the mud was red). (Eric Saunders)

Students' common room at Charlottetown. (Eric Saunders)

Left: Bruce Daymond with the first real fall of snow at Charlottetown, Prince Edward Island, October 1941. *Right:* Bruce with Mr W. Steinway of Steinway Pianos outside LaGuardia Airport, New York, 19 November 1941. (Bruce Daymond)

entertaining us with meals and outings. We found a Miss Danahy in charge of the RAF Visitors Committee. She gave us all sorts of information and suggestions for doing things, including providing free tickets to almost any place we wanted to see. We took some tickets for Carnegie Hall and went along to hear Albert Spalding, the violinist.

Bill had connections that resulted in us meeting Mr W.R. Steinway of Steinway pianos. We met him at his showroom and he drove us to LaGuardia Airport, the New York air terminal, which was the largest in the world. We were then taken to the Steinway factory and introduced to some of the executives.

On one of our outings we were hailed by the Smiths, a married couple, who saw the 'Australia' labels on our uniform shoulders. They were Australians: he from Mosman and she from Bundaberg.

No. 15 Course, No. 31 General Reconnaissance School, Charlottetown, Prince Edward Island, 13 September – 15 November 1941. Most of the Australian group is in the middle row: (left to right) Pilot Officer Weaver, Pilot Officer Canning, Sergeant Wheeldon, Sergeant Wheeler, Sergeant Blackley, Sergeant Wright, Pilot Officer Bruce Daymond, Pilot Officer Campbell, and Pilot Officer Glenwright. Pilot Officer Clark is fifth from the left in the back row. Instructors are in the front row. (Bruce Daymond)

We went back to their apartment, where we drank and yarned for a few hours. They gave me a souvenir kangaroo. It was a cunning toy with a baby kangaroo poking out of its pouch. This became my lucky mascot. I flew with it throughout the war and treasured it all my life.

At the completion of our leave, we were sent to a large military camp at Debert, about 15 miles from Truro, Nova Scotia. The camp was only six months old and sorting out its programme. We comprised No. 3 Course, composed of my No. 15 Course from Charlottetown, seven students from No. 16 Course there, and one RAF type. The course was to convert us to Hudsons. After ten hours solo on Hudsons, and another ten hours flying with a second pilot, with most of the flying on cross-country flights of varying length, we

Bruce Daymond with his lucky kangaroo mascot in 1942 and 2001. The mascot was given to him by an Australian couple in New York in November 1941. It travelled in the navigator's compartment on every flight and had the names of each location Bruce visited written on it. Bruce Daymond retained the mascot for the rest of his life. (Bruce Daymond)

were then to ferry a Hudson over the Atlantic. Instead of continuing the conversion, Bill Campbell and I were sent to RCAF No. 1 'Y' Embarkation Depot, Halifax, for transport by ship to the UK.

On 6 December, I received an airmail from the family. Unfortunately, it contained one shocking piece of news. Rolla Cooke, a great friend of mine from university, had been killed on 4 November while returning from a night patrol in England. He was with RAF 145 Squadron (flying Spitfires) and his death was accidental. He was 24. His wife, Betty, was to have a baby in early December. After the death of Jimmy Unsworth, also an accident, that made two close friends the air force had claimed. I wondered then how many more were to die before the end of the bloody war.

While waiting at the depot, I ran into Vern Dyason,[21] who had been at university with me. With him was Tom Allen, who used to live just across the road from us at Vaucluse in Sydney. Both of them had been drafted to leave for England that day. When an officer came around looking for somebody else to go on the draft, I asked if there was any chance of me joining them. As I would have been the only Australian left on the station, he took pity on me and I was included.

(E) **MONEY (Cont'd)**

103. GLAD IF YOU COULD SEND SOME MONEY.
104. HAVE RECEIVED MONEY.
106. HAVE YOU RECEIVED MONEY.
106. HAVE YOU SENT MONEY.
107. THANKS FOR MONEY RECEIVED.
108. HAVE NOT RECEIVED MONEY.
109. UNABLE TO SEND MONEY.
110. SORRY CANNOT SEND MONEY.
111.
112.
113.
114.

(F) **CONGRATULATIONS**

115. CONGRATULATIONS ON ANNIVERSARY BEST WISHES.
116. CONGRATULATIONS LASTING HAPPINESS TO YOU BOTH.
117. GLAD AND PROUD TO HEAR OF YOUR DECORATION EVERYBODY THRILLED.
118. LOVING GREETINGS AND CONGRATULATIONS.
119. GOOD LUCK KEEP IT UP.
120. I WISH WE WERE TOGETHER ON THIS SPECIAL OCCASION ALL MY BEST WISHES FOR A SPEEDY REUNION.
121.
122.
123.
124.

(G) **WAR DAMAGE**

125. ....INJURED AND IN HOSPITAL.

NOTE
THE NAME TO BE INSERTED AND TRANSMITTED IMMEDIATELY AFTER THE TEXT NUMBER.

126. INJURED AND IN HOSPITAL.
127. SORRY TO HEAR OF DAMAGE HOPE ALL WELL.

(G) **WAR DAMAGE (Cont'd)**

128. SORRY TO HEAR OF INJURY AND HOPE NOT SERIOUS.
129. SORRY TO HEAR OF INJURY AND HOPE PROGRESS FAVOURABLE.
130. SORRY TO HEAR OF INJURY AND HOPE SOON BE BETTER.
131.
132.
133.
134.

(H) **MISCELLANEOUS**

135. VERY HAPPY TO HEAR FROM YOU DEAREST AM FIT AND WELL.
136. HEARING YOUR VOICE ON THE WIRELESS GAVE ME A WONDERFUL THRILL.
137.
138.
139.
140.

(I) **BEREAVEMENT**

141. SORRY TO TELL YOU......DIED.
142. SORRY TO HEAR......DIED.

NOTE
THE NAME TO BE INSERTED AND TRANSMITTED IMMEDIATELY AFTER THE TEXT NUMBER.

Expeditionary Force Messages

Commencing June 1st, 1941, the use of standard text is authorized in EXPEDITIONARY FORCE MESSAGES (EFM) destined to Egypt, and to the United Kingdom and other countries of the British Empire; except India where existing free text service will continue for the present. To Newfoundland the regular rates apply.

60 cents per Message

(Plus Government Tax 5 Cents)

This cancels and supersedes the E.F.M. service which provided for messages of sender's own composition. Senders may select one, two, or three, of the texts given overleaf for transmission in any one telegram, for the same charge.

Messages not covered by the standard text will be accepted but charged for at the rate applicable to one of the other classes of service.

Further information may be obtained from any

CANADIAN PACIFIC TELEGRAPH OFFICE

Mark your messages **"VIA IMPERIAL"** and file with any CANADIAN PACIFIC TELEGRAPH OFFICE

When telephoning messages, please specify **"VIA IMPERIAL"**

Sample of the range of Expeditionary Force Messages, in which a text is attached to each number and the sender was allowed to select one, two, or three texts. It was an economical way of communicating, but very impersonal.

Early on 15 December, during a heavy snow storm, we were driven to Pickfords Wharf and taken with our baggage by launch to our ship, *Gdynia*. She was built in 1934, in Goteborg, Sweden. She displaced 2,700 tons, and could make 30 knots. On the way to our ship we passed a Catapult Armed Merchantman[22] and also dozens of other ships, including two submarines, and two of the over-age

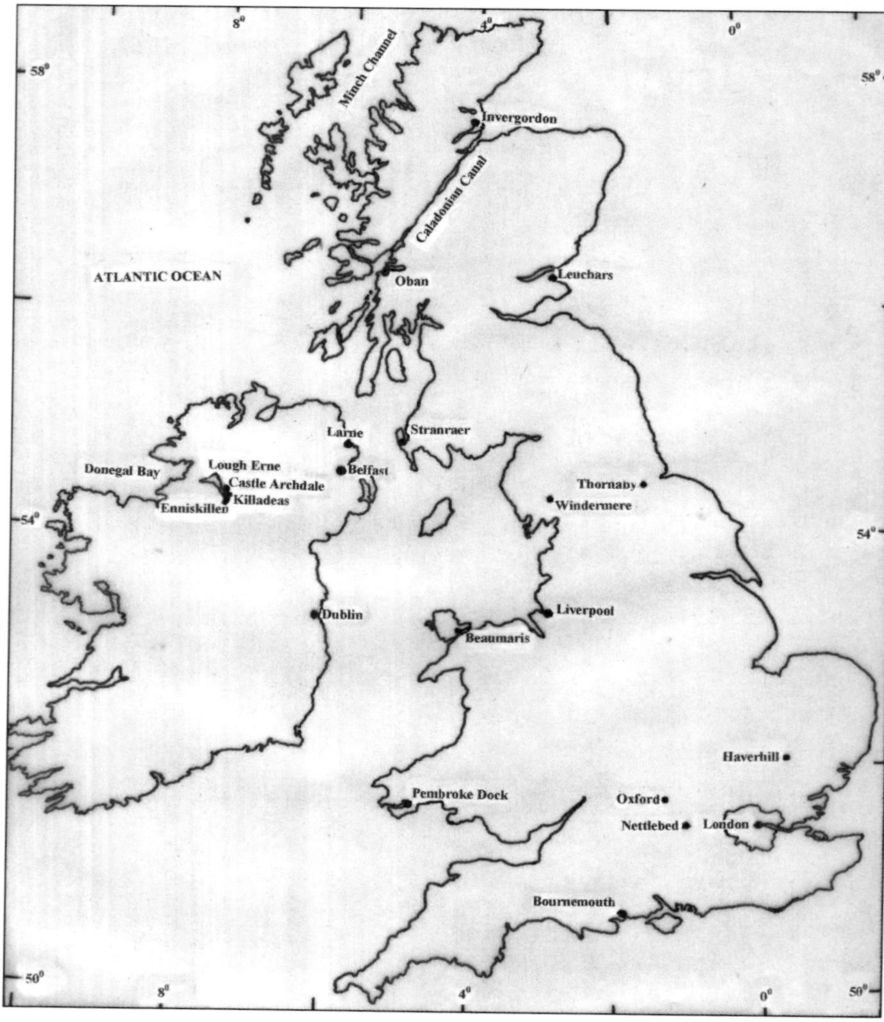

Map of the United Kingdom showing the locations of places named in the text.

destroyers acquired from America under the destroyers-for-bases deal.[23] Our convoy comprised forty-eight ships, of which twenty-five were carrying aviation spirit, benzine, or oil.

There were only ten passengers, all pilots, on the ship. We were allocated five two-berth cabins, which were very nice indeed. The ship departed soon after we boarded. The charming captain introduced himself and produced a bottle of excellent Scotch whisky.

Unlike most EATS graduates, who travelled to the UK like sardines in over-crowded troop transports, we travelled to war in the style of a pre-war pleasure cruise. The food was Swedish and superb. Lunch was usually a terrific salad affair, including herrings and meats of all sorts. That was followed by another course of something like pork chops and potatoes. We usually went and slept after lunch.

On Christmas Day the captain informed us there were supposed to be ten U-boats[24] ahead of us. He also confirmed the rumour that the chief engineer was missing. He was pretty drunk on Christmas Eve, although he had stood his watch from 4–8 am. The ship was thoroughly searched and he was declared lost overboard. Some of the lads had heard him talking and said he was anti-British as he had slung off at the British armed forces. We never found out if he fell overboard or was pushed.

For several days we anchored off Liverpool as the port was congested with shipping. From *Gdynia*'s bridge I saw one of the Catapult Armed Merchantmen launch its Hurricane. The fighter's motor was warmed up and shortly afterwards the ship steamed through the column of the convoy to get upwind. There was a roar from the plane's motor, a huge flash of flame from the catapult, a large explosion, and the Hurricane was in the air.

On New Year's Day we finally went ashore in Liverpool. We travelled by train to London and were taken to the Strand Palace Hotel. After a pub and nightclub crawl, we got back to the hotel at about 3.30 am.

Chapter 3

In limbo at Personnel Despatch and Reception Centre, England

(2 January – 17 April 1942)

We travelled by train to the RAAF's No. 11 Personnel Despatch and Reception Centre, Bournemouth, an English seaside town that had been taken over by the military. It was a fine sort of place, with plenty of parks, guest houses, and hotels.

The procedure at the Centre involved spending the first week or so catching up with administration, doing a night vision test to assess how well one could see in dim light or the dark, and getting the lay of the land. The daily routine involved reporting to the Centre's parade ground in the town square for a short parade and then having the rest of the day free. Personnel were given a week's leave, after which they returned to Bournemouth to await postings to an operational training unit or to a squadron. We were told that we could expect to spend from two to six weeks at the Centre.

Together with John Boland and Tom Allen, I went to London for a few days to catch up with family friends, sort out my financial affairs, get some tailoring done by Gieves Ltd on Piccadilly, and enjoy myself.

The Lady Frances Ryder and the Dominion and Allied Forces Hospitality League in Bournemouth were extremely helpful in suggesting where we should go on leave. They arranged for Tom and me to stay with the Stobart family at Pickering in Yorkshire. We travelled on the famous Flying Scotsman with John Muirhead and Vin Mansell,[1] who were on my course at Macleod. Mr Stobart met us at Pickering station and drove us to his home in Thornton-le-Dale, a little village about 2 miles from Pickering. The Stobarts were gracious hosts and we ate well, slept well, and had great fun tobogganing.

After a lovely stay, it was back to Bournemouth for more waiting, during which we attended morning parades and lectures, were subjected to the occasional route march, took part in rifle range practice, chatted up women, and went to parties, the cinema, and a pantomime. We also went sight-seeing, did a lot of reading, and received and wrote letters. During the rest of my time at Bournemouth, I ran into a number of men I had not seen for a while. They included Ian Ross,[2] Bruce Sharkey,[3] Dave Bloomfield,[4] and Bruce Buls.[5]

In late February, after nearly two months at Bournemouth, I received my posting to No. 6 Operational Training Unit at Thornaby-on-Tees, a Canadian Hudson outfit. I was disappointed with the posting because it was not to flying boats and I was the only Australian posted there. Being the only Aussie on a Canadian course sounded pretty bloody to me. We were a mixed bag and there was confusion about our skills. Some had 130 hours on Hudsons, some like me had none, and some had not done a general reconnaissance course. The chief ground instructor imagined that we all had at least 100 hours on Hudsons and we had only come to this unit to crew up. It staggered him to find that the majority had no Hudson time at all. And when he found that some of the crowd had not done a general reconnaissance course, he all but passed out. It was a hell of an administrative mess.

As I was not qualified on Hudsons, I was sent back to Bournemouth. However, I was able to have a weekend's leave on the way back. I used the opportunity to catch up with Mr Malcolm and Mrs Nance Bond, old family friends, at Halfridge, their estate near Nettlebed, outside London. I was met at Henley station by Mrs Bond and Mrs Peggy Pammenter. Peggy was married to Mrs Bond's nephew, Ken Pammenter, an army officer who was away in camp. The Pammenters had a flat on the Bonds' estate. Peggy was accompanied by Vicky, her 1-year-old baby.

Over that lovely weekend I went to the pictures with Mrs Bond and Peggy, caught up with the Bonds' news, walked round their 1,500-acre estate, and did some sight-seeing, including a wonderful day visiting Oxford with Peggy as my guide.

I was back at Bournemouth on 10 March. It seemed that the authorities did not know what to do with me, so they sent me off on another week's leave. I arranged to go back to Halfridge to help out on the farm. I did a lot of walking over the estate with Mr Bond and Peggy and helped with the fencing. I was enjoying myself so much that I sent a telegram to Bournemouth asking for a week's extension of leave, which was granted.

I did some local sight-seeing at Henley with Mrs Bond and Peggy, as well as wandering alone around the estate and neighbouring lands. In those two visits, I fell in love with Peggy, a married woman with a baby, and Peggy fell in love with me. One afternoon, Peggy and I took Vicky on a long pram outing and en route we talked over a hell

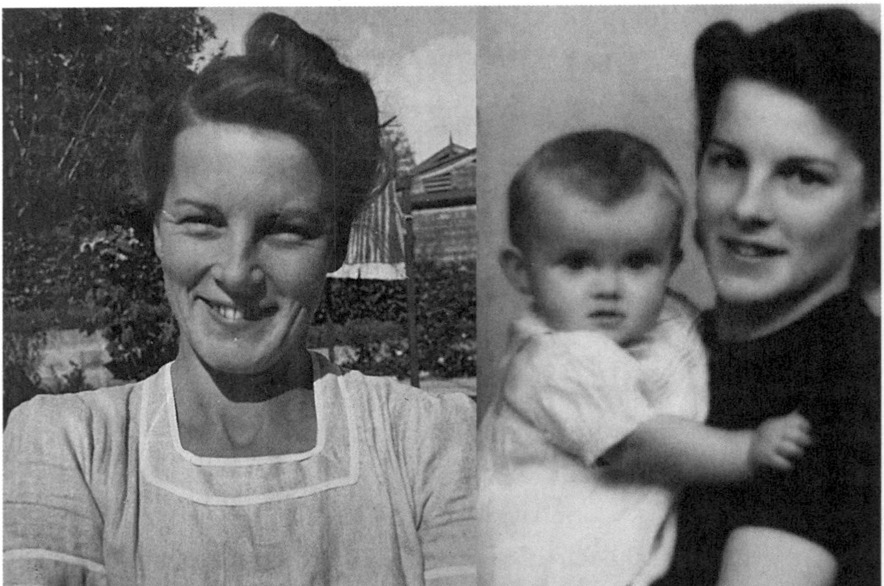

Left: Peggy Pammenter. *Right:* Vicky and Peggy Pammenter, 1942. (Bruce Daymond)

of a lot of things that had been troubling us. Then Peggy and I went to London, sight-seeing, going to the pictures, and dining out.

One evening, Air Marshal Sir Leslie Gossage, Commander-in-Chief, RAF Balloon Command, came to dine with the Bonds. He was an awfully decent old bloke and easy to talk to. We had a damned fine dinner, including poultry and wine. After dinner, I swapped a scarf with my initials on it for a yellow one of Peggy's.

In late March I left Halfridge for Bournemouth after spending two of the happiest weeks of my life. At RAAF HQ, I found out that a posting for me to the operational training unit at Invergordon for 30 March had been cancelled. This was rather unpleasant news as I had already spent three months in limbo. And so, back to filling in time with parades, lectures, route marches, cinema, drinking, physical training including swimming, dancing, tennis, golf, writing letters, sight-seeing, sorting out my clothing allowances, and going mad with boredom, while other chaps came and went. I heard the dreadful news that poor old Rex Marre, from whom I had a letter only a month before, had been killed on 15 March, aged 24, in an accident while with RAF 3 Squadron (flying Hurricanes) in the UK. He was one of the best of men.

After fifteen weeks at the Centre, I received welcome news that I was being posted to RAF 209 Squadron at Pembroke Dock, Wales. It was an RAF Coastal Command maritime reconnaissance squadron, equipped with Catalina flying boats. Its role was long-range anti-submarine patrols and convoy protection.

Before I left the Centre, I had several days in London, where I caught up with Jack Davenport and his brother Phil, Dave Laurenti, Alan Ada, and Cliff O'Riordan.[6] I had two wonderful days with Peggy, who was staying with friends. Peggy and I managed to see a lot of each other. Seeing her again sent me off as badly as ever. I had hoped it wouldn't have been so bad.

I was lucky to have spent time in London during the Blitz. There was an almost spiritual feel to the city, as it was truly the heart of

Bruce Daymond (rear left) with Sergeant Alan Ada and Pilot Officer Jack Davenport (at rear), and Pilot Officers Dave Laurenti and Phil Davenport (at front), at Waterloo station, 17 April 1942. Alan Ada was killed nineteen days after the photograph was taken. Dave Laurenti was killed in a Sunderland crash on 12 August 1942, which is explained in Chapter 4 of *They Shall Not Pass Unseen*, an account of 461 Squadron RAAF written by Ivan Southall. (Bruce Daymond)

the war effort. The city throbbed with the activities of winning the war. Always subjected to bombing raids, the city nonetheless bustled with bright, cheerful men and women in the uniforms of every Allied nation. Undeterred, they socialised and went about their business with an air of confidence. In particular, there was the great courage and indomitable will of the civilians. They accepted hardships and shortages without complaint. They had been through week after week of nightly fire of explosive bombing and the destruction of almost a third of the city. They spent nights crammed together on the floors of basements and the Underground and then came out to face a full day's work. Amazingly, many said later they enjoyed that period.

17 April was a sadly memorable day for me. Jack and Phil Davenport, Dave Laurenti, and Alan Ada came to Waterloo station to see me off to Bournemouth. Alan Ada was killed nineteen days later, and Dave Laurenti died in a Sunderland crash on 12 August 1942.

Chapter 4

209 Squadron, UK, East and South Africa

(18 April 1942 – 3 April 1943)

I travelled with four others by train on 18 April from Bournemouth to RAF Pembroke Dock, a large, pre-war, permanent seaplane and flying boat station. The officers' mess was more like a hotel than anything else and the quarters were absolutely wizard.

On arrival, we were told we were to convert to Catalinas before the squadron relocated somewhere in the Indian Ocean, but no one could tell us where. The ground staff had sailed shortly before we arrived, in the *Duchess of Belford*, to be ready for our arrival by air.

Wing Commander Dicky Drew, aged 32, was the squadron's CO and my flight commander was Flight Lieutenant John Barraclough AFC, a huge cove, aged 24. I was one of eleven second pilots posted to 209. Shortly after we arrived, Barraclough introduced us to the Catalina.

During the Second World War, Coastal Command operated two long-range flying boats in large numbers: the Sunderland and Catalina. The Sunderland was designed and built by Short Brothers in the UK for the RAF. It was a derivative of Short's Empire model civil flying boat. It was introduced into service in 1938, had four engines, was almost palatial in size, had an endurance of around thirteen hours, a range of 1,800 miles, a crew of nine to eleven, and was armed with up to twelve 0.303-inch Browning machine guns. A total of 749 of all marks were built. At least thirteen RAF and two RAAF squadrons operated them.

Right: 209 Squadron coat of arms. (Eric Saunders)

Below: Squadron Leader Barraclough on the dorsal strake of Canadian-built Catalina Mark II 209/M, RAF serial VA703, in Pembroke Dock before he and his crew flew her to Mombasa in June 1942. Barraclough's second pilot, Tommy Eakins, is standing behind him. The airmen on the wing were winching a pannier to attach under the main plane. These panniers were used to carry spare parts from Pembroke Dock to the squadron's new base in Mombasa. (Eric Saunders)

Consolidated's 1935 Model 28-5 flying boat, known to the Americans as the PBY and as the Catalina by the British, was slow, strangely beautiful, thoroughly reliable, tough, and much loved by the men who operated her. While considered obsolete by 1939, the Catalina was the right aeroplane at the right time and went on to serve with the armed forces of many countries.

The Catalina was literally a flying boat. Once waterborne, it became a boat that required a secure mooring. One mooring line is attached to the snubbing post beside the bow turret and the other to the open stowing compartment in which the anchor was stowed when not in use. Below that is the chine rail, on which the crew stood when mooring the boat. Some routine servicing could be carried out while on the water with special scaffolding, seen here attached to sockets in the starboard engine and the main plane (wing). Another scaffold can be seen resting above the bow turret forward of the pilots' windscreen. In addition to the man in the sun about to climb onto the main plane, two others are working in the shade on the port (left) engine. The window below the port engine is in the wireless operator/navigator's compartment. The radar aerials can be seen below this window. There are three depth charges under each wing and the landing lights can be seen in the leading edge outboard of each engine. Note the dressing of the propellers, which were positioned to minimize the danger to traffic coming up from the water. The faded round patch under the cockpit window is the Donald Duck mascot. The aircraft was a Catalina Mark I, RAF serial Z2142, WQ-Q. It was delivered early in 1941 and allocated to 209 Squadron. It was struck off charge in September 1944. (Eric Saunders)

The RAF evaluated and ordered the Catalina in July 1939, with the first deliveries arriving in early 1941. The Catalina served with great distinction in twenty-one RAF squadrons and they operated the type from the Arctic Circle to south of South Africa.

She had a wingspan of 104 feet, was 63 feet 10 inches long, and 18 feet 10 inches high, with a wing area of 1,400 square feet. She was powered by two Pratt & Whitney Twin Wasp R-1830-92 radial, air-cooled engines of 1,200 horsepower. The engines were mounted on the main plane,[1] which was supported above the hull on a pylon and braced with two struts, attached either side of the hull. The propellers were Hamilton-Standard Hydromatic constant-speeds that could be fully feathered[2] and were located either side of the cockpit.

Catalina cockpit showing the layout of the instruments and the control wheels. In the RAF, the aircraft captain was the senior pilot, who flew from the left-hand seat. The right-hand seat was occupied by the second pilot. The large rudder pedal bars can be seen in front of the pilots' seats. (Denis Saunders)

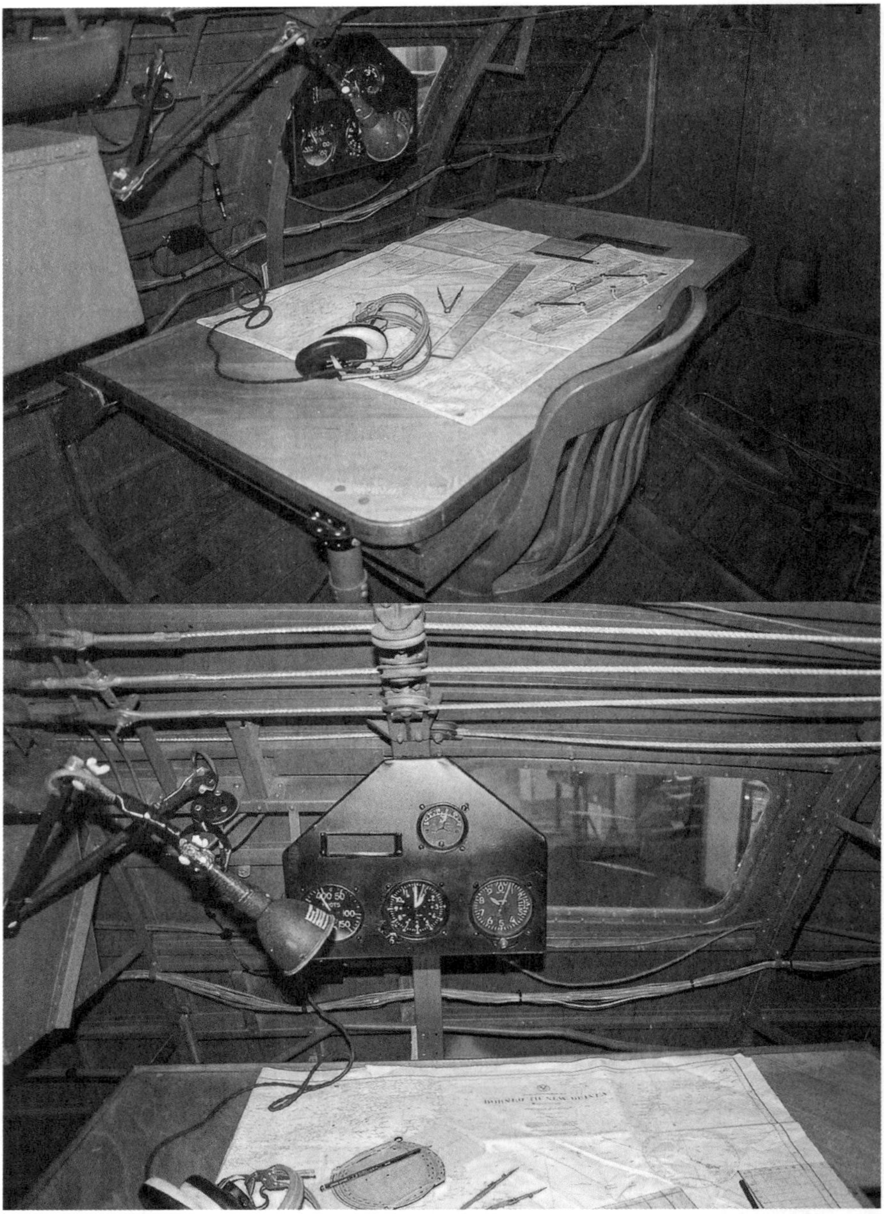

Upper: Catalina navigator's station. The moveable light is obscuring the navigator's instrument panel. *Lower:* Navigator's instrument panel and instruments and the window to the right of the instrument panel. Above the instrument panel are control cables for the tailplane. (Denis Saunders)

Catalina instrument panel in the engineer's station. The engineer sat inside the pylon separating the hull and the main plane. (Denis Saunders)

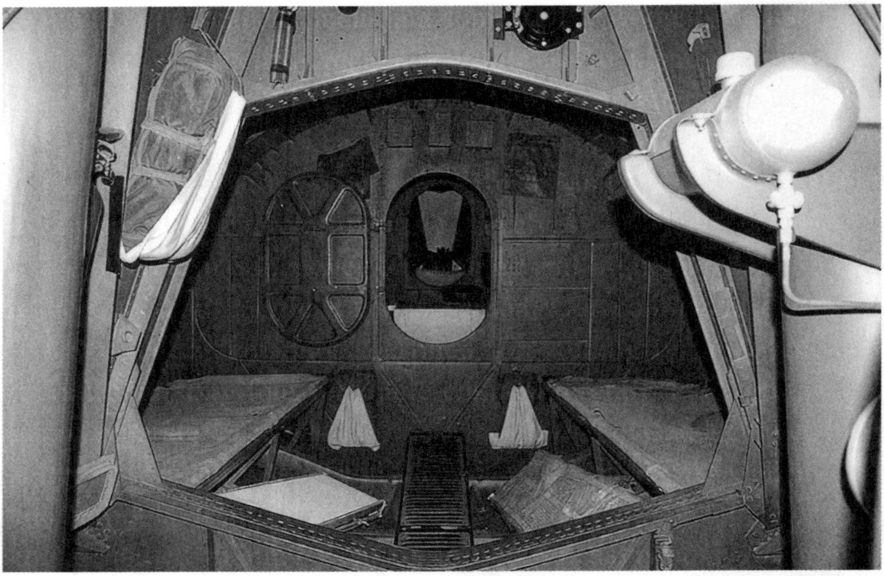

Catalina bunk compartment: essential for long flights. The watertight door for the compartment is shown on the left of the hatch, as is the catwalk covering the bilge. (Denis Saunders)

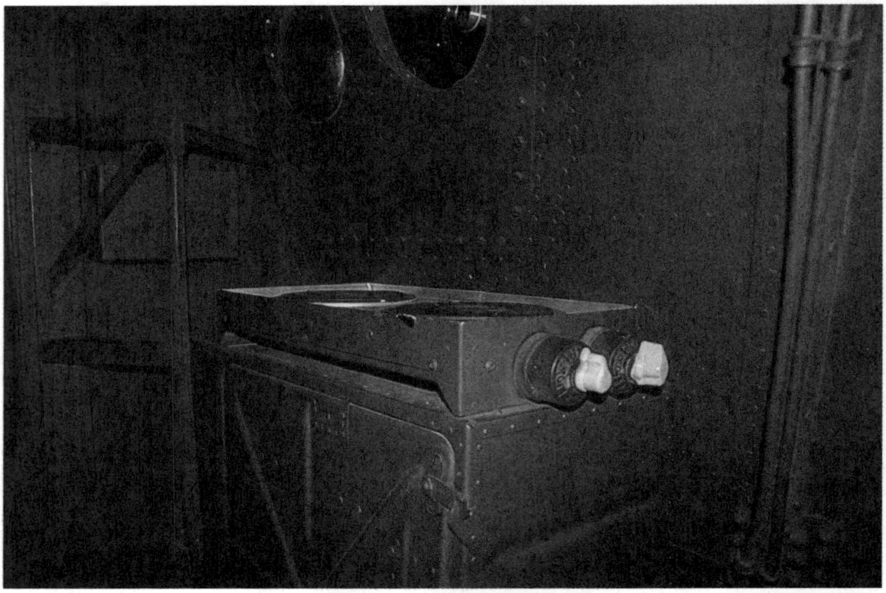

Catalina galley with two electric hot plates. (Denis Saunders)

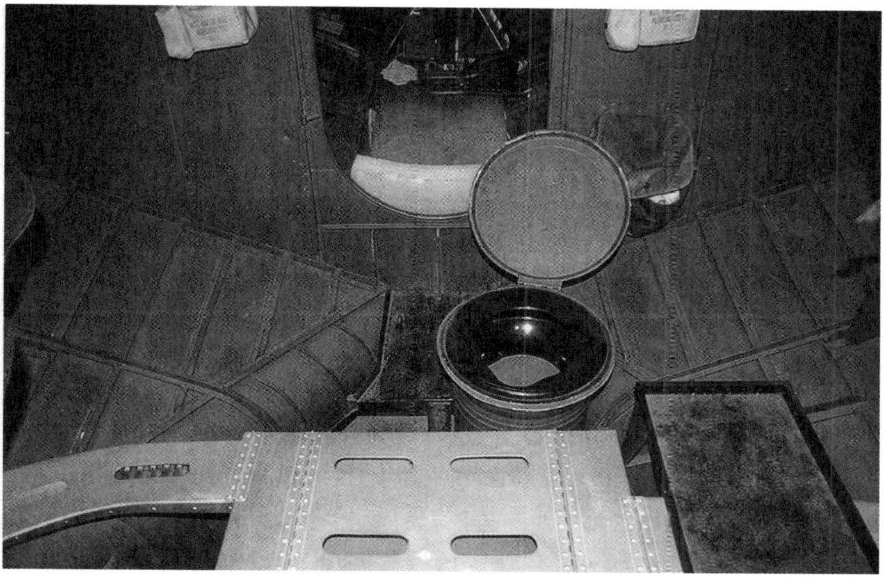

Catalina toilet, located at the rear of the aircraft. The compartment to the rear of the toilet contained the tunnel hatch. (Denis Saunders)

Catalina starboard blister. Excellent visibility was provided with a blister on each side of the aircraft. (Denis Saunders)

Catalina boat details. *A:* The snubbing post for attaching mooring lines is beside the bow turret. The chine on which the crew stood while mooring is the vertical ledge just above the water line. It has two cleats for attaching mooring lines. The anchor is resting on the chine. The detail is taken from a US Navy amphibian PBY-5A; the mooring fittings were the same for RAF flying boats, but the turret equipment was not. *B:* The mooring ring at the left-hand top of the port float is shown. The Catalina float design was unique as they were retracted in flight to form the wing tip. The crossed retraction gear can be seen in the triangular gap of float arms. *C:* Mooring ring under the fuselage, below the tailplane. *D:* The detachable access ladder and starboard blister are shown, as is the stirrup-shaped hole, which is the bottom of the flare shute on the underside of the fuselage. The step at the stern of the boat's hull is shown to the left of the access ladder. (Denis Saunders)

It was a versatile long-range reconnaissance aircraft because as a flying boat it could operate without runways, remain in the air for long periods, and, with the two blisters either side of the hull, it had excellent visibility. The fuel tanks, located in the main plane, held 1,452 imperial gallons. The maximum take-off weight was 34,000 pounds, although with operational aircraft this was often exceeded. The maximum speed of the Catalina was 170 knots, but the typical cruising speed was around 96 knots. Its maximum range exceeded 3,000 miles and it could stay in the air for over twenty-four hours.

The RAF operated her with a crew of nine: the aircraft captain, who was the senior pilot; a second pilot; a navigator; two flight engineers; three wireless operators/air gunners; and a rigger. For the comfort of the crew, it had a compartment fitted with bunks, a galley with a two-burner electric stove, and a toilet.

My first few days on the squadron were interesting: getting to know my fellow aircrew, attending lectures, learning semaphore, making sure all my equipment and clothing were in good order, being subjected to a complete medical examination, and receiving vaccinations for my pending overseas posting.

During our second evening on the station, the CO and flight commander joined us after dinner and bought us a few beers. It was a friendly action on their part. Although we were still under training, we seemed to be regarded quite differently than if we were at training schools. From then on, we were treated as members of the squadron.

Initially, there were nine pilot officers and two sergeants posted as second pilots to the squadron. However, only nine were required for the squadron transfer to the Indian Ocean. The British class system[3] decided who would go, with the sergeants sent off the squadron. This seemed unfair as, if given a choice, two of the officers would rather have stayed in England. The remaining nine were split into three groups of three, each with an instructor. Flight Lieutenant David Fitzpatrick was in charge of my group, which included Pilot Officer Mike Barry, a South African, and Pilot Officer Frank Henderson, a Canadian.

We spent as much time learning to fly Catalinas as Fitzpatrick could fit in. We were taught how to feather the propellers if an engine packed up, the procedure for engaging the Sperry automatic pilot[4] in flight, single-engine flying and landings, night flying procedure, flare path layout for flying, and glide landings. The technique for glide landings was to descend to 400 feet, throttle right back, and maintain airspeed at 85 knots plus. We were told to maintain an air speed of not below 85 knots: any speed below 85 knots was potentially fatal.

At about 50 feet, the stick was pulled back slightly, and the aircraft flown under control onto the water. Because they were boats once on the water, we had to learn nautical skills: casting off, mooring up, taxiing on water, handling during windy conditions, dealing with tides, and tying knots and other rope work.

In late April I went solo in 209/S AH543. I must confess it did not give me as much of a thrill as I had imagined. The best feeling of all was going solo in the Tiger Moth thirteen months previously. Even the Anson solo had a little more excitement about it. Three days later, I pulled an awful boner. Mike, Frank, and I spent the afternoon doing various drills with Fitzpatrick in W8418. The first was water handling in a strong wind. Then, at 4,000 feet, we practiced putting in the automatic pilot and feathering and unfeathering the propellers.

Left: Flying Officer John Inglis, captain of 209/S, RAF serial AH543, in the UK before going out to Africa, May 1942. (Bruce Daymond) *Right:* Flight Lieutenant Ken Murray, captain of 209/J, RAF serial W8415, in Mombasa in 1943. He was credited with sinking the last U-boat of the war, off Sullom Voe in Catalina 210/X JX249, on 7 May 1944. An account of the operation is given in *Flying Cats* by Andrew Hendrie. (Eric Saunders)

Three of the crew of Catalina 209/Q at Pembroke Dock, Wales, May 1942. Left to right: Sergeants Stoner, Howell, and Maguire. (Bruce Daymond)

We had feathered the propeller on the port engine and I was supposed to unfeather it and start the engine. Instead of unfeathering the port engine's propeller, I feathered the one on the starboard engine, which promptly stopped. There we were, with both engines stopped and both propellers fully feathered. How the blazes I could have done such a bloody stupid thing, I still can't understand. It was a momentary and humiliating lapse of concentration. Fitzpatrick was able to get them both started again, thanks to good generators. I was subdued for the rest of the afternoon.

Shortly after, we had another bad day. The electric starter on the port engine of 209/J W8415 was unserviceable. Frank was in the pilot's seat while Mike and a fitter climbed onto the main plane to crank the starter. I was in the engineer's compartment, ready to engage the starter. As cranking was terribly heavy work, after numerous failed attempts to get the engine going, a wireless operator and I went to help the other two crank. Eventually the engine started. Frank opened the throttle and left it open. The blast of air from the propellers was terrific. Mike was picked up and blown down the main plane. He landed on the blister, put his foot through a panel and saved himself from being blown into the water. I was also blown over but managed to grab the wireless operator and saved myself. Fitzpatrick blew Frank up for not closing the throttle, but not as much as he did later when we were trying to taxi away from the buoy, only to find ourselves still moored to it! Boy, did he get mad! The same day, there was a dreadful accident at the fort on top of the hill. During a lecture on disposal of landmines, two mines exploded, killing nineteen and injuring ten.

During the afternoon of 1 May, we had some real excitement in 209/O AH548. Fitzpatrick told me to climb to the cloud base at about 6,000 feet. We had almost got there when the starboard engine failed and the control wheel was pushed out of my hands. Fitzpatrick had the engineer cut off the petrol, feathered the propeller, and switched off the engine in less time than it took to relate this sentence. We headed back to base and popped off two Very lights to have a boat standing by to tow us. Fitz executed a nice single-engined landing. The trouble was caused by a broken fuel line. We didn't know why the engine didn't catch fire with petrol being pumped out under pressure onto a hot engine. Having only one engine running made manoeuvring on the water rather difficult.

Life in the officers' mess could be chaotic. One night, Squadron Leader Barraclough told me that it was both the CO's and his birthday. He asked me to round up the rest of the crowd and bring them to the mess. This I did and a drinking party ensued. Squadron Leader Tim Belcham, who wasn't popular with the old members of the squadron, made himself very unpleasant by throwing beer mugs around. Barraclough, at a late stage of the evening, got a headlock on him and, when released, this cove ran outside and came back with a loaded revolver, threatening to blow Barra's guts out if he ever did that again. And by God he meant it.

On 4 May I went on leave to Halfridge, where I spent a lovely eight days. The countryside was in full spring bloom. Pink cherry blossom dotted amongst the seemingly endless number of shades of green trees made a perfectly lovely picture. And then, on arrival at Henley, seeing the river practically motionless with punts ready on the banks, all combined to give a perfect atmosphere of peace. War, with all its noise and horror, seemed in another world. I had heard of the beauty of England in the spring, but I never realised it would be as lovely as it was in 1942. Wandering through the woods at Halfridge revealed many lovely scenes and shades which couldn't be caught by my camera. During that idyllic leave I helped at the farm, inspected the estate with Mr Bond, did some sight-seeing in Reading, Windsor, and the surrounding countryside, and spent a lot of time with Peggy, including some lovely walks to the Carpenter's Arms or the White Hart for a few beers, and some lovely walks home.

In late May, nearly seventeen months after I started at Bradfield Park, I was about to go to war. I was assigned as second pilot to Flying Officer Eric Saunders (RAAF), a graduate of EATS who had just completed his captain's course. Our navigator was Flight Sergeant Vincent, with a lot of operational experience. Our wireless operator/mechanic was the squadron signals officer, Pilot Officer Vic Field. The rest of the crew were sergeants. In addition to our crew, we were to carry two maintenance people as passengers to Mombasa.

I was sent on special duty to Coastal Command HQ in London to collect some documents for the squadron. I had an overnight stay in London and Peggy was able to get to the city. This was the first time Peggy and I were able to have an evening alone together and it would be the last for ages. We went to the dinner dance at the Savoy and had a simply grand time. Dancing to Carroll Gibbons' band was wonderful. I took Peggy to where she was staying, stayed an hour or so saying goodbye, and met up with her the next day. We had lunch and sat in Hyde Park for our last few minutes together. At the time, I wondered if this time it really would be the last. She was a grand girl and we got on with each other so excellently. In one way I hoped this parting would finish it, for if we kept on like this, being so terribly fond of each other, we would run into a nasty packet of trouble. The plain fact was I had met her two and a half years too late.

Towards the end of May I received a letter from Stewart Brundell,[5] in which he wrote that Alan Ada was missing from an operational trip over the Bay of Biscay. I wrote at the time:

> How fervently I hope he is alright, that he may have been picked up and now be a prisoner of war. I can't bear to think of poor old Alan being killed. We trained for so long together. It's not too good when really intimate friends go. The list of them is mounting – Jim Unsworth, Rolla Cooke, Rex Marre and now Alan. Do let's hope it is not true.

Unfortunately, it was true.

Table 1. Details of 209 Squadron Catalina transfers from Pembroke Dock, Wales, to Mombasa, Kenya, in June 1942 and the fate of the aircraft. The blank rectangle indicates no data is available.

209 Squadron individual aircraft code	Catalina model	RAF serial	Aircraft captain	Second pilot	Aircraft's fate
J	Mark I	W8415	Flying Officer Ken Murray	Pilot Officer Rolf Luck	Struck off charge, 28 September 1944
K	Mark I	W8428	Flying Officer 'Jeep' Balfour	Pilot Officer Ted Mangan	Crashed, Kisumu, Kenya, 1 August 1944
L	Mark II	VA713	Flying Officer John Wyllie	Pilot Officer Frank Henderson	Crashed on take-off, 8 September 1942

209 Squadron individual aircraft code	Catalina model	RAF serial	Aircraft captain	Second pilot	Aircraft's fate
M	Mark II	VA703	Squadron Leader John Barraclough	Pilot Officer Thomas Eakins	Wrecked in a gale, 14 July 1943
N	Mark II	VA715	Flying Officer William Hossent	Pilot Officer Jack Kennedy	Struck off charge, 4 August 1944
O	Mark I	AH548	Flying Officer Ronald Roberts	Pilot Officer Ted Taylor	Damaged, Seychelles, 1 November 1944
P	Mark II	VA727	Flight Lieutenant David Fitzpatrick	Pilot Officer Michael Barry	Blown up by own depth charges, 2 September 1942
Q	Mark I	Z2142	Flying Officer Eric Saunders	Pilot Officer Bruce Daymond	Struck off charge, 28 September 1944
S	Mark I	AH543	Flying Officer John Inglis		Ditched in neutral territory and impounded, 13 October 1942

On 2 June, the first three Catalinas departed for Gibraltar on the first leg of their transit to Mombasa, Kenya. They were (captain and second pilot) John Wyllie and Frank Henderson taking Wing Commander Drew in 209/L (arrived Mombasa 15 June), David Fitzpatrick and Mike Barry in 209/P (15 June), and Ken Murray and Rolf Luck in 209/J (16 June). The next four were John Inglis and unknown in 209/S (27 June), Ron Roberts and Ted Taylor in 209/O (27 June), Jeep Balfour and Ted Mangan in 209/K (22 June), and Bill

Hossent and Jack Kennedy in 209/N (17 June). The last two departed on 14 June and were John Barraclough and Tom Eakins in 209/M (22 June) and Eric Saunders and me in 209/Q.

I was supposed to hitch a ride to Beaumaris, Anglesey island, on 6 June with Squadron Leader Belcham. I was to meet Saunders and the rest of our crew there to collect our Catalina. My transport was AH545 of 119 Squadron. She was formerly 209/Z, the aircraft that found the *Bismarck*. She had an etching of the *Bismarck* on the bow, and also two submarines which she had found. She had a whopping great Leigh Light[6] slung under the starboard wing. The weight of the searchlight kept the starboard float under water. We slipped the buoy and taxied around, but then discovered that there was a whacking great leak from the main fuel cock, so the trip was off. Had we taken off and a spark from the wireless had caught this petrol, we would have disappeared in a sheet of blue flame. So I had to catch a train to Beaumaris.

We took over Z2142 WQ-Q at the Saunders-Roe works just outside of Beaumaris. There was an army of people cleaning her up and she looked like a new pin. One of the Saunders-Roe people painted a mascot of Donald Duck with a telescope to his eye on the bow.

Nose art, Catalina-style. *Left:* Bruce Daymond in the cockpit and the Disney character Donald Duck with a telescope, painted on the side of 209/Q. *Right:* The Disney character Goofy with a baseball bat, smacking a submarine, painted on the side of 209/M. (Eric Saunders)

We spent the afternoon doing compass swings on the three compasses, running up the engines, and checking the early air to surface vessel radar unit. We then flew the one and a half hours to Pembroke Dock, where an inspection revealed her engines were in good order, but the hull had a few leaks.

Before we left for Africa, we did a final test including circuits and bumps in Angle Bay, Milford Haven. We had Lieutenant Franklin of the Fleet Air Arm on board as a guest. Saunders let him do a take-off

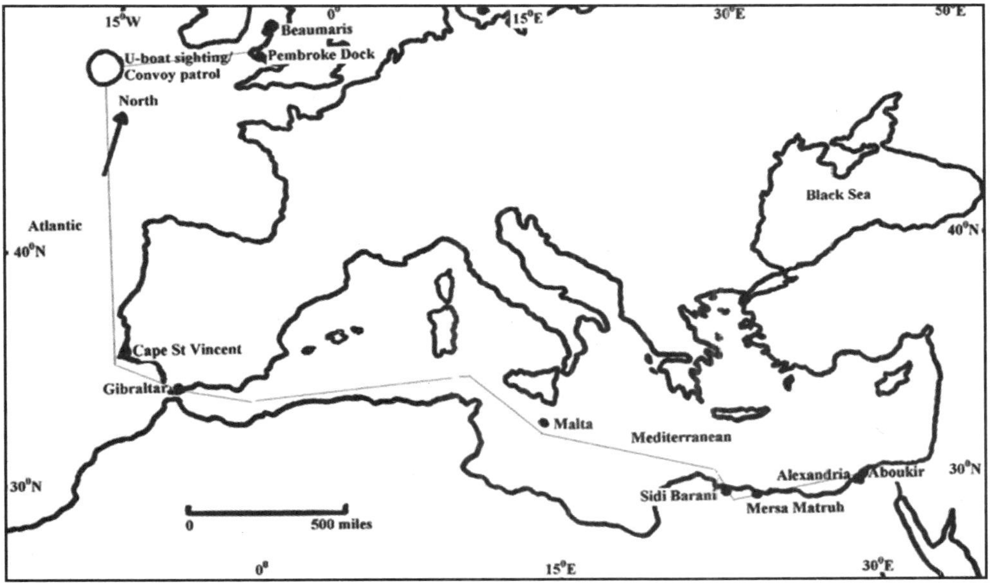

Map showing the first two stages of the track (thin line) of 209/Q on its transit from Pembroke Dock to Mombasa between 14 and 25 June 1942. The first stage, from Pembroke Dock to Gibraltar, included a convoy patrol and a sighting of a U-boat. That stage took 20 hours and 40 minutes. This was Bruce Daymond's first operational sortie and until then he had never spent more than 3 hours in the air in a single flight. The second stage was from Gibraltar to Aboukir, near Alexandria. This took them nearly the length of the Mediterranean and lasted 20 hours and 25 minutes. The next stages are shown on another figure. These consisted of Aboukir to Wadi Halfa (6 hours), Wadi Halfa to Khartoum (3 hours and 55 minutes), Khartoum to Kisumu (10 hours and 45 minutes), and finally, Kisumu to Mombasa (4 hours and 10 minutes). The total flying time was 65 hours and 55 minutes.

and landing. He made an excellent job of both considering he had never been in a Catalina before. He was used to flying Supermarine Walrus amphibians. On completion of our tests we topped up our fuel to 1,500 gallons. We came back on the step from Hobbs Point to get the feel of a heavy take-off. The boat was fully loaded except for personal kit. We also carried part of the beaching gear the squadron needed at Mombasa.

I commenced my first operational flight at 11 pm on 14 June as Eric Saunders did his first heavily laden take-off. We took nearly a mile before becoming airborne. During the first part of our transit to Gibraltar we escorted a convoy south-west of Land's End. Just before we reached the convoy we saw a U-boat on the surface. There was a swirl of water as it crash-dived. Unfortunately, we had no depth charges. We circled the area for some time, but saw nothing further of the submarine. Not far away we found a corvette and passed on our U-boat sighting using the Aldis Lamp.

Flight Sergeant Vincent, navigator of 209/Q, holding a sextant in the open port blister. The access ladder has fabric backing on the top two steps to prevent damage to the aircraft's skin. The lettering 'Cupola must be raised & lowered very slowly or glass will shatter' is under the blister. This is unusual as the writing did not feature on later models. The access hatch to the next compartment can be seen on Flight Sergeant Vincent's left. (Bruce Daymond)

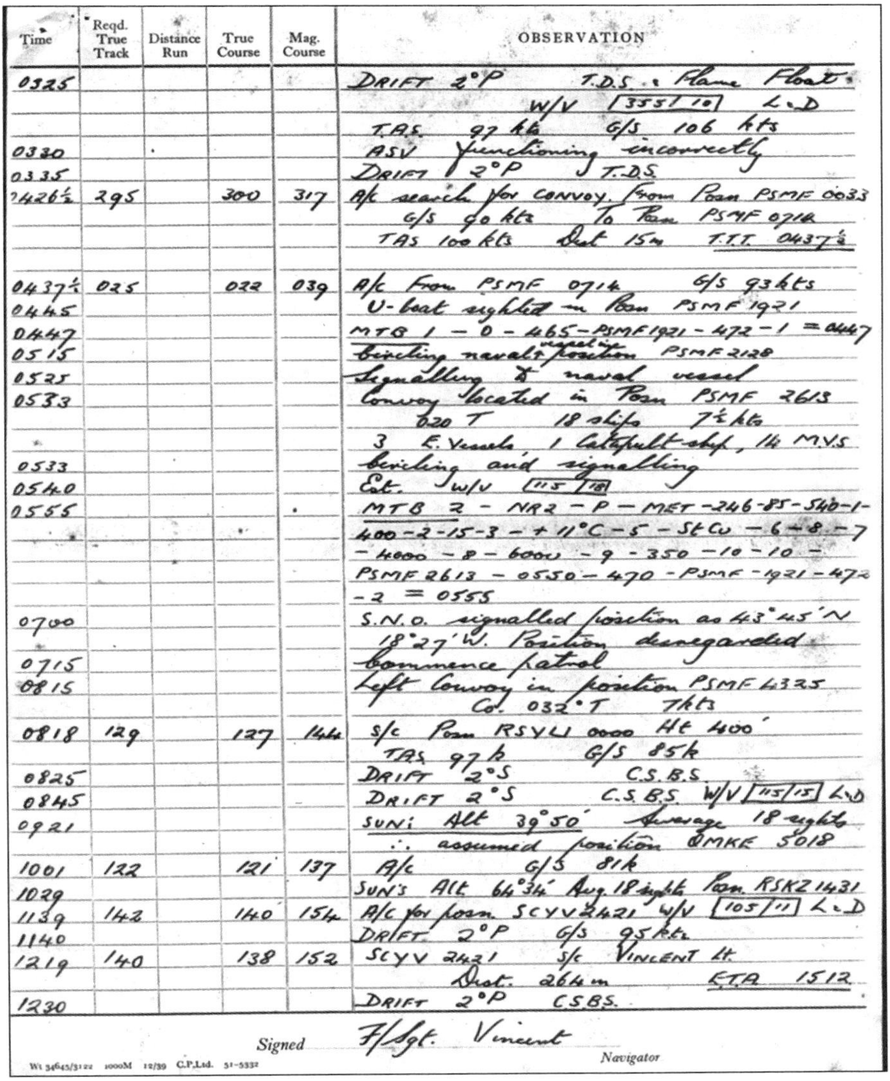

Time	Reqd. True Track	Distance Run	True Course	Mag. Course	OBSERVATION
0325					DRIFT 2°P T.D.S. : Flame Float.
					W/V 355/10 L.D
					T.A.S. 97 kts G/S 106 kts
0330					ASV functioning incorrectly
0335					DRIFT 2°P T.D.S.
0426½	295		300	317	A/c search for convoy. From Posn PSMF 0033
					G/S 90 kts To Posn PSMF 0714
					TAS 100 kts Dist 15m T.T.T. 0437½
0437½	025		022	039	A/c From PSMF 0714 G/S 93 kts
0445					U-boat sighted in Posn PSMF 1921
0447					MTB 1 – 0 – 465 – PSMF 1921 – 472 – 1 = 0447
0515					Circling naval vessel in position PSMF 2128
0525					Signalling to naval vessel
0533					Convoy located in Posn PSMF 2613
					020 T 18 ships 7½ kts
					3 E. Vessels, 1 Catapult ship, 14 M.V.S
0533					Circling and signalling
0540					Est. W/V 115/18
0555					MTB 2 – NR2 – P – MET – 246 – 85 – 540 – 1 –
					400 – 2 – 15 – 3 – + 11°C – 5 – StCu – 6 – 8 – 7
					– 4000 – 8 – 6000 – 9 – 350 – 10 – 10 –
					PSMF 2613 – 0550 – 470 – PSMF – 1921 – 472
					– 2 = 0555
0700					S.N.O. signalled position as 43°45′N
					18°27′W. Position disregarded
0715					Commence patrol
0815					Left Convoy in position PSMF 4325
					Co. 032°T 7 kts
0818	129		127	144	S/c Posn RSYU 0000 Ht 400′
					TAS 97 k G/S 85 k
0825					DRIFT 2°S C.S.B.S.
0845					DRIFT 2°S C.S.B.S. W/V 115/15 L.D
0921					SUN: Alt 39°50′ Average 18 sights
					∴ assumed position QMKE 5018
1001	122		121	137	A/c G/S 81 k
1029					SUN'S Alt 64°34′ Avg. 18 sights Posn. RSKZ 1431
1139	142		140	154	A/c for posn. SCYV 2421 W/V 105/11 L.D
1140					DRIFT 2°P G/S 95 kts
1219	140		138	152	SCYV 2421 S/c VINCENT Lt.
					Dist. 264 m ETA 1512
1230					DRIFT 2°P CSBS.

Signed F/Sgt. Vincent Navigator

Wt 34645/3122 1000M 12/39 C.P.Ltd. 51-5332

One page of the navigation log kept by Flight Sergeant Vincent for the flight in 209/Q captained by Flying Officer Eric Saunders, with Bruce Daymond as second pilot, from Pembroke Dock to Gibraltar on 14/15 June 1942. Navigation was done entirely by using the sun and stars. The navigator also needed to establish the strength and direction of the wind to work out how much the aircraft was drifting off track and compensating accordingly. Drift was established by sighting on a flame float dropped from the aircraft. The Catalina was a slow aircraft and, as shown in the log, ground speed varied from 85 to 105 knots. Note the sighting of a U-boat at 0445 hours.

Some aircrew had been on patrol since the war began and never seen a U-boat and I saw one on my first operational trip. We picked up the convoy of fourteen ships, one Catapult Armed Merchantman, and three naval escorts at about 7.30 am and stayed with it for three hours.

We approached Gibraltar from Europa Point, about 10 miles out. After madly flashing the letter of the day and firing off a recognition

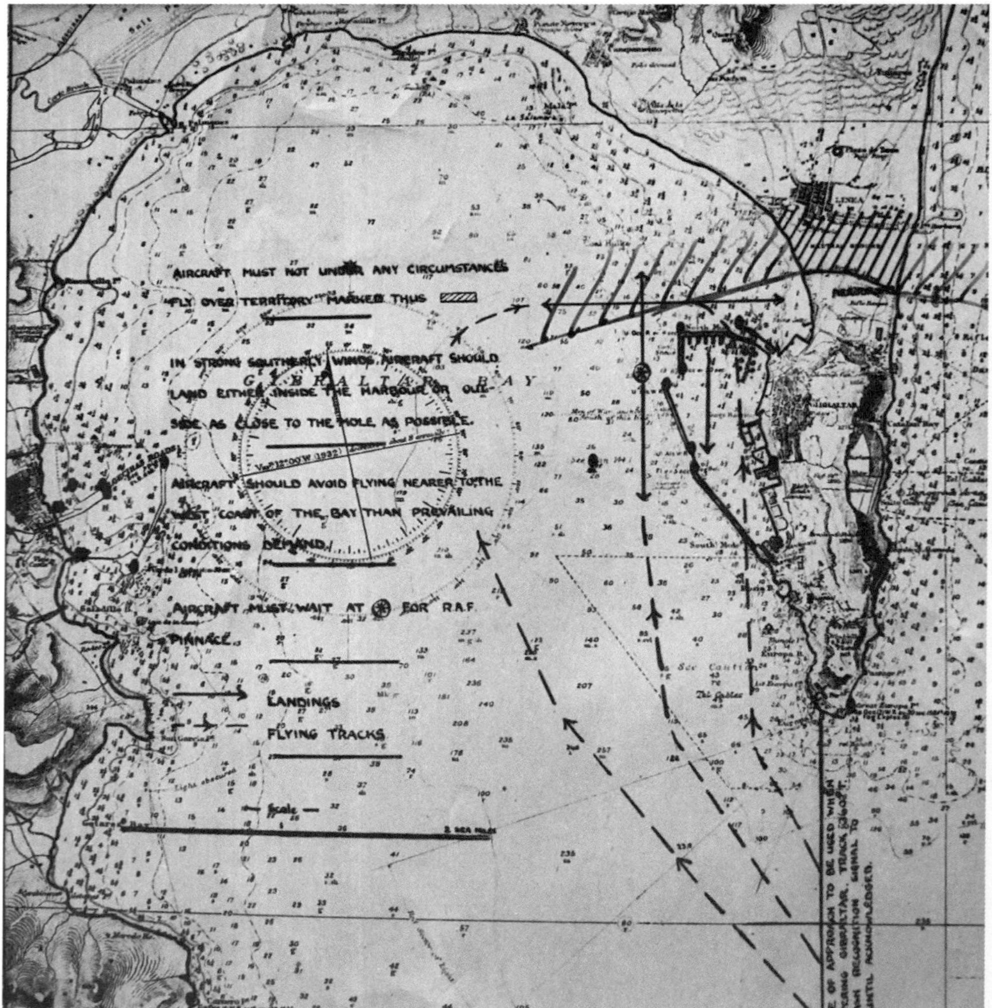

Chart for flying boats operating in and out of Gibraltar. (Eric Saunders)

cartridge to avoid being fired on, Saunders made a bouncy landing, during which I whacked my forehead on the tail trimmers. We were led into the harbour by a pinnace and moored up, twenty hours and thirty minutes after slipping moorings at Pembroke Dock.

We were supposed to depart for Alexandria the next afternoon but, due to a combination of faults, we could not. The starter on the starboard motor would not work. The spreader on the mooring buoy got caught on the rigger's step and tore a hole in the hull below the waterline. We patched the hole with plasticine and taxied into harbour, but found the automatic pilot had a leak in it. That was the last straw. We could not conduct an eighteen-hour trip without 'George' so we moored up.

Our boat was repaired five days after we left Pembroke Dock. After a taxiing test to see all was OK, the notorious Gibraltar swell prevented our becoming airborne until our third attempt. And then only after a large wave washed over the bow, windscreen, and cockpit roof, completely obscuring our vision, and thoroughly drenching us because of inefficient seals on the overhead hatches.

We did not want to pass near Malta during daylight as it was under constant air attack, so we cruised along at 85 knots. It was a perfectly lovely day with bright sunshine and a calm blue sea. I remember one of the old RAF types telling me: 'My boy, I used to take drift sights on the bottom of the Mediterranean.' The water was so clear I could believe him. We passed Malta at 1 am about 30 miles to port and saw some flashes, probably because the island was under air attack.

We made landfall at Sidi Barrani in North Africa and alighted at RAF Aboukir, on a peninsula about 17 miles from Alexandria. We found Ron Roberts with his crew in 209/O still at Aboukir. They had had a forced landing at Mersa Matruh, sprung some rivets, and had been at Aboukir for about ten days while their boat was being repaired.

After two days we flew over the fertile Nile Delta, past the pyramids, to Wadi Halfa on the Nile. The next day we flew to Khartoum. I did

The Rock of Gibraltar from the air, June 1942. (Bruce Daymond)

Pyramids of Giza and the Great Sphinx, photographed on the transit from Aboukir to Wadi Halfa, 22 June 1942. (Eric Saunders)

the take-off as the boat was relatively lightly loaded. Flight Sergeant Vincent had 'Gyppy tummy'[7] but was able to navigate. We landed on the Nile at Gordon's Tree, about twenty minutes from Khartoum. I supervised the refuelling. This was quite an event as it was carried out by a chain of labourers handing up 4-gallon tins of petrol and we needed the contents of 228 tins. The petrol was filtered through a piece of chamois. The next day we flew to Kisumu[8] on Lake Victoria. Vincent's health got worse and he spent the trip on one of the bunks so Saunders did most of the navigation. Vincent was seen by a doctor and taken to hospital with a suspected bout of typhoid.

I did the navigation to Mombasa. Kisumu was 3,726 feet above sea level and to clear the mountains en route to Mombasa we had to climb to 8,000 feet. During our flight we saw a train, so we dived down on it at a hell of an angle, with the mooring up horn blaring. The passengers asleep on the bunks must have come to wondering if their last moments had come.

Left: Refuelling on the River Nile at Khartoum using 4-gallon petrol tins, brought out on a barge which can be seen off the port blister. Refuelling required the contents of 228 tins. The starboard blister is open and the round handle for moving the blister cover can be seen to the lower left. *Right:* The loop antenna can be seen between the motors and the exhaust ports, without flame dampers, on the top of the engine. (Bruce Daymond)

Mombasa Harbour was full of ships, including HMS *Indomitable*, an Illustrious class aircraft carrier. Our accommodation was not too hot, and a let-down after Pembroke Dock. Most of the squadron's ground staff were berthed on the P&O ship *Manela*. Boat captains and senior officers were accommodated in the officers' mess at Port Reitz Hotel. However, poor second pilots slept in a cottage with three, four, and five beds to a room, no cupboards, no sheets, and no pillows.

With our arrival, 209 Squadron was fully operational at Mombasa to conduct anti-submarine and convoy patrols and other activities as directed by Air Headquarters East Africa. The next day we went on our first patrol south to islands north of Madagascar. However, we had to turn back after about four hours as the fuel pressure gauge on the starboard engine was reading high.

An aerial view of Mombasa and Kilindini Harbour. (Bruce Daymond)

While Mombasa was our main base, we were sent on detachments to other temporary bases. Our first detachment was on 5 July, when we were supposed to go to Dar-es-Salaam, Tanganyika.[9] However, we had not been in the air more than five minutes when the automatic pilot servo unit above the navigator's table burst, spraying the occupants with hydraulic oil. We had to return to base as we couldn't have 'George' unserviceable during a ten-day detachment at Dar-es-Salaam. The next morning, I flew the two-hour trip to Dar. Pilot Officer Ken Neill,[10] an Australian, was our navigator as Vincent was still in hospital in Kisumu. En route, we flew over Zanzibar from north to south.

Eric Saunders' crew in front of the Hotel Kisumu while in transit from Pembroke Dock, Wales, 24 June 1942. Rear rank, left to right: unidentified, Sergeant Maguire, Sergeant Stoner, unidentified, Pilot Officer Vic Field, and Bruce Daymond. Front rank, left to right: unidentified, unidentified, and Sergeant Howell. (Eric Saunders)

Dar-es-Salaam was an attractive place. There were only four or five permanent officers on the RAF station. The rest were the 209 Squadron detachment. When not flying, we served as strike boat, i.e., if any urgent job came in we had to take off immediately and deal with it. We also censored mail before it could be posted. Off duty, we wrote letters, chaffed each other, wrestled, listened to the wireless, and derived

The crew of 209/Q, June 1942: (A) Flying Officer Eric Saunders (aircraft captain), (B) Sergeant Fulton (rigger), (C) Sergeant Howell (engineer), (D) Sergeant Richardson (rigger), (E) Sergeant Stoner (wireless operator), (F) Sergeant Thomas (engineer), (G) Sergeant Maguire (wireless operator), and (H) Flight Sergeant Vincent (navigator). Vincent has an observer's brevet above his left pocket; the O was later changed to an N to reflect they were navigators. (I) Sergeant Woolley (wireless operator/mechanic). Bruce Daymond was the second pilot. (Bruce Daymond)

Three 209 Squadron Catalinas on the 'trots' (line of moorings) at Dar-es-Salaam. (Eric Saunders)

great pleasure from photos of provocative women in *The Sketch*.[11] It seemed to me that women always seemed to form the main topic of conversation among men when they were isolated from women.

A few days before we arrived, Rolf Luck in 209/J collided with a barge and ruined one float, the propeller, and the reduction gear of one engine. In order to get the boat back to Mombasa, Barraclough attempted a single-engine take-off. We watched as he spent the afternoon trying to get airborne, but he could not get enough speed to come unstuck.

From Dar we flew operational patrols. Our first was sixteen hours, during which we flew a couple of hundred miles down the coast and did a creeping-line-ahead patrol[12] of the Moçambique Channel, between the mainland and the Comoro Islands. When we returned to base, we shot up the camp. This shooting up was the legalised procedure to let the signals officer know that an airraft was commencing or returning from patrol. The regulations stated: 'Fly over at 100 feet.' We thought this was a misprint for 1,000 feet, however we decided that until it was corrected, 100 feet and less it was going to be. On one occasion, John Inglis just cleared some palms.

Our second patrol was a creeping-line-ahead anti-submarine patrol. Flying through the night at 3,000 feet over the sea, hundreds of miles from land, calmly eating a meal in the blacked-out navigator's compartment, never failed to send a tingle of excitement of adventure through me. Landing early in the morning after an eighteen-hour patrol could be breathtaking, with lovely dawns and banks of cloud that one could almost believe that one could walk on the surface of, if one stepped out of the aircraft.

On 20 July we flew Q back to Mombasa, while John Wyllie and his crew in L and Bill Hossent and his crew in N flew to Pamanzi at the start of another of 209's detachments. Pamanzi island in the Comoro group, at the north end of the Moçambique Channel, was an excellent base from which to conduct long-range reconnaissance and prevent submarines using the northern part of the Moçambique Channel. Flying boats could watch over the whole of this area, including the Portuguese East African coastline, where Japanese submarines called from time to time to meet Axis agents, who arranged replenishment provisions and stores.

When we flew into Mombasa the place looked like a regular Portsmouth. Two of the latest aircraft carriers and three battleships, *Warspite*, *Royal Sovereign*, and *Resolution*, were in harbour. I thought if the navy could spare such a formidable array for Mombasa, then the naval strength must have been far greater than we imagined. I hoped

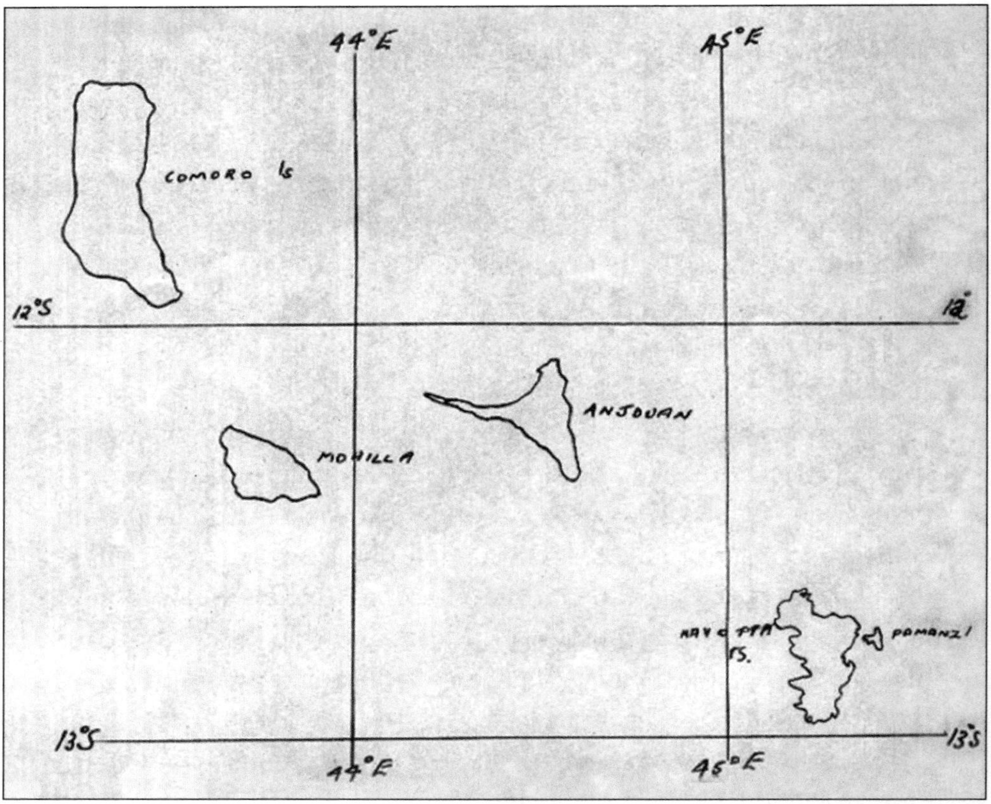

Bruce Daymond's sketch of the Comoro group of islands: the town of Dzaoudzi was on the western side of Pamanzi island.

Dzaoudzi on Pamanzi island, August 1942. The officers' mess was on the headland at the left of the photograph. A Catalina was moored slightly to the right of the centre of the panorama. (Bruce Daymond)

Approaches to the harbour and Pamanzi island (to the right of the photograph), 2 July 1942. The wing support strut is at the top right of the photograph and part of the radar array is at top left. (Bruce Daymond)

Officers' mess, Pamanzi island. (Eric Saunders)

the presence of this strength was going to lead to something as I was busting for a bit of real action.

We returned to Mombasa to have extra bomb carriers fitted to enable Q to carry eight 250-pound depth charges instead of the four 450-pounders she was carrying. After she had been modified, we loaded her with 1,150 gallons of petrol, bags of equipment, and fourteen people for our trip to Pamanzi, about 700 miles south of Mombasa. Our passengers included Ron Roberts, his crew, and Squadron Leader Barraclough. As Barra was on board I imagined that either he or Saunders would do the take-off, seeing as the boat was so heavily laden. However, just as we were about to leave the buoy, he said to Saunders, 'Let's see what sort of a cock-up young

Catalina taking off from Pamanzi. It was carrying eight depth charges. (Eric Saunders)

Daymond can make of this take-off.' Saunders piped up saying that I had never done a heavily laden take-off and well he might too for he had hogged the take-offs and landings ever since we had been together. Away we went and there was a difference between a heavily laden boat and the one I'd been used to. Barra seemed reasonably satisfied despite the bounce.

As we approached Pamanzi, a surf was breaking on the reef which circled the small island and there was a wizard sunset. HMS *Albatross*, a seaplane tender, was there, as were two destroyers with which we were to cooperate while on detachment.

Pamanzi was lovely. One could walk across it in less than five minutes. We were based in Dzaoudzi, the town on Pamanzi. The army

209/Q (in the foreground) and 209/N in formation over the Comoro island group. This photograph was taken by one of Ken Murray's crew from 209/J when the three aircraft flew in formation from Diego Suarez to Pamanzi on 20 September 1942. 209/N was Bill Hossent's boat. 209/Q was normally operated by Eric Saunders and his crew. However, during September 1942 it was operated by Ron Roberts and his crew as their boat, 209/O, was unserviceable. (Eric Saunders)

mess occupied the former Government House and our officers' mess was in a small house on the top of a cliff facing south. It was an absolutely wizard position and it would have made an absolutely super holiday spot.

Our accommodation depended on our duty. When we were strike boat, we slept aboard *Albatross*, and when not on duty we slept in the cottage we had done up as our mess. We had our meals on board the ship. We also refuelled our boats from the stern of *Albatross* using 4-gallon tins.

When John Inglis and his crew arrived in S, Pamanzi boasted five flying boats, although three were unserviceable, reducing our operational efficiency.

For night operations we had a flare path made of rafts supported by four petrol cans. On each raft was a petrol box, on which was a petrol can containing paraffin. A gooseneck pipe went into a casket containing cotton waste that was ignited to make the flare.

On 2 August, Barraclough arrived from Mombasa bringing bags of equipment with him. After lunch aboard *Albatross*, all the RAF personnel went ashore with all this baggage. So began our life on

Swimming party, Pamanzi, July 1942. (Eric Saunders)

Native labour carrying petrol cans ashore at Pamanzi. Each wooden box contained two 4-gallon cans of petrol. All refuelling was done by manhandling the cans from a tender on to the aircraft's main plane; the fuel was then poured into the tanks, filtered through a chamois. A full fuel load could require over 350 cans. (Eric Saunders)

Flying Officer Ken Murray carrying a battered petrol tin on the wharf at Pamanzi, July 1942. The object on the wheelbarrow is unknown. The two men handling the wheelbarrow appear to be smoking. Note the assortment of head-gear. (Eric Saunders)

Dzaoudzi: sixteen officers living in a little cottage on the top of the hill, and forty-five airmen living in what used to be the old administration building.

To make our base more effective, each officer was allocated a task to supervise: some looked after the airmen's and sergeants' messes, others stores, others the water supply, etc. I was given the job of sanitation officer, organising the lavatory, ablution, and garbage situations in consultation with the medical officer from the King's African Rifles.

In early August we got news from Mombasa of the close shave Ken Murray and his crew had had in J. They had taken off on a trip to the Seychelles and had gone about 20 miles out to sea when oil was seen pouring out of the port engine. They turned around, did a night landing without any flares, and just as the aircraft touched the water the port engine seized and one of the cylinders blew off.

Using over 1,500 gallons during an operational patrol, our aircraft consumed enormous quantities of fuel, and so petrol was a major item on every supply ship. When unloading the petrol boxes, the pier was a veritable hive of activity for several days as the labourers unloaded 25,000 boxes. This was done to the accompaniment of much singing and chanting in true African style.

Tom Eakins was Barraclough's second pilot. He had been allowed to fly N to Kisumu from Mombasa, and then to Pamanzi, as captain of the aircraft. This illustrated the luck of who one was crewed with. The flight commander, with his experience, gave his second pilot considerable scope. I was crewed with Saunders, a relatively junior captain, so as a step in the right direction, I was allowed to move Q from one buoy to another! Discussing this lack of opportunity with Eric after the war, Eric told me he was conscious of this, but he was trying to get as much experience as he could, as he was only one short jump ahead of me in experience.

In mid-August we were sent to Diego Suarez, Madagascar to collect some passengers and transport them to Mombasa. The water was smooth, with no ripples, and we had a phenomenally long run before we could break free.[13] During landing we literally had to pick our way through the wrecks sunk in the harbour. Our passengers were 'brass hats' of the highest order: Lieutenant General R.G. Sturges (Royal Marines), Brigadiers L.A. Dimilon and M. Lush, and R. Hoskins, a Foreign Office type. When we taxied for take-off Lieutenant General Sturges found one of his dispatch cases was not on board, so we had to moor up and collect it. He was most profuse in his apologies. Our passengers took it in turns to sit in the second pilot's seat and appeared to enjoy the flight. They were the most awfully jolly old birds. Sergeant Thomas turned on a wizard luncheon for them: something they didn't expect for they had brought sandwiches. Just before getting to Mombasa some of us fired off a drum of ammunition each. It was my first experience of air firing. The target was the aircraft's shadow on the water and I got the odd few bullets into it.

Assortment of marine craft, Mombasa, 1942. The boats were used to ferry the crews to and from their aircraft, two of which can be seen moored in the background. They were also used to set the flare paths for night flights. (Bruce Daymond)

Back in Mombasa Flight Sergeant Vincent rejoined us as navigator, about six weeks after we left him in hospital in Kisumu. On 14 August we engaged in anti-submarine exercises with two destroyers, a couple of corvettes, and a tame O class submarine. We had to work with the surface vessels to find the submarine and shoot it up. We conducted this exercise several times, returning to base between each exercise. When the submarine was surfaced, most members of the crew had practice picking her up on the radar. At one stage she submerged, but we could see her quite plainly when we were between the sun and the submarine. On our final run back to base, we indulged in some wizard low flying with me at the controls. We skimmed the top of the waves for 25 miles.

One day Ted Mangan, Ted Taylor, six NCOs, and I went out on the destroyer decoy to get the naval point of view on submarine exercises. We were picked up by naval pinnace and taken to the destroyer, which was lying alongside the aircraft carrier *Formidable*. Leaving harbour was quite a business. As we passed each naval vessel, the whole crew came to attention on the blowing of the bosun's whistle. As the harbour was chock-a-block with naval ships, we had a busy time. At sea, firing practice at an aircraft drone was carried out, and then Asdic[14] hunts for the tame submarine took place. The destroyer had an automatic plot of its own course and the course of the submarine was judged from the Asdic readings. We conducted many attacks. Another destroyer, the *Foxhound*, was also engaged on the exercise. The submarine had three red floats tied to it to indicate its position. These were not terribly prominent from any considerable distance, but did help as a means of checking up on the Asdic operators. Altogether it was an interesting and instructive day. As we steamed into harbour, we went through all this standing to attention business again and finished the day by drawing up alongside a tanker for refuelling.

Peggy's birthday was on 21 August and I celebrated the occasion in true style. In fact, by the end of night there were very few people who didn't know that my-reason-for-living was having a birthday.

On 26 August, the CO decided that as Ron Roberts' boat, O, had been unserviceable since it arrived in Mombasa, he and Eric Saunders would share Q, with Ron operating Q for the next eighty hours' flying. Ron's boat had been beached and was being repaired using parts taken from Ken Murray's J, which was also unserviceable.

Eric Saunders was sent to Pamanzi, leaving me in Mombasa. One day I went up as a passenger in Q, with Ron Roberts as captain and Ted Taylor as second pilot, to do some photography. Flight Sergeant Vincent was the camera operator and I acted as bomb-aimer or 'guider' over the area. We were up for an hour and five minutes and it nearly proved to be the last flight for the seventeen people on board. The first approach to alighting was ruined by a destroyer coming into harbour, so we went around again. Coming in a second time, Ted

Mombasa Harbour, with a Catalina and two Fleet Air Arm Walrus amphibians on the hardstand in June 1943. The congestion in the harbour can be seen, with many ships of varying sizes and a 209 Squadron Catalina moored. Flying boats had to contend with this congestion while taking off and alighting and this could be hazardous. The Catalina on the hardstand was 209/J. It was being used for spare parts to keep 209/O operational. It was subsequently made serviceable. (Eric Saunders)

The 104-foot wingspan of the Catalina dwarfs that of the two Fleet Air Arm Walrus amphibians nestled each side of it. The man standing behind the port engine shows how large the propellers were. (Eric Saunders)

didn't throttle back enough and we sailed on just above the water for nearly a mile. When she did hit the water, it came with such a heavy thud that we bounced right off. I heard the engines roar madly and looked out to see the starboard float almost amongst the rigging of a hospital ship. Ron said afterwards that he didn't know how we missed it. It was only by madly dipping the port wing that we got away with it.

I was duty captain on 2 September, when at a couple of minutes to three there was a terrific bang. I looked up to see 209/P VA727 enveloped in a cloud of spray. The first bang was instantly followed by a second, a third, and a fourth. P was hurled into the air as four of her depth charges exploded. She broke in half. Flames spread quickly and reached from the moorings almost to the shore. The whole station tore along to see what was happening. Tragically, Sergeant Dawson and Corporal Hughes of the rigging section were on board. A dinghy had taken them out and was going to wait alongside. However, Dawson told the dinghy driver he needn't wait. The dinghy had gone about 30 yards from P when the first depth charge exploded. The fire died down after ten minutes, but began again shortly after and burned for another hour. The first item to be recovered was a Mae West[15] and the mascot, a little black stuffed dog. Later, navigation books were recovered and, perhaps strangest of all, the fitter's chair. As this was metal, we thought it was blown rather than washed ashore. The two riggers would not have known much. As there was a danger posed by the unexploded depth charges, I sent a seaplane tender on patrol to keep any small boats from venturing nearer than 200 yards. The tragedy was caused by a faulty set of bomb racks and releases. After the disaster, the Air Ministry grounded all Canadian-built Catalina Mark IIs fitted with American bomb racks. The Wing Commander tasked me with getting the naval people cracking on the salvage of P in the hope some of it would be useable. Unfortunately, the engines were not, as they had been in the water too long. Two naval officers from HMS *Valiant* conferred with me and after being told of the possibility of unexploded depth charges, they were not too anxious to recommend diving operations. The navy succeeded in dragging most of P into shallow water. The parts recovered included the port wing, which was split in many places, and that portion of the hull aft of the bunk compartment. However, the navy failed to make the mooring safe for shipping, because they were unable to recover the starboard wing with the unexploded depth charges.

Two days after the tragedy, the bodies of the two lads were washed up. Both had been killed by concussion and had died instantly. As one was a Roman Catholic and the other an Anglican, there were two funerals held the same day. Walking behind the coffins was not so hot as they stank to high heaven.

On 8 September, the squadron was struck by another tragedy. Catalina L VA713 crashed on take-off from Pamanzi. Flight Lieutenant Wyllie, Flying Officer Rich, Pilot Officer Henderson, Pilot Officer Hall, and Sergeants Broomfield, Lamond, White, Aberley, Sheppard,

Funeral service for either Sergeant Dawson or Corporal Hughes, who were killed when 209/P was destroyed by depth charges on 2 September 1942 in Mombasa Harbour. (Bruce Daymond)

and Davies were all listed as missing, believed killed. Subsequently, the bodies of Rich, Hall, Broomfield, White, and Davies were recovered. The aircraft started its take-off at 4.19 am with the engines running smoothly. When the aircraft passed the last flare, it appeared airborne. Then the tail light went out and the engines cut. A few seconds later there were five explosions and the petrol caught fire. While searching for the bodies, John Wyllie was found. However, when his Mae West was grabbed, it became detached and his body sank.

The adjutant, the intelligence officer, and I spent the afternoon of L's crash going through the kit of the four officers killed. It was a pathetic job looking through their letters to see if there was any relevant service matter in them. In Ken Rich's case, the mother of a lad with whom he trained wrote to Ken's mother saying that her son had been killed and that she'd like Ken to know. Poor old Trapper Henderson had a letter from his mother, the same sort of loving letter

Left: Pilot Officer Eric Hall (RAF). *Right:* Pilot Officer Frank (Trapper) Henderson (RCAF). They were killed on 8 September 1942, when Canadian-built Catalina Mark IIA 209/L, RAF serial VA713, captained by Flight Lieutenant John Wyllie crashed on take-off from Pamanzi, killing all on board. (Bruce Daymond)

we all receive from mothers, asking him to take care of himself. Because the bodies of the remainder weren't recovered, they were posted officially as, 'Missing, believed killed.' This was cruel to their families for it allowed them to entertain false hope whereas the rest of us knew they were dead.

One night after this accident I saw the film *Saturday's Children*, a story of a young married couple who didn't have much money, with the husband going into the office day after day and getting nowhere. It set me thinking about the future. We were all hoping like hell for peace to come so we could go back to civvy life. But what would peace have to offer? In the majority of cases, nothing but a dull grinding routine that stamps out all initiative. Tied down by family responsibilities and not being able to do as one wants. Grouse as we did about service life, there was no denying that it had excitements to offer, and not only in wartime. Even in peacetime, squadrons were moved around the world. One could see interesting places. We were doing that, but were not really satisfied. I wondered if one ever strikes a happy balance. The old saying 'distant fields look greener' was only too true. But perhaps this restlessness was something brought on by the war: or was it a phase of youth? All these years later, I still don't know.

One day I managed to arrange a flight with Sub Lieutenant Richardson in a Fleet Air Arm Blackburn Skua (L2973) practicing dive bombing. I was issued with a parachute and strapped into the back seat, which faced aft. We did nine dive bombing practices from 4,000 feet, descending at 210 knots. At the start of each dive Richardson throttled the motor back, dropped the left wing, and, whizz, I was hurtling down backwards. The pull-out glued me firmly to the seat. From my position the target ship seemed to be right underneath the aircraft before the dive was done.

With time on our hands, I often had discussions with some of the lads, Barry, Mecklem, and Roberts, in particular, about the war and its aftermath. I wrote at the time:

> Suppose, for instance, that peace were declared tomorrow and that we were all home within a month. After the joy of being with parents, wives and friends was over, how long would it be before we all became as dissatisfied and restless as hell? Wanting to get back to the companionship of the war? I don't think it would be very long – say about six weeks. And what is one going to do with the rest of one's life, once peace comes? Going back to ordinary, humdrum, everyday jobs is going to be very difficult for many thousands. The idea of going back to a desk in the

> Accounts Department of Qantas just fills me with horror. I couldn't stick it. And there would be thousands like me. What are we all going to do? Of course such situations arose after the last war – the problem was there but the solutions were not always happy. These things make one think and think deeply. In fact they're rather terrifying. The future is not bright.

With the detachment at Pamanzi concluding, Q and S returned to Mombasa and we got Q back from Ron Roberts. We were sent out to search for a submarine which had been sighted not far from Mombasa. Des Hosking came along as third pilot and it was just as well he did for when we plugged in 'George,' the aircraft did a violent dive. We twiddled the up knob, but this only resulted in steepening the dive. We tested it a few times, always with the same result. It meant we had to fly the bitch all night, taking an hour each at the controls. At about 10.30 pm the radar packed up. We left it for half an hour and then tested it again with the same result. We eventually received a message from the operations room to cease the patrol and land at Dar-es-Salaam. We set course and crossed over Zanzibar. Eric pulled off a fine landing by the flares at 2.15 am. We returned to Mombasa the next day.

John Inglis and his crew in S struck trouble on a transit flight from Mombasa to Durban. They were forced to land on a lake north-east of Lourenço Marques in neutral Portuguese East Africa on 13 October. S was holed and ended up in 5 feet of water. The crew destroyed the radar, all other secret equipment, and the code books. John and his crew were picked up by a BOAC boat which was on a test run and they were taken to Durban. There was a bit of a stink as the crew should have been interned by the Portuguese.

On 13 October, we flew Q to Kisumu for a major overhaul. We had no navigator, so I looked after that department. We climbed to 12,000 feet and set course for Mount Kilimanjaro. We saw it from

Mark I Catalina 209/S, AH543, captained by John Inglis, force-landed on a lake north-east of Lourenço Marques on 13 October 1942 while on transit to Durban. As this was neutral Portuguese territory, the aircraft was taken over by the local authorities. A full account of this episode is given in *Wings of the Dawning* by Arthur Banks. The aircraft was camouflaged and lacked the squadron code letters, WQ. (Eric Saunders)

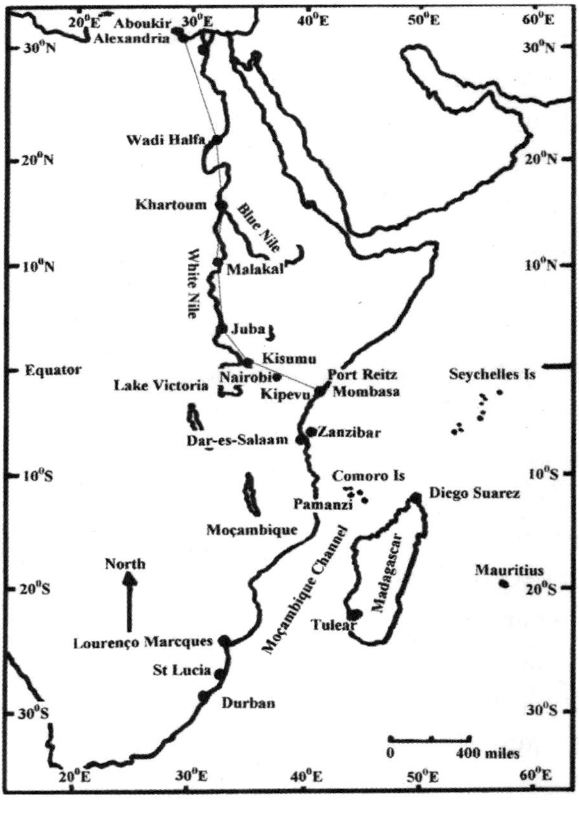

The East African coast and Indian Ocean, showing locations mentioned in text. The thin line indicates the approximate track of 209/Q on the African part of its transit from Pembroke Dock, via Gibraltar and Aboukir, to Mombasa. The strategic importance of the Comoro Islands in relation to control of the Moçambique Channel is obvious.

nearly 100 miles away. It looked magnificent: a solitary peak rearing high above the sea of cumulus cloud. It was truly a grand sight with its snow-capped peak and I made good use of my camera.

Having handed Q over to the maintenance people, Eric and I went on leave by train to Nairobi, where we stayed at Torr's Hotel. We met up with the two South African Air Force types we brought up from Dar-es-Salaam to Mombasa the previous week, and had a session from 12 to 2 pm with them. They arranged some women for us that night. We went out to the WAAF (Women's Auxiliary Air Force) mess for a few drinks before going to the dinner dance at Torr's Hotel. The lass I was with was in the Women's Territorial Service. She was the answer to months on a desert island, thank God!

We had two days in Nairobi, sightseeing and generally enjoying ourselves. We then took a train to Molo, where a colleague had arranged for us to stay with Mrs Molly Ryan, an Australian, who lived there with Tony, her 6 foot 4 inch Irish husband, a bloody fine bloke. They regularly hosted Australian service people at their home, *Garryowen*. During our leave we walked, and played tennis, and played golf on the course reputed to be the highest in the British Empire at 9,000 feet. All three activities left us extremely puffed because of the altitude, and prone to falling asleep after lunch. We also socialised, went to the cinema, went horse riding, played poker, and read a lot. One of the books I read was Philip Gibbs' 1942 novel *The Long Alert*. It was an account of a Canadian soldier's life in England while waiting for the invasion. He falls in love with a married woman, though married himself. As I wrote at the time: 'Many of the situations reminded me only too vividly of my lot. Darling Peggy, God knows she's never out of my mind for an hour. How soon will I forget her, as forget her I must?'

On returning to Kisumu, we took Q and headed for Mombasa. We flew over Lake Victoria, fired 700 rounds into the water, shot up Kisumu, and then set course for Molo. We shot up the Ryans'

Left: Molly and Tony Ryan hosted service personnel on leave at their home in Molo, Kenya. (Eric Saunders)

Below: Molly and Tony Ryan's house, *Garryowen*, Molo, Kenya. (Eric Saunders)

Eric Saunders and Bruce Daymond hamming it up at Molo, Kenya. (Eric Saunders)

Above left: Molly Ryan and Bruce Daymond at Molo railway station, Kenya, 31 October 1942. (Eric Saunders)

Above right: Eric Saunders standing on the port horizontal stabilizer of 209/Q in Durban Harbour. Note the pull-out steps either side of the vertical stabilizer, and the Catalina moored astern of Q. (Eric Saunders)

house, threw a message to them, then set course for Mombasa. I was delighted to find a huge wallop of mail waiting for me in Mombasa: twenty letters, five cables, three parcels, and six newspapers.

In early November we took off to join a detachment in Durban, South Africa. We flew via Pamanzi, taking Tom Cairns as third pilot. He was charged with conducting a reconnaissance of St Lucia Bay, north of Durban, to assess its suitability for squadron operations. At Pamanzi I got an awful fright when I moved the boat from the refuelling buoy to a mooring buoy. I was in charge of the move, with a crew of Tom Cairns, Sergeant Howell, and a maintenance type. We missed the buoy on the first approach, but failed to retrieve the drogues[16] before the next approach to the buoy as the trip lines were well and truly wound round the main line. The boat headed for the

Detail under the starboard wing of 209/Q from the blister compartment. From left to right are the struts supporting the main plane, four depth charges, and the radar array. (Eric Saunders)

shore fast and full port engine was just enough to counteract the cross-wind and the drogues. I thought that the drogues would break at any minute, but fortunately they didn't. Once out in the open water, it took us nearly quarter of an hour to recover them.

We flew to Durban on 5 November, taking Flight Sergeant Vincent with us as he was not improving in the hospital at Pamanzi. It was hoped that a stay in a big hospital at Durban plus a change of climate would fix him up. Eric did the take-off, which was his first fully laden night take-off and my first in a flying boat. The flare path consisted of three flares 700 yards apart. We taxied the length of the flare path, then beyond the last flare before turning to take off. We were airborne by the second flare, circled back over the island, set course, and climbed to 5,000 feet. We made landfall about an hour's flying north of Durban. We circled the city and landed in what we thought was the correct channel. On alighting, a launch whizzed up alongside, threw us a towline, told us to switch off our engines, and they towed us to the BOAC moorings. Evidently, we had only 3 feet 6 inches of water under our keel and it was high tide. If we stayed there, we would have been stranded when the tide went out.

On arriving in Durban, we were told we had four days of operations. We felt it was about time work came our way. The next day I was struck with 'The shits' – and how! I couldn't go out on operations. A medical officer bunged me into Addington Military Hospital. After ten days in hospital I was discharged. I moved from the Royal Hotel to the RAF officers' mess in town at Congella. Our boats were all moored at Salisbury Island in Durban Harbour. The Congella mess was convenient for going out to dinner, cinema, night clubs, etc. Salisbury Island was not, as it was in the middle of Durban Harbour and used to be a holiday resort. All the RAF types were billeted in what must have been quite a nice beach cottage before the war. The aircraft were moored outside the back door of the cottage, which faced out across the harbour to the city. Squadron Leader Barraclough was housed in a doll-like house which served as an orderly room with Bungey Hart as adjutant.

We took off on 20 November to search for a ship believed to have been torpedoed off Lourenço Marques. We did a square search, but found no signs of wreckage. While we were out, Ken Murray and his crew in J had a good day. They were on an anti-submarine patrol and came across a large patch of red oil, wreckage, and four rafts, three of which contained survivors. They dropped their aircraft's rubber dinghy as one of the rafts appeared to be in a bad condition. They also dropped seven Mae Wests, biscuits, and a 2-gallon tin of water. The survivors were rescued by a destroyer the next day. This was the first bit of joy the squadron had had for ages.

The next day we took off to search for survivors of the SS *Scottish Chief*,[17] a tanker that had been torpedoed two days earlier. After doing many legs of a square search, we sighted two rafts tied together. The five survivors waved like blazes and all appeared to be fit. Fortunately, a convoy we sighted earlier was only 8–10 miles away so we were able to signal the position of the rafts to HMS *Jasmine*, the convoy escort. We flew back and forth from the corvette to the rafts to give moral support to the survivors and to lead the *Jasmine* to the rafts. We photographed the survivors in the rafts and again when they were beside the corvette. We felt we had done something worthwhile at last. These five survivors, together with the seven located by Ken Murray and his crew, were the only survivors of the twenty-six crew of the *Scottish Chief*.

Subsequently, we received a copy of the message to our HQ from the captain of the *Jasmine*.

> FROM: CO HMS *JASMINE*
> DATE: 29 NOVEMBER 1942
> TO: STAFF OFFICER AIR INTELLIGENCE Ref No 78/12
>
> Very many thanks for the photographs you sent me of *Jasmine* rescuing survivors. They are of great interest to the ship and I would like to say how grateful we were for the magnificent assistance given by the Catalina aircraft and would ask you to convey our congratulations to them for their fine work in finding the rafts.
>
> (Sgd) Cecil D.B. Coventry
> Lieut Cdr RNR Rtd

The next day we searched for survivors of the SS *Dornington Castle*. We took extra water cans, which we were to drop if we sighted them.

Five survivors of the torpedoed tanker SS *Scottish Chief* awaiting rescue by the Flower class corvette HMS *Jasmine*. The survivors had spent two and a half days on the rafts. Catalina 209/Q led the corvette to the rafts and circled them as they were rescued on 21 November 1942. (Eric Saunders)

Survivors of SS *Scottish Chief* being taken aboard HMS *Jasmine* (K23), 21 November 1942. (Eric Saunders)

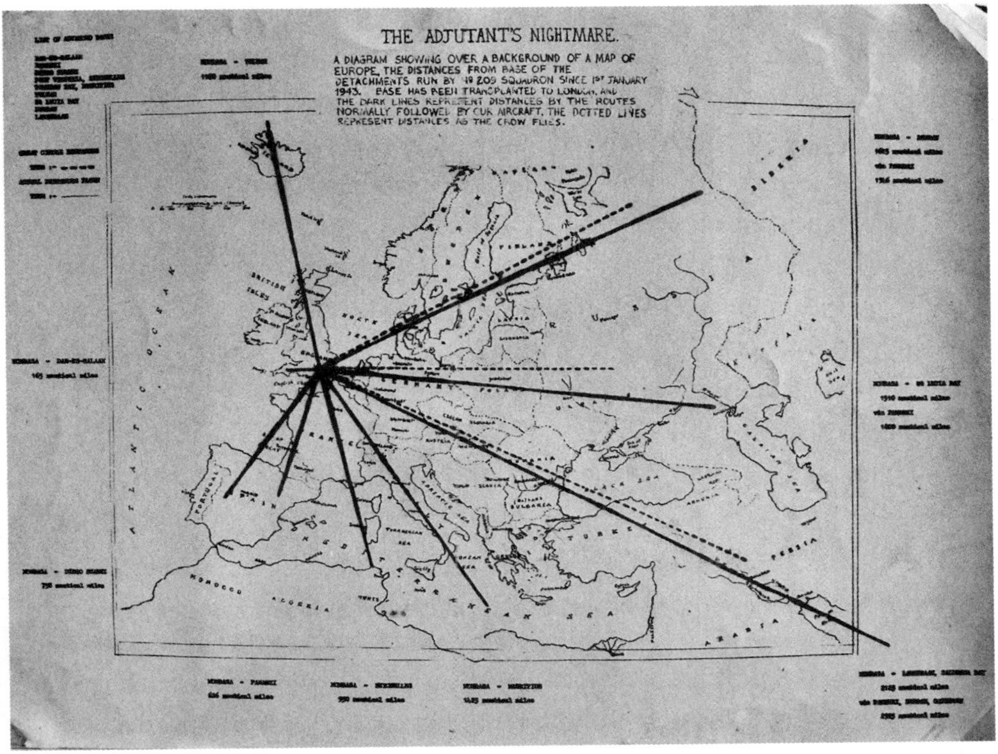

'The Adjutant's Nightmare. A diagram showing over a background of a map of Europe, the distances from Base of the detachments run by No. 209 Squadron since 1st January 1943. Base has been transplanted to London, and the dark lines represent distances by the routes normally followed by our aircraft, the dotted lines represent distances as the crow flies.' The text around the sides of the figure starting at the top left-hand corner and working anti-clockwise reads: 'List of advanced bases: Dar-es-Salaam, Pamanzi, Diego Suarez, Port Victoria, Seychelles, Tombeau Bay, Mauritius, Tulear, St Lucia Bay, Durban, Langebaan. Great Circle Distances Thus – dotted lines: Actual Distances Flown Thus – unbroken lines. Mombasa – Dar-es-Salaam 165 nautical miles. Mombasa – Diego Suarez 758 nautical miles. Mombasa – Pamanzi 626 nautical miles. Mombasa – Seychelles 950 nautical miles. Mombasa – Mauritius 1,425 nautical miles. Mombasa – Langebaan, Saldhama Bay 2,125 via Pamanzi, Durban, Cape Town 2,925 nautical miles. Mombasa – St Lucia Bay 1,510 nautical miles via Pamanzi 1,800 nautical miles. Mombasa – Durban 1,625 nautical miles via Pamanzi 1,546 nautical miles. Mombasa – Tulear 1,180 nautical miles.' (Eric Saunders)

Off we stooged and searched, but saw bugger all. After an hour in the air we received a signal from base telling us to land and spend the night at St Lucia Bay. This would give us an extra hour in the search area. I was wild about this, for about twenty minutes before we were ordered to take off, I had arranged to take Jean Williams to dinner and a dance. I was unable to cancel it before we left. There were no moorings so we had to anchor. While the rest of the crew whizzed off to the Estuary Hotel, about 12 miles away, Thomas, Maguire, Richardson, and I stayed aboard on anchor watch.

We got back to Durban to find a huge load of mail for us. There were thirty-one letters for me, the most ever at one time. I was able to make it up to Jean Williams and fixed a date in lieu of the previous night's failure. Jean was the most marvellous dancer I had ever been with. She was as light as a feather.

We were off in Q at dawn on 29 November on an anti-submarine patrol and shipping reconnaissance off Lourenço Marques. We picked up a convoy off Inhaca Island and did an anti-submarine sweep ahead of the convoy. A couple of hours into the flight, we received a signal from base asking us to tell the ships to keep together as there would be a destroyer meeting them before dark. We met the I class destroyer HMS *Inconstant* off St Lucia Bay at about 4 pm. She was going flat out and looked a lovely sight. It was a 13-hour trip, giving me a total of 466 hours on Catalinas, of which 113 were on operations.

On 1 December, Q and N conducted an anti-submarine sweep to look for the U-boat that had torpedoed the troop ship *Llandaff Castle*[18] the previous day. We took off at 6 pm along Maydon Channel, and turned on the step along Maydon Wharf with a 2-mile take-off run. We began our square search off Delagoa Bay. The navigator found on about the second or third leg that an astro fix had put us nearly 60 miles from his dead reckoning position. We altered course, trusting his fix, and eventually came out exactly where we should have been. We didn't see a bloody thing all night. The moon rose about 2 am and provided damned good light for searching. We arrived back

SS *Adviser* in Durban Harbour. It was torpedoed by *U-178* on 15 November 1942 and escorted for 11 hours by 209/Q, captained by Eric Saunders. The temporary repairs with wood and other material can be seen in the gaping side. Bruce Daymond was in hospital at the time and not on this flight. (Bruce Daymond)

at Durban about 8 am to find cloud right down on the deck. After stooging about for some time, we eventually landed outside the boom in the open sea. There was quite a swell running and we bounced about five times on alighting.

Catalinas 209/N, VA715 (Catalina Mark IIA), on the beach, and 209/K W8428, moored in Durban Harbour. A man is working on the hull at the bow of N. The boats could be beached, worked on, and re-floated by the tide without having to use a slipway and beaching gear. Heavy oil stains can be seen on the main plane behind each engine. This staining was characteristic of the reliable Pratt & Whitney Twin Wasp air-cooled radial engines. (Eric Saunders)

Whenever we got the opportunity, we socialised as much as we could, partied at private houses, went to night clubs, the country club, the cinema, played golf, swimming, shopping, etc. The Durban locals were very friendly and hospitable.

We were despatched on 12 December to find a U-boat believed to be heading south from Lourenço Marques. Intelligence thought it was moving to intercept a convoy leaving Lourenço Marques and to get amongst one leaving Durban on 14 December. We took off at 6.45 pm and ran into equipment trouble. Both generators packed up, making it impossible to carry out the radar sweep or use the radio and the stove. By starting the auxiliary power unit, we used the radio to get a message to base. We received a signal from base telling us to discontinue the patrol as it was a waste of time without radar and to land at St Lucia Bay. We had to wait, circling St Lucia for quite a while, as the flare path wasn't ready. We all slept on board so it was easy to get away first thing. After taxiing back on the step for take-off, I closed the throttles, let her swing into wind and then opened up for take-off. The engines roared but we didn't move. We were stuck on a sandbank! On an even keel we must have had just a few inches clearance, but when pulling the stick back and opening the throttles the tail went down and we stuck fast. However, by letting her come back on an even keel, we were able to taxi off. We got back to Durban quickly and moored up, but the pennant became detached from the buoy and a few minutes later we found ourselves drifting gently towards the shore. We were saved by the bomb scow. As Q was due for an eighty-hour inspection, we just taxied her onto the beach.

After her inspection we couldn't do a flight test as a washer on the priming pump had broken and maintenance had sent to Pretoria for a replacement. With no washer, it was impossible to get any petrol on to the cylinder walls for priming. Eric got hold of a cork from a beer bottle top and made a temporary repair washer so we were able to get off an hour or so later. We diced around for an hour or so, did a bit of low flying over the water, and the crew fired off 100 rounds from each gun.

On 20 December we investigated a suspected convoy of thirty to thirty-eight ships reported south-east of Port Elizabeth. We headed south over land. The country was lovely with huge gorges, from which up-currents every so often tossed the aircraft around no end. We had been out about an hour when we got recalled to base.

We turned for home at Point St John and from there on we were flying for pleasure, rather than for operations. We gave a couple of members of the crew some dual flying and then we indulged in low flying along the beaches, being waved at and waving to everyone we

A Fleet Air Arm Walrus about to alight near a Catalina moored in Durban Harbour. The Catalina is armed with six depth charges and the propellers are correctly positioned. (Bruce Daymond)

passed. Base didn't know exactly why we had been recalled but it looked as if someone in naval headquarters had 'boobed' badly. We guessed that the 'enemy' convoy was one of ours which some clot had forgotten to check up on while it was in his sector.

Rolf Luck and I were tasked on 23 December with organising the crews of Q and N for an evening work party to unload a bomb scow bringing equipment from Salisbury Island to the pier on the mainland. I asked Flight Sergeant Vincent to pass the order to the two crews. Vincent came back at 5.30 pm to tell me that the crews of Q and N were not coming. They told him they knocked off at 5 pm. He should have put them on a charge but didn't. I told him to tell both crews to be on the pier at 6 pm otherwise there would be trouble. At 6 pm only Q's crew arrived. Bill Hossent then put N's crew under open arrest. The charge was heard the next day by Wing Commander Barraclough and the crew were remanded for a hearing by the Group Captain. The sergeants' point of view was that for months they had been asked to do manual tasks such as unloading boats, etc., while airmen were doing nothing. In this there was some truth, for in not many places would one see a sight like the unloading of the scow the previous evening, when six officers and eight senior NCOs humped stuff around while a leading aircraftman sat in the front seat of the truck.

We flew Q to St Lucia on 28 December. I did the heavy load take-off; it was quite a fair one. However, my landing at St Lucia was far from good. We shot up the Estuary Hotel and then flew at zero feet up to the moorings, 13 miles north. En route we saw two lots of hippos wallowing in the river. I spent the night on anchor watch with sergeants Howell, Stoner, and Richardson.

The next day we took off at 9 am on an escort of a troop-carrying convoy. We had a full operational load of eight depth charges and 1,450 gallons of petrol. We set course eastwards to meet the 'boys up north'. They were nearly 500 miles out to sea and we expected to contact them at 2.30 pm. However, the convoy was not in the position given and it was almost 4 pm before we sighted them. There were only two troop

Durban Harbour, late 1942. The aircraft from which this photograph was taken was departing, flying over the harbour mouth. Salisbury Island is on the left of the photograph. Note the shipping, through which flying boats had to take off and land. (Eric Saunders)

transports, but how they were escorted! Two cruisers – HMS *Gambia* (Fiji class) and HMS *Frobisher* (Hawkins class) – two destroyers, and one corvette. We did our anti-submarine patrol around the ships until 11.30 pm, when we set course for home. There would have been some very happy people in the Union of South Africa if they knew how close to home these lads of the 1st South African Division were. The division had been fighting in North Africa for two and a half years.

We ran into dirty weather on the way home, with lightning everywhere. As it was unsafe to land at St Lucia, we received a message from base to stay up till dawn, instead of our scheduled time of arrival of 3.30 am. In order to conserve fuel, we jettisoned our depth charges from 5,000 feet. With 27 inches of boost and

A fine profile view of Squadron Leader Barraclough's 209/M off East Africa. The serial number VA703 shows clearly, as does the aircraft's letter M. The squadron code letters WQ are on the hull in the shade of the main plane. On the bottom of the fuselage, below the letter V of the serial number, the attachment for the aft mooring lines can be seen. The aircraft was not carrying depth charges. The stern of the flying boat's hull is directly below the rear of the blister and this was known as the step. (Eric Saunders)

1,650 revolutions, we hung in the air as slowly as we could, using only 41 gallons of petrol an hour. This was excellent consumption for a big flying boat. A few hours later we received another message from base to say that St Lucia was now OK for landing. So, we set course and landed at 5.25 am after twenty-one hours in the air. We had a spot of fun before touching down. We got mixed up in an electrical storm with lightning and driving rain. We had a purplish glow of St Elmo's fire off the end of the radar aerials. We spent the night at the Estuary Hotel, St Lucia, and then had to return to Durban as a battery had burst during our flight and we needed more depth charges, and also a piece of Perspex for one of the blisters.

When we got back to Durban, Flight Lieutenant Forgham, the station engineering officer, examined Q's starboard float. The bushings were badly worn and the float rattled. Forgham thought she was safe enough for flying in the short term, but he doubted whether she would get to the next major inspection, about 130 flying hours away, without our having trouble with the float. Q was one of the first Catalinas delivered to the RAF. She had operated with 209 Squadron in Iceland before we took her over, so after heavy operational use, she was tired and in need of major work, including a new set of engines.

Having tried unsuccessfully to get into the Stardust Club, I spent New Year's Eve with Ron Roberts, Jo Thorpe, and Dot Parker at Jo's flat on the Berea. At about 3 am on New Year's Day, Ron, Jo, Dot, and I made another assault on the Stardust Club and this time we were successful. We danced until about 5.15 am, when the

Port oblique view of 209/Q moored at Salisbury Island, Durban. Mooring lines are attached to the bow and the port float. The anchor compartment is open. A man is sitting on the rigger's scaffolding. The round marking on the hull below the cockpit window is the Donald Duck mascot. The camouflage paint can be seen on Q and K, the boat moored astern. (Eric Saunders)

209/Q moored at Salisbury Island, Durban. Mooring lines are attached under the tailplane, and from the bow and port float. The loop antenna can be seen between the engine nacelles on the top of the main plane and the extension mechanism for the port float can be seen. Note that the blister compartment is open. Part of RAF serial Z2142 can be can be seen below the tailplane. The aircraft's squadron individual code Q is obvious. (Bruce Daymond)

powers-that-be turned on two shockingly bright lights as a signal for everyone to go home. Dot and I went back to her flat, woke up Ginger, her husband, and the three of us had a welcome breakfast of bacon and eggs. I picked up Ron at the Mayfair and we reached camp about 8.15 am. New Year's Eve was quite a contrast to last year, when I went to bed at 10 pm aboard the little Swedish ship *Gdynia*, anchored just off Liverpool.

In early January we flew back to St Lucia. While there, we stayed at the Estuary Hotel, 12 miles from Eastern Shore, where the boats were moored. The road between the two consisted of two-wheel tracks only, running over swamp-like ground. It was so bad the journey took an hour. Refuelling arrangements at St Lucia were not as primitive as Wadi Halfa, where we used 4-gallon tins and native labour. At St Lucia, the bomb scow was loaded with ten 44-gallon drums and the fuel was put into the aircraft using two hand rotary pumps, again with native labour.

It was a fisherman's paradise. Rolf Luck and I took a boat around to the estuary to do some unsuccessful shark fishing. On the way, we saw a large crocodile waddle off the mud flat into the water. It stayed there, with just a portion of its head above water, and fixed us with a glassy stare. We wandered a couple of hundred yards up the beach and had a surf. It wasn't a good surf for the beach was too steeply sloping. We both got terribly sunburnt.

We set off from St Lucia in Q on 11 January on a convoy escort patrol for the troop transport *Nieuw Amsterdam*. I did the heavy take-off with 1,450 gallons of petrol on board. Apart from a rather shaky period, when the starboard wingtip looked as if it might go into the water, my take-off was more or less OK. On our way we had a scare. I was in charge when suddenly a huge air bubble appeared on the surface. This was quickly followed by a long brown shape. For a second or two we thought it was a U-boat and on went the bomb selector switches. However, we soon saw that it was an extremely large whale. We found the *Nieuw Amsterdam* at 6.15 pm. She had no escort and was doing about 22 knots. We escorted her until about 1 am, when we headed for St Lucia. The weather for the whole time we were in the air was absolutely wizard. Dawn came up about 5 am and it was lovely. The dark first changed to grey, and then quickly through pale pink to bright red. It was more like a sunset than a dawn. We landed at 6.30 am after twenty hours in the air.

To help ferry squadron personnel, the Fleet Air Arm had loaned the squadron an amphibian Supermarine Walrus, X5900, flown by Sub Lieutenant Jimmy McIvor. It was a fun machine and we all itched to fly it rather than be passengers. It was very useful at St Lucia as it spared us the ghastly commute by truck. On our return from our *Nieuw Amsterdam* escort, the Walrus flew in piloted by Jeep Balfour and John Barraclough and did some terrific shooting up. It came down over us many times. On one occasion, a float cleared our heads by no more than 18 inches. We had previously resolved not to duck

Eric Saunders' crew in Durban. Left to right: Sergeant Stoner (wireless operator), Sergeant Thomas (engineer), Sergeant Richardson (rigger), Sergeant Woolley (wireless operator/mechanic), Sergeant Maguire (wireless operator), Flight Sergeant Vincent (navigator), and Bruce Daymond. (Eric Saunders)

for we knew that was what Jeep and Barra were trying to make us do. It took three ferry trips to get our crew back to the hotel.

The next day we took off at 9 pm to escort the *Nieuw Amsterdam*. Jimmy McIvor came with us. We found her two hours out of St Lucia, escorted by two destroyers. It was a lovely moonlit night, in which the silhouettes of the ships were plainly seen. Some cumulus cloud came in after a time and we climbed to 4,500 feet to carry out our patrols, which were forty-minute left and right-hand circuits above

Crew of 209/Q in Durban Harbour. Flight Sergeant Vincent (navigator), Sergeant Stoner (wireless operator), Sergeant Woolley (wireless operator/mechanic), Bruce Daymond, Sergeant Richardson (rigger), unidentified, Sergeant Fulton (rigger), Sergeant Maguire (wireless operator), and Sergeant Howell (engineer). Both Sergeant Richardson and Bruce Daymond are holding their mascots. A waterproof aluminium Catalina case is sitting on the hatch. (Eric Saunders)

Ken Murray's crew of 209/J in Durban. Back row left to right: unidentified, Rolf Luck (second pilot), Ken Murray (aircraft captain), Bungey Hart (navigator), unidentified. Front row: unidentified, unidentified, unidentified, unidentified. (Eric Saunders)

the ships. At that height the ships' wakes showed clearly. We stayed with the convoy all night and escorted it into Durban. When we landed at Congella at 8.15 am, we had logged thirty-one and a half hours escorting the *Nieuw Amsterdam*.

When not on duty, I lazed around reading, writing letters, bringing my diary up to date, swimming, playing golf, liaising with the navy and drinking in their wardrooms, catching up with Dot Parker, Jo Thorpe and other locals, and visiting hotels and night clubs, particularly the Stardust.

We were supposed to take Q to St Lucia, but the starboard engine would not start. Water was coming through the carburettor so we tried switching to cross-feed to locate the trouble but with no success. The faulty carburettor was badly corroded as a result of the strainer

SS *Nieuw Amsterdam*, carrying more than 6,000 troops. Photograph taken on 11 January 1943 from 209/Q. (Eric Saunders)

cock not having been drained regularly. With fuel tanks half full, there was a lot of condensation inside and the water needed to be drained off. The strainer cock had been stuck for months and despite it having been put on the engineer's sheet on the last two eighty-hourly inspections, it had not been attended to. The carburettor was serviced and the engine started but only ran on the fuel from the priming. No petrol from the carburettor was getting through. The carburettor was taken off again and sent to the workshops to have the trouble located.

The engineers took it to pieces and found further defects and poor old Q was unserviceable. She was beached at Salisbury Island while her carburettor was being repaired. While she was beached, her hull was scraped. The quantity of barnacles removed from her hull would have slowed our take-off runs by seconds. There we were with plenty of land time and no aircraft to relieve the boredom.

The saga of Q's maintenance continued. A new carburettor sent from Mombasa was the wrong type, so the engineers took the rubber diaphragms out of the new one and put them into the faulty one. However, the old bitch still refused to start. The engineer officer

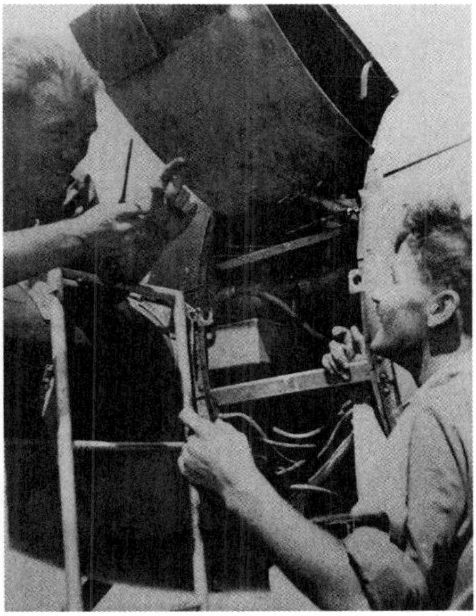

Above left: Sergeant Thomas, engineer in 209/Q, looking out of the window of the engineer's station in the pylon between the hull and the main plane. (Eric Saunders)

Above right: Sergeant Howell (engineer, 209/Q) talking things over with Corporal Strachan (maintenance section) while working on Q's port Pratt & Whitney Twin Wasp radial engine in Durban, December 1942. Note the scaffolding attached to the main plane to allow access to the engine while the boat was on the water. (Bruce Daymond)

thought the spark plugs were oiled up so he had those in the lower cylinders changed. Still no joy, and what was more, there was no fuel pressure. All the plugs were changed. After changing the plugs, we ran both engines, using the port fuel pump to get the starboard engine going. The carburettor was adjusted correctly, but the fuel pump was giving trouble. On being dismantled, the vanes were found to be rusty.

The plume astern this 209 Squadron Catalina indicates she was taking off. Both floats are just off the water and are about to be raised in the standard British technique, unlike the American technique, which involved raising the floats after the aircraft left the water. (Eric Saunders)

All Catalinas carried rubber dinghies. One day I suggested to Eric Saunders that we should do a dinghy drill. So, after lunch, aboard the aircraft, Q's crew stripped to underpants or bathing togs. After the 'abandon aircraft' signal was given, we all went to the blister compartment to prepare the dinghy. Sergeant Maguire unfortunately turned the inflation air bottle on before we had our dinghy over the side. The dinghy inflated while inside the aircraft and practically jammed the compartment. Had it been necessary to have left the aircraft, I'm afraid most of us would have been trapped inside.

I volunteered to go St Lucia in early February to stand by the flare path for a few days. I flew there with Jimmy McIvor in the Walrus. He let me fly it at zero feet most of the way. With little to do, I went for a walk one afternoon to a local village and saw the human-driven ferry in action. This was an iron arrangement fixed to some overhead wires. About a dozen labourers were required to haul the thing across the river. It moved painfully slowly, especially when there was a

Left: Bruce Daymond on the port end of the main plane of 209/Q in Durban Harbour. The wing span of the Catalina was 104 feet. The canvas cover over the cockpit is obvious, as are the exhaust ports on top of each engine and the black oil stains behind each engine. Two men can be seen standing in the open port blister and there are two Catalinas moored behind. *Right:* Bruce Daymond standing on one of 209/Q's engines. He was about 1.8 metres tall and provides an indication of the size of the propellers. (Eric Saunders)

Left: The human-driven ferry at the Estuary, St Lucia, Zululand. *Right:* The Estuary Hotel, Zululand, February 1943. This was used as accommodation when operating from Lake St Lucia, 12 miles north of the hotel. (Bruce Daymond)

Rolf Luck with harpoon (left) and Jeep Balfour holding a revolver while shark fishing at St Lucia. (Eric Saunders)

cross-wind or a strong current. It took about twenty minutes to go 300 yards, if that. As Jack Whittaker said, 'After 2,000 years of progress it comes to this!' Being bored silly, I hitched a ride back to Durban in the Walrus.

After three happy months on detachment, with Q serviceable, we said farewell to the Union of South Africa on 8 February. Once in the air, we shot up the officers' mess and said farewell to Durban. We set course for Pamanzi and landed there after a twelve-hour flight.

The next day we flew to Mombasa. Sitting in the pilots' seats, Eric and I read books the whole way, except that after five hours out, I got so thoroughly brassed off that I took us down to the deck and indulged in a spot of low flying for a quarter of an hour or so. I did the landing at Mombasa and bounced. Among the gallery watching the landing was the CO, who asked 'if the wireless operator had landed it'.

Left: Bruce Daymond on the stern of one of the marine craft going out to lay the flare path before a night take-off from Pamanzi, July 1942. Great care was taken to clear all driftwood from the take-off path. *Right:* Bruce Daymond on the wharf at Pamanzi, August 1942. (Bruce Daymond)

Left: Left to right: Eric Saunders (with camera slung from his shoulder), Jack Whittaker, and Jeep Balfour. All three were wearing the baggy shorts known as Bombay bloomers. *Right:* Eric Saunders at the controls of 209/Q. He was wearing a Mae West life preserver. The hatch above the pilot opened by sliding it back. (Bruce Daymond)

As Q was due for her fourth major inspection not long after we returned to Mombasa, we flew her to Kisumu for maintenance and then went on leave. Eric and I were accompanied by Jack Whittaker, who had joined our crew as the navigator. We headed for Nairobi, where we stayed for a couple of days before going to Molo to stay with the Ryans. We took a passenger train to Nakuru, and then a slow goods train in which we rode in the smelly guard's van to Molo. It took three and a half hours to do the 30 miles to Molo.

We had a lovely, relaxing time at *Garryowen*. Once again, the Ryans were superb hosts. I lazed around, sorted out my photograph album, visited neighbours for drinks, read a lot of books, wrote letters, shopped, went horse riding, played golf, tennis and poker, and one day, together with Molly, I drove Tony and three of his friends out to a camp for a four-day fishing expedition.

Left: Bruce Daymond and Jack Whittaker. *Right:* Jack Whittaker and Eric Saunders. They were in the smelly guard's van in which they travelled at 10 miles per hour from Nakuru to Molo. (Bruce Daymond)

The rest of our crew were billeted around the Molo district. Sergeant Maguire told me that Q would not be finished her major inspection as her new engines had not arrived. Given the number of things that happened to Q, either on the ground or discovered on inspections, there was little doubt we were the luckiest Catalina crew flying. The engineers discovered on the latest major inspection that both fuel pumps were on the point of seizing: a fine thing to have happened on our way up from Durban, or anywhere in the air for that matter.

After a wonderful eleven days, we left the Ryans and returned to Kisumu. At Kisumu I heard that Mike Barry had passed through Kisumu the day before we arrived. He was off to England to do his captain's course. Tom Eakins, Barraclough's American second pilot, had left to join the US forces. I was cheesed off to hear of other second pilots leaving for their captain's courses and me with no clue when my turn would come.

Eric, Jack, a cypher type, and I were the only passengers on 1 March on the BOAC Empire class flying boat *Canopus*, G-ADHL, from Kisumu to Mombasa. There we found a new training programme

Above left: Bruce Daymond in the starboard blister of 209/Q. The pivot point for the Perspex blister can be seen to the left of his head. The main plane, one of its supporting struts, and the starboard engine can also be seen. *Above right:* Sergeant Richardson (rigger) in summer flying gear in the blister compartment of 209/Q. They were en route to Kisumu, February 1943. (Bruce Daymond)

Opposite above left: Sergeant Ginger Thomas (engineer) in the blister compartment of 209/Q, en route to Kisumu, February 1943. *Opposite above right:* Bruce Daymond in the second pilot's seat. The open cockpit hatch and the base of the pylon supporting the main plane can be seen at the top of the photograph. (Bruce Daymond)

Opposite below left: Refuelling 209/Q from a barge. The open hatches in the cockpit, the bow turret, and the mooring cleat (the two dark, triangular marks) on the chine, to the lower right of the photograph, can be seen. Sergeant Stoner is standing on the bow holding the fuel line. *Opposite below right:* Sergeant Richardson on the bow of 209/Q during refuelling. He is sitting on the canvas hatch cover because of the hot metal. The Donald Duck mascot below the cockpit window can be seen. (Bruce Daymond)

had been instigated with major changes in crews. Eric and I were separated. I became Bill Hossent's second pilot, Jack Kennedy, Bill's second pilot, joined Eric, and Sergeant Howell was transferred from Eric's to Bill's crew.

I wrote a two-page airgraph to Peggy, after writing to the family and Dot Parker. It was a year previously that I met Peggy and Nance Bond on Henley station. What an emotional shaking followed for Peggy and me. It hadn't died down by any means and I was sure it would flare up if we were ever to see each other again.

I was about to board the bomb scow to go swimming on 11 March when, from the duty captain's hut, an Aldis Lamp signal was flashed: 'Is Mangan there, strike alarm.' Ted was captain of the strike boat on which I was second pilot. I tore up to the flight commander's office and was told that there was a suspicious motor vessel off the coast and that we were to investigate. Further instructions would be flashed as we were running up the engines. We gathered the crew together, slipped moorings, and received an Aldis message to do an anti-submarine patrol off Mount Kilimanjaro and to return to base at once! It had been a test to see how quickly we could get organised.

At long bloody last, I was promoted to flying officer. My promotion was back-dated to 1 March last year. That meant I was due for twelve months' back pay. It also meant that I became due for promotion to flight lieutenant fourteen days earlier.

Ted Mangan and I, with the rest of the crew, were sent to Kisumu by train to bring K back to Mombasa. When we got to Kisumu, Eric Saunders and his crew were still waiting for Q to be serviceable. Ted and I took K for a test flight, but found the main pennant on the buoy and the aircraft pennant firmly wrapped around the cable of the buoy. Try as we could, we could not get it loose. Because of the fear of crocodiles, no one was keen on diving into the murky water. After lunch a power-boat towed the aircraft round the buoy a couple of times to free the pennants. The test flight turned out OK. Both Ted

Mount Kilimanjaro, East Africa, off the starboard side of 209/Q en route from Mombasa to Kisumu. Part of the aerial array can be seen under the main plane. (Eric Saunders)

and I did a landing and take-off. We flew K back to Mombasa using navigation of the crudest sort. We had no protractor to measure off the track, so we merely guessed it. We also had no deviation card for the compass. However, Mount Kilimanjaro provided a damned good landmark two hours out and we found ourselves dead on track.

One day, I had a good look over one of the new Catalinas with which the squadron was re-equipping. She was a Catalina Mark IB, 209/P FP273, and was assigned to Eric Saunders and his crew to replace tired old Q.[19] The new boats had ten bomb racks instead of eight and they had an opening window in the front windscreen. It also had a dead reckoning compass and the pilots' instrument panel was rearranged.

Doug Dolphin, of RAF 230 Squadron (flying Sunderlands), arrived from Dar-es-Salaam on 29 March. He was being sent to the

HMS *Blackmore*, a Type II Hunt class escort destroyer. Photograph taken from 209/Q while *Blackmore* was on convoy escort out of Durban, March–April 1943. (Eric Saunders)

UK to do his captain's course. I was told by the CO that I was also being sent to the UK.

On my last day with 209 Squadron, Eric Saunders took me up in P for a four-hour creeping-line-ahead patrol to allow me to get to 600 operational hours. I saw the two new drift recorders in action. They were the astigmatic and pelorus and the navigators swore by them. However, our navigator pulled a boner and f****d up the patrol by giving us a completely wrong course.

There was a hell of a piss-up in the mess to send me off. I had many jugs of water poured over me and I looked like a drowned rat. It completely messed up my nicely organised laundry arrangements. We all ended up in the rafters of the mess, singing like blazes.

Chapter 5

Operational Training Unit, Northern Ireland

(4 April – 26 December 1943)

On 2 April, after nearly a year with 209 Squadron, I said farewell to all the 209 Squadron types, 90% of whom were bloody wizard blokes. I boarded BOAC's Empire flying boat *Champion*, G-AFCT, under the command of Captain Travers, for my transit to England. We flew to Kisumu, then across the top of Lake Victoria to Port Bell and spent the night in the lovely Imperial Hotel, Kampala. The next day we refuelled at Laropi. There was no sort of habitation, just the Nile River running through the jungle. Between Juba and Malakal, the aircraft suddenly dived to about 100 feet to show the passengers a herd of elephants in a swamp adjacent to the river. We had lunch at Malakal, then on to Khartoum. The next day we flew to Wadi Halfa for morning tea. On leaving Wadi Halfa, the starboard inner engine developed an oil leak and we were forced to land at Luxor to fix the problem. We then flew to Cairo.

Because we were flying to England via Lisbon in neutral Portugal, we could not travel that sector in uniform, so we had to look like civilians. I had a suit of civilian clothes made, for which the RAF paid £8. I chose a grey flannel job which looked reasonably respectable. I was also issued with a new passport that listed me as a government official. The whole thing was a bloody ramp, for the Portuguese Consul in Cairo must have known the passport was for a member of the armed forces.

Four days after lobbing into Cairo, we were on our way on the secret Liberator communication service. Among the passengers on

Wildlife spotting, flying boat style: two giraffes photographed from a low-flying Catalina. (Bruce Daymond)

Liberator G-AGFN, under the command of Captain Vesey, were a naval captain, commander, lieutenant commander and lieutenant (Fleet Air Arm), a wing commander, an embassy bloke, another civilian, Doug Dolphin, and me.

We landed at El Adem, 20 miles south of Tobruk, Cyrenaica. We took off just after midnight in a blacked-out aircraft. We landed at Algiers, and then on to Lisbon. We taxied beside a German Douglas DC-3 with a huge swastika on the tail. We went through Customs and on the other side of the barrier were Huns, also going through the Customs before emplaning. I stared at, and was stared at by, a blond fräulein. Everybody seemed to see the humour of the whole situation.

The next day we were at the airport by 8.15 am. There was an Italian Savoia-Marchetti 75 passenger aircraft about to take off. It seemed damned silly being mixed up with one's enemies. But there was no animosity, for we were respectable government officials, clad in our best, and only, civilian clothes. Probably the Huns and the Ities were also service people. While crossing the Bay of Biscay, our skipper had us doing watches in the tail turret for U-boats and enemy aircraft, but we saw none. We landed at RAF Lyneham.

On the train to London I changed into my uniform. Passing through Reading was too much for me. It was too near Nettlebed. I got off and caught another train to Twyford and to Henley. I rang Nettlebed and Peggy answered the phone. I was so excited I could hardly speak. She was at Halfridge by herself as the Bonds were away. And so, to Peggy. I was still as much in love with her as ever. We sat talking and recalling our joys of twelve months ago until 4 am. God, it was good to be back, but things between us could not go on like this. I thought I would have to stay away from her or I would put up the most terrific 'black'. We all but went over the edge as it was.

The next day I reported to the Ex-Overseas Disposal Section at West Kirby. I was told that I could go on a fortnight's leave and could stay on leave until my posting came through. I spent the first part of my leave exploring the lovely Lake District. I wandered on foot, on a bicycle, and by bus, using the Riggs Windermere Hotel as my base. I went to London to do some shopping and visited Australia House to sort out pay and promotions. Then I went to Halfridge. Ken Pammenter, Peggy's husband, was there on leave from the army. We went to the pictures together, did some work around the estate, went to some dances, and spent some time in the White Hart. After a couple of days, Ken's leave was up and he returned to his barracks in York.

Two years after I completed Elementary Flying Training School, I caught a train to Paddington, taxi to Euston, train to Stranraer, Scotland, and a ferry to Larne, Northern Ireland, and on to RAF Station Killadeas, on Lough Erne. I had just settled in my cabin on the ferry when Doug Dolphin[1] came in. He was going to do his Sunderland captain's course at RAF Castle Archdale, also on Lough Erne.

When I got to RAF Killadeas, the adjutant and chief instructor told me I was not needed until 18 May and sent me back on leave. Heading back on leave, I hitched a ride on Catalina FP105, captained by Pilot Officer Nelson, doing an exercise over Donegal Bay. The landing at Stranraer was a bad one. We taxied around the bay for nearly half an hour before a dinghy took me off and dropped me at the pier. I caught a train to London, where I did some sight-seeing while waiting to link up with the Bonds, who were also in London.

The Bonds' estate grew timber and the Forestry Department needed their timber for coal mine pit props. Miners refused to work if mines contained concrete or steel props, for these gave no warning before breaking and allowing walls or ceilings to collapse. Before the war timber came from Norway and Russia, but due to the war, England had to produce her own. During 1942 the UK produced 600,000 tons more timber than its previous production, and in 1943 the minister asked for another 400,000 tons beyond that: i.e., a million tons above normal. Halfridge, at around 1,500 acres, contained 10% of the timber required from the whole of Oxfordshire.

Peggy and I saw as much as we could of each other, both working on the estate, going to dances, pubs, the cinema, and to London, where we went out to dinner, shopped, and went to the Grosvenor House Hotel for the afternoon tea dance. We spent an absolutely wonderful night at the Savoy. Carroll Gibbons' band was in fine form. Such tunes as 'Dearly Beloved', 'Time Goes By', 'Darling' and one or two others I know remind me of that wonderful night. Lord Louis Mountbatten, Chief of Combined Operations, had a party sitting at a table near ours.

I spent the morning of 16 May at Halfridge, packing and spending as much time with Peggy as possible. I wrote in my diary:

> Whatever is the outcome to be of our love? I hate to think for as things now are there can be nothing but strife. Why, oh why, must we both be so hopelessly in love with each other when we are not free to follow it through?

Of course what should be done is clear but neither of us wants to do it.

I arrived at Killadeas on 17 May for my captain's course and reported to Flight Lieutenant Vernon, the adjutant of the training wing. He told me that four students on the course were operationally qualified Sunderland captains and five were Catalina second pilots. The idea was to push us through the Catalina captain's course in a month. The Sunderland chaps were decidedly cheesed off with having to convert to Catalinas. That afternoon I met Flying Officer Jock Gilbert, who was assigned as my navigator. He had been in Bomber Command since the beginning of the war.

Captains under instruction on Captain's Course No. 7, Killadeas, Northern Ireland. Rear rank, left to right: Flying Officer Potter, Sergeant Garside, Flying Officer Vowles, Flying Officer Bradford. Front rank: Flying Officer Street, Flying Officer Deller, Flying Officer Bruce Daymond, Flying Officer Muffitt, and Flying Officer Nicholson. (Bruce Daymond)

The purpose of No. 131 Coastal Operational Training Unit was to assemble Catalina crews and put them through as much operational training as could be crammed into them, appalling Irish weather permitting. The captain and crew were constantly assessed as to their suitability for service. Once the crews passed the course, they were assigned to operational squadrons.

I was in the air in FP110 on 19 May with Sergeant Ted Garside, an ex-Sunderland pilot. We cracked off at 8.45 am and I spent the one and a quarter hours I was in control doing glide landings on Lough Erne. We moored up at 12 pm and were back on board again by 2 pm for more glide landings, engine-assisted landings, and single-engined landings.

I spent the whole of 21 May flying. For the first hour and a half I was with Flying Officer Quinn, an instructor, and Sergeant Garside in FP106. Quinn demonstrated stalling both powered and off the glide. It was a beautiful feature of the Catalina that she gave bags of warning of a stall, in that she shuddered like hell. When she stalled there was nothing vicious about it, no dropping of a wing and a tight spin, but merely a sinking of the nose. Quinn went ashore and Garside and I went solo in AH538, doing glide, engine-assisted, and single-engined landings.

One day the water was rough, so I prevailed on Squadron Leader Cooper, the course commander, to take advantage of the bad conditions and allow me to practice full stall landings on rough seas. He complied, and under instruction from Flight Lieutenant Potier DFC, I spent the afternoon bashing the hell out of AH538's hull.

The course consisted of many lectures, as much flying as could be fitted in, commando training, and route marches. Squadron Leader Edwards was our chief flying instructor. He took Sergeant Garside, Flying Officer Ted Muffitt, a Canadian ex-Sunderland type, and me up for bombing practice in W8414. We dropped twenty-three bombs: singly, a stick diving from 500 feet, a stick diving from 3,000 feet, and then judgement of yards ahead of a U-boat's diving swirl. It was jolly good exercise.

During the course, we also did glide landings, stall landings, landings off the bounce, powered landings, single-engined landings, night circuit procedure, instrument flying, low flying, circuits and bumps, time in the Link Trainer, and gunnery practice.

We did get time off, during which we were able to sail on the lough, cycle into Enniskillen for drinks and meals, get together in the mess or at local hotels, and attend the occasional dance.

I flew with my full crew for the first time on 12 June in FP245 with instructor Fight Lieutenant Arthur Smallman DSO. The crew were: Sergeant Brown (second pilot), Flying Officer Gilbert (navigator), Sergeant Lewis (engineer), Sergeant Allen (rigger), Leading Aircraftman Walker (wireless operator/mechanic), Sergeant Hunt (wireless operator), Sergeant Foxall (engineer), and Leading Aircraftman Hawkins (engineer). I thought they would turn out to be

Bruce Daymond's crew (No. 4 on No. 7 Course). Rear rank, left to right: Leading Aircraftman Hawkins, Sergeant Allen, Leading Aircraftsman Walker, and Sergeant Lewis. Front rank: Sergeant Foxall, Sergeant Brown, Bruce Daymond, Flying Officer Gilbert, and Sergeant Hunt. Leading Aircraftsman Walker died of tuberculosis in 1944. (Bruce Daymond)

Bruce Daymond's crew (No. 4 on No. 7 Course) in front of the officers' mess (now the Manor House Hotel), Killadeas, Northern Ireland, late 1943. Left to right, back row: Sergeant Lewis (engineer), Flying Officer Bruce Daymond, and Sergeant Allan (rigger). Middle row: Sergeant Brown (second pilot), Flying Officer Gilbert (navigator), Sergeant Walker (wireless operator/mechanic), and Sergeant Hunt (wireless operator). Front row: Sergeant Foxall (engineer), and Sergeant Hawkins (engineer). Bruce Daymond is wearing the dark blue RAAF uniform, in contrast to the lighter blue coloured RAF uniforms. (Bruce Daymond)

a pretty reasonable crew, for there was no apparent bolshie element among them. Time proved me right.

The Republic of Ireland, which was neutral during the Second World War, provided a narrow air corridor between Lough Erne and Donegal Bay to allow armed RAF aircraft a short commute to patrol the North Atlantic. Without access to this corridor, aircraft would have wasted a lot of time accessing their patrol areas, dramatically decreasing their efficiency. The provision of this corridor was not in accord with Eire's neutral status. The one bad feature of Ireland was its weather, which washed out a lot of our planned flying practice. I had never seen a country like Ireland for wet weather.

We conducted an operational flight exercise in FP240 on 23 June, taking off at 3 pm accompanied by Squadron Leader Cooper. It was a total of five hours and the exercise included air firing and an attack on a flame float representing a U-boat. I was pleased the crew coped well.

I received a letter from Rolf Luck that brought me up to date with 209 Squadron news. Barraclough[2] was no longer CO as he had moved to 246 Wing. Bill Hossent had left 209 Squadron and was at Invergordon, Scotland. Jack Kennedy and his crew were lost on an operational trip.

Our next operational flight exercise was the first without an instructor. We flew FP106 to two sea positions, to the island of Islay, conducted a reconnaissance off Bowmore, landed there, then back to base via Tory Island. The crew coped well, despite the navigator making a boob in one spot.

One day we had an interesting three-and-a-quarter-hour session. For the first hour we were attacked by a Miles Martinet and the crew fired at it with the cine gun. Once or twice I took evasive action and threw the Martinet miles off. But as it was an exercise for the gunners in range estimation, I could not indulge in evasive action too often. The cine gun over, we stooged out to Inishmurray in Donegal Bay and did a compass swing. Then, to conclude the afternoon, we did a couple of radar QGH approaches.[3]

Mike Barry and Gordon Millem finally pitched up at Killadeas, where they joined the course after mine. Both demonstrated the vagaries of transit postings. Mike left Mombasa at the end of February and Gordon in early March. Both arrived in England around the same time as I did, and I did not leave until the beginning of April.

Peter Duff, en route to RAF 210 Squadron (flying Catalinas) at Hamworthy, told me that U-boats were staying on the surface in packs and shooting it out with aircraft. Before working in packs, only the odd one stayed on the surface to fight. U-boats were armed with 20mm cannon and while they were unsteady gun platforms, lots of cannon made aviating around them much more hazardous.

In the middle of July, I went to Dublin on leave with Ted Muffitt and Doug Disney. As Eire was neutral, we had to shed our uniforms and travel in civvies. We stayed at the Hibernian Hotel. It was wizard to see a city without a black-out. Sauntering out on our first morning in Dublin, I agreed with the opening lines of the song 'In Dublin's fair city, where the girls are so pretty' as there were some smashing-looking women in Dublin. I revised my opinion of Irish girls, vague as it was. I imagined them to be dark, but there were as many blondes as not, and lovely figures most of them had too.

Ted, Doug and I went for a horse ride in Phoenix Park late one afternoon. Ted rode a big hunter that was hard to handle. He was ex-Royal Canadian Mounted Police and a former member of their specialist unit, the Musical Ride, so he had the horse under control. We had a damned good race around the park for an hour and a half.

Flight Lieutenant Vernon had relatives in Dublin. Through them I met and had lunch with Mary Lillis. She was extremely attractive, with a grand figure, and dressed well. It was a great pleasure to talk to such a sensible lass. For talk we did, from 1 to 9.30 pm. She appealed to me immensely. She had just finished a novel that was in the hands of a publisher. It was the story of an Irish girl who went to London for the 1937 Season, then on to Europe, and escaped from Vienna when the Germans invaded. Mary said it was not her autobiography, despite the fact all these things happened to her.

I was back on the train to Belfast on 22 July after a grand week. I vowed that I would go back like an arrow if any forty-eight-hour passes showed up on my return to Killadeas. Mary Lillis was really something special. We got on damned well, and over our long talk over dinner I told her all about Peggy and myself. Though why the hell I should have let that out, I didn't know. When I got to Belfast, I whizzed off a telegram to Mary: 'What can I say except thanks for an evening in which so much was accomplished. Or was it?'

I was given more leave and headed for London. There, I found out that Ken and Peggy Pammenter were having a holiday in

Bournemouth, so off to Bournemouth I went. Ken and Peggy had scouted out Irene Shräger, a guest at their hotel, for me. The four of us went to a very pleasant evening dinner dance. Irene and I went for a walk and sat up talking till after 4 am. I was in favour of having other lasses and Ken around the place when Peggy was about, for it helped us try to get over this business which was so hopeless.

On 1 August I was back in London and met up with the Killadeas types returning from leave. I gathered the boys had certainly been giving it a lacing while in London. Jack Lever spent a lot of his leave at some bomber station and went on a bomber raid to Hamburg, during which 2,300 tons of bombs were dropped. He said he had never been so scared in his life. He saw a Vickers Wellington bomber flying alongside them just disappear in one bloody great explosion as its bombs blew up. Comment from the crew he was with was: 'Ha, ha, ha, Wimpey's[4] had it.'

When we got to Killadeas, we found there was no prospect of our getting anywhere for some time. The flying training unit at Oban, Scotland, refused to accept any more crews as they had no aircraft. So basically, we did 'make work' duties, such as engine testing, or anything to keep us occupied. After cooling our heels, all my crew were sent on leave, yet again. So, on 11 August, together with Sergeants Lewis, Allen, and Walker, I took the train to Dublin to spend my forty-eight-hour leave. When I arrived, I rang Mary Lillis, but she was unable to get me in at the Hibernian Hotel and kindly asked me to stay with her family. I had a wonderful couple of days with the Lillises and slept very comfortably on the sofa in their lounge. On my last evening we went out to dinner and caught up with some of Mary's friends. When I left for the train, Mary kept saying, 'Why can't you tell the Air Force you're not coming back till later?' I wished I could have done so, for there was a cocktail party organised that night and a race meeting the next day.

On 17 August I was over at Castle Archdale for an operation briefing at 1 pm. The job was an anti-submarine escort in FP134 for the troop transport RMS *Aquitania*. It was a very pansy briefing with all typed gen[5] in manila folders. I did a good heavy load take-off with a full load of fuel and six depth charges. The weather going out was OK, stratocumulus, but at 6,000 feet we were in bright sunshine above the stuff. At 10 am we located the ship on radar, slightly to starboard at 65 miles. Jock reckoned that the ship was 50 miles ahead of the position which we had been told at the briefing. We did a creeping-line-ahead patrol, or rather a variation of it in which we flew fifteen minutes ahead of the ship, fifteen minutes to the starboard side, ahead ten minutes, thirty minutes at right angles to the ship's course, ten minutes on a reciprocal bearing to the ship's course, and then fifteen minutes back, which should have brought us on the ship's port beam. But the ship was bagging along quicker than we calculated and we finished up well behind her. So, on gaining contact I signalled, 'What is your course and speed?'

He came back, 'Course 250 speed 20 knots.' This time we did a pukka creeping-line-ahead. The weather was closing down, with cloud-base about 200 feet. We came back to the ship once or twice. We saw another ship, which we thought was the SS *Deseado* from the flags she was flying. The radar went unserviceable so we couldn't find the *Aquitania* to tell her, 'I go.' Off patrol at 10.15 pm and so began the five-hour bog home. We climbed to 6,000 feet and were still in cloud. However, after a few miles, we were above it. Jock couldn't get any drifts but got a few astro shots and a bearing from Buster, a long-range cathode-ray station in the south of England. We arrived over base to find 8,000 feet of cloud above it. We could get no joy from the radar, so after bogging around for one and a half hours, we came in on the radio beam. It was a lot of cloud to come down through. At 2,000 feet, for a second or so, we saw the flare path so we knew we were OK. I did my first night landing from an operational trip. We taxied slowly back to the Killadeas moorings as the sea was rough. That was a fourteen-hour stooge, the first operational trip with Coastal Command for Jock, and the first operational trip for the rest of the crew.

RMS *Aquitania*, taken during Bruce Daymond's first operational trip as aircraft captain. (Bruce Daymond)

I went on leave to Halfridge on 19 August and caught up with Peggy. I was with her on her birthday two days later. The leave for my crew and me was extended on 29 August for a week. I spent some time in London catching up with relatives. On my way back to Halfridge I was sitting in the train at a station when I caught sight of Peggy walking past the window. With a wild leap and a yell of 'Peggy!' which fairly startled the rest of the occupants of the carriage, I dragged her inside. God, how good it was to see her again. We were a couple of starry-eyed kids the whole trip back. Never had I felt like it with anyone else. And there we sat, holding hands and hoping like blazes that everyone else would get off the train. For the remainder of my leave, Peggy and I gathered blackberries and mushrooms, went to the White Hart or the Carpenter's Arms for drinks, and tried to spend as much time together as we could, including my staying in her flat when the Bonds were away.

Peggy and I had a final trip to the White Hart on 5 September and it developed into quite a party. The next day she came down with me to the station. It was the first time she was able to see me off by

The White Hart, Nettlebed, Oxford, one of Bruce Daymond's favourite pubs, in December 1943. He had a note in his photograph album that stated 'hundreds of American bombers were returning from a raid as I took this'. (Bruce Daymond)

herself. I wrote at the time: 'Farewell Peggy – when, oh when shall I see you again. Thank you for the happiest days of my life.'

When I got back to Killadeas, I was met with jeers from all at having to return. I was told Peter Duff of No. 6 Course wrote himself off on a night take-off at Poole after he rejoined his squadron. Jock Gilbert had been promoted to flight lieutenant, but I was still a flying officer. When I asked the adjutant and the chief flying instructor about flying duties, they told me they could offer nothing except sitting on our arses with more boredom ahead. Several operations planned for me were scrubbed because of bad weather.

I collected a wizard bunch of mail in mid-September. I received two aerographs from Mother, and Eric Saunders wrote at long last. He had fallen for Joan Morrison, a member of the Female Aid Nursing Yeomanry in Mombasa, and he was thinking of popping the question. He and his crew had been to the Seychelles, Mauritius, and Tulear. Howell, the engineer on old Q, had got his commission.

As part of keeping the troops occupied, Ted Muffitt and I were sent as navigators in FP191 with Squadron Leader Cooper to Felixstowe to collect another Catalina. We got as far as the Welsh coast when we ran into some very low rain and cloud which completely obscured the mountains. After stooging about for some time, Cooper decided that it was no go and we set course for Beaumaris on Anglesey island. We were met by Saunders-Roe officials and given lunch at the company's dining hall and stayed the night in the old Bulkeley Arms, a wizard spot, even though most of the guests were all but dead. We had a pretty fair session at The Old Bulls Head just across the road. This reminded me of the pleasant time I had at Beaumaris the previous year when I was with Eric Saunders' crew and we picked up 209/Q.

The next morning, we flew to Rhyl and on to Felixstowe. I did the navigation and was pleased with my results. It was interesting flying over England and seeing the number of aerodromes we passed. It was truly amazing: the whole country was nothing but one big aerodrome.

Felixstowe was covered with balloons, so we landed outside the harbour boom and taxied through. Felixstowe was a pre-war, permanent RAF station and had a good, comfortable mess, WAAF waitresses and batwomen. The CO would not allow flying boats to remain on the water overnight, so up the slip ours came. They had a dirty great crane which lifted the whole aircraft out of the water. I had never seen this operation before: 'airborne at the buoy'.

After refuelling the next day, we had to go through all the business of lowering the boats back onto the water. I was part of the crew that had flown to Felixstowe to collect Catalina W2152 and fly her to Killadeas. Once we got airborne, we carried out an air test. The synchroscope[6] was unserviceable and the radio channels needed tuning. We returned to Felixstowe to have them fixed and then headed for Killadeas. However, we had no functioning navigation gear, so we 'navigated' by following Cooper in FP191. Without having to worry about navigation, I was able to get a good view of the countryside. The industrial haze over the Midlands was certainly no myth. The weather over the Irish Sea was pretty sticky and got worse as we flew over Ireland. As we neared base I asked for the radio range, only to be told that it wasn't switched on. We put the radar on but it was all to cock as well; however, we landed safely.

While waiting for operations, we embarked on the latest programme for idle aircrew, i.e. chopping wood and collecting old tins and other bits of salvage lying around the camp. This work was a command order and was being carried out at Castle Archdale and the idea had been extended to all personnel at Killadeas. It would not have been so bad if all personnel had to do it, but it was pretty humiliating for officers and senior NCOs to be chopping wood while aircraftmen and aircraftwomen walked past and smiled in amusement. On this occasion I blessed Killadeas weather because 'rain stopped play'.

We went on an operational flight exercise in FP191 on 19 September. It consisted of going to Point A in Donegal Bay, flying north to 55°N, and doing a creeping-line-ahead patrol westward.

We flew through a front most of the time. The cloud base was never higher than 400 feet and at times was as low as 100 feet. I did not turn back because I thought it would be good navigational experience for Jock. Most of the crew were airsick. We threw out a flame float for a dummy submarine attack and even though I turned immediately it was lost in the murk before we got to it. We climbed through the muck as we approached land. After bogging on for some time, on the port side, through a hole in the clouds, we saw a beach. Down we went to get our bearings. We discovered that we were on the north coast and a hell of a long way from where we should have been. We had a sticky time before we eventually got down. There was a flap in the operations room when we returned. RAF Northern Ireland had been on to the operations room saying that we had grossly infringed Eireann neutrality, so we had to give all details of weather conditions. Squadron Leader Cooper was panicking to know why we hadn't immediately used the emergency flight plan provided.

I received an aerograph from Jack Whittaker, who informed me of yet another tragedy in 209 Squadron. Ron Roberts,[7] Vic Field and John Inglis had been killed. I found out later that they were all killed when R crashed off Mombasa, during an exercise on the night of 20 August 1943.

I was summoned before Squadron Leader Edwards at the end of September to explain the seventeen holes in the tailplane of FP531, caused by fragmentation of bombs while practicing several days earlier. Did I know we were

Flight Lieutenant Ron Roberts (RAAF) was killed on 20 August 1943 when his flying boat crashed into the sea during a low-level night exercise off Mombasa. A full account of this tragedy is given in *Wings of the Dawning* by Arthur Banks. (Eric Saunders)

not supposed to come below 50 feet? I did. Well, how could I account for the damage? All I could say was that one of the bombs scored a direct hit on the platform and this probably caused the damage.

In early October, Vowles, Aiston, Potter, me, and our crews were selected to travel to Invergordon by train to bring four Catalinas back to Killadeas. We took the ferry to Glasgow and then a train through Perth, Gleneagles, and Pitlochry. The Scottish Highlands were lovely, although there wasn't really enough sun to show off the heather to its best advantage. The trees were in their best autumn tints. How lovely they were, especially round about Pitlochry.

The Catalinas we collected were Mark IVs and had Westinghouse radio equipment rather than the Bendix we were used to, so we had to familiarise ourselves with the new equipment. Just before we departed, meteorology told us there were patches of cloud down to 600 feet along the Caledonian Canal. However, the weather was OK over Ireland. The controller decided to scrub the trip because of the low cloud, as parts of the Caledonian Canal were so narrow that it was impossible to turn an aircraft. The Wing Commander came in and said that we had to leave, for if we didn't, there was a possibility of our being bogged down for a week in Invergordon. He told us to land in the canal if it got too bad, turn around, take off down wind, and return to Invergordon. It brought to mind the famous saying: 'Take off, I say. Take off. I'm the Controller here, I'll take the risk.' However, the trip proved uneventful. In fact, it was enjoyable. We flew AH541 over Culloden Moor, down Loch Ness, and into Oban. From Oban, Charles Potter formatted with me most of the way to Killadeas, with Jack Vowles and Freddie Aiston behind.

In mid-October, we flew FP191 to Greenock. It was a beautiful sunny day, one right out of the box for Killadeas. The crew was late in coming on board so I tore a hell of a strip off them. They had a great failing and that was lack of punctuality. Jack Vowles also took an aircraft, so we flew in a loose formation. We passed over Larne, Ailsa Craig, and into Greenock.

From Greenock I went to Edinburgh. I had arranged to see Jack Davenport there, but he had just got engaged and insisted that I go to St Andrews to see him and dine with his fiancée's family and his old CO. I met him at RAF Leuchars and he took me to St Andrews, where I met his fiancée and her family. She was charming. She graduated from the University of St Andrews the next day and her family had come over from the west coast for the ceremony. So all-in-all, it was a pretty cheery party. Wing Commander Bob Holmes,[8] CO of 455 Squadron, Jack's old squadron, was in the party. When it was over the Wing Commander, Jack, and I drove back to the officers' mess at Leuchars, then moved on to Sandford, the home of Mrs Walker at Wormit, where Jack and his brother Phil were spending their leave. I spent the night with them and then the next night at RAF Leuchars.

On returning to Killadeas, the driver of the RAF transport broke the news that Squadron Leader Cooper and eight others had been killed the day before. Their Catalina spun in from about 2,000 feet. It was a mystery how two of the crew survived because the machine was in tiny pieces. I found out I had been promoted to flight lieutenant.

We were off on an operation in FP105 on 23 October. In addition to my crew, I had Jimmy Quinn DFC as screen skipper and Moose Haugen DFC as screen navigator. They were on board to assess my and Jock's performances. The job was an eighteen-hour convoy escort to fifty-seven ships, two aircraft carriers, and seven escort vessels. We were towed to the main lough and took off at 3.00 am. It was my first full-load night take-off. It was nowhere as terrifying as I had expected, with the moon rising just before we took off. We closed with the convoy at 9.30 am. Although we were supposed to contact the senior naval officer by radio, we could get no answer. Nor did we have any more joy with the Aldis Lamp. After taking nearly half an hour to circle the convoy as we flashed all the escort vessels for instructions, we began our patrol. Two American-built escort carriers, HMS *Biter* and HMS *Tracker*, were in the centre of the convoy, which was westwards-bound. We stayed with the convoy till 2 pm. We left them about 27°W and altered course on one of Moose's sun-sights. We sent our estimated time of arrival and asked for the barometric pressure and cloud base at Killadeas. We got on to radio range and were getting onto the beam when Quinn took out 'George' and headed for the lights of a town which he thought was Bundoran, but which turned out to be Sligo. It was a wizard night and I saw Bundoran and Ballyshannon in the distance as we altered course visually. I did the night landing. The water was as smooth as glass. We overshot the flare path but Quinn told me to land straight ahead. It was OK as the flare path was facing right down the lough. We taxied back on the step[9] to Killadeas. We moored up after eighteen hours five minutes from 'engines on' to 'engines off'.

I began my first operational trip as aircraft captain in FP105 on 28 October with no accompanying superiors. Our task was to escort the SS *Laurentic* inward bound. We were towed from Killadeas to the flare path at Castle Archdale. There was quite a sea running down the lough and I got terribly wet running up the engines. The take-off was OK but quite rough for one's first solo, fully loaded effort. We were in cloud at about 800 feet. An hour or so out from base, we ran into some shocking weather. Drift was 20° starboard at one stage and 13° port half an hour later. When about an hour from the *Laurentic*, we had trouble with our radio direction gear, which we wanted to use to find the ship, so we used the radar and chased a 'blip' for a while, but it faded off the screen. We set course for the ship's dead reckoned position and I sighted it at 9.30 am. The weather was good with visibility about 15–20 miles. We made our recognition signals and asked for patrol instructions. She gave none so I set off 20 miles ahead of the ship, 10 miles across and 15 back. We got back after quarter of an hour so went 30 miles ahead and eventually, as the weather improved, up to 40 miles ahead. The ship looked to be the *Aquitania* not the *Laurentic*. Intelligence had no photos of the latter and the ship looked just like the *Aquitania* we had escorted in August. She was loaded with troops. We stayed with her for nine and a half hours, eventually leaving her at 7 pm just as we ran into low cloud. Back in Donegal Bay, the weather was bad again. We took one and a half hours to clear our estimated time of arrival message. Radio range was unserviceable and the wireless operators could not pick up the beacon on the radar. I asked for a priority radio QGH approach and eventually got down on this. It took longer than it should have done for there was another kite in the air doing a QGH also and he was jamming our magnetic course. Although told to change to another frequency, he didn't. The landing was OK, but by God, what a sea! When on the water, our troubles began. A dinghy came alongside and smashed off one of the radar aerials. We were towed back to Killadeas. I was thoroughly exhausted after the intelligence people had finished with us. After an eighteen-hour trip, to have to concentrate like hell on getting the aircraft down through cloud with mountains nearby put the finishing touch for me.

Later, I wrote and submitted a report on the damage by the dinghy to the radar aerials. I was summoned to Squadron Leader Ogle Skan's office to discuss the incident. I was blamed for the damage because I had not ordered the rigger to go into the bow. I did not know whether the dinghy was one of ours or was from Castle Archdale and I was not prepared to take a line. One good tip I did get was that on a bad night, or really at any time, it was a good idea for the rigger to have a heaving line ready in the bow in case the line from the dinghy isn't caught.

I went on leave on 1 November, heading for London and then to Bognor Regis to stay for a few days with Ken and Peggy Pammenter. Ken was stationed there with the Commandos and expected to be going overseas shortly. He had to go to London early the day after I arrived to get himself outfitted with khaki drill for his overseas posting, which was imminent. Peggy, Vicky, and I had a late breakfast and then went for a walk to the centre of town for coffee and shopping. I showed Peggy a lovely cottage that I had passed the day before to see if she agreed that it was a whizz. Our tastes in most things were practically identical and that made our situation a lot harder to take, knowing that it could never be. I spent a lot of time with Ken and Peggy before heading for London and then on to accept Lloyd Butler's[10] invitation to visit him at Stradishall, a permanent RAF base, near Haverhill, Suffolk, where I stayed in the officers' mess. It was every bit as good as Pembroke Dock. Lloyd was acting flight commander of RAF 149 Squadron, flying Stirling bombers. The serviceability of these kites was not too hot. Out of five or six, only one or two were OK. Despite their huge size, one had to be a contortionist to make one's way from the door to the cockpit. I had almost forgotten the difficulty of crawling around a landplane after the spaciousness of a flying boat. Lloyd took me on a test flight in N6089. In contrast to the crew usually taken on a boat test flight, all we had was an engineer, Lloyd, and myself. One seemed to be a hell of a long way up when sitting in the cockpit while the aircraft was resting on the ground. We did a spot of local flying in EF332. I found the Stirling very different in the aileron controls compared to a Catalina. The former was very sensitive.

When back in London I was joined by Peggy as Ken had gone overseas. Not long after she arrived, I got a telegram from Halfridge saying I was recalled from leave. Peggy and I managed to spend one evening at the Mayfair and then the Coconut Grove in Regent Street. We spent much of that night talking over our love affair and how we could straighten it out. She saw me off on the train to Stranraer. The ferry crossing was very rough and loads of people were sick.

I saw Duffield at Belfast station. He gave me the sad news that Ted Muffitt (aged 34, RCAF), Doug Disney (aged 35, RCAF), Ken Hipwell (aged 29, RAF), and the rest of their crew had been lost. They took off in FP120 on an operational flight exercise on 2 November and all base heard from them was a position signal. It was thought that while doing practice bombing, they must have dived in. Whether due to the glassy surface of the sea and the 'mush' of a heavily laden boat, or blown up by their own bombs, we never knew. Air Sea

Rescue aircraft were sent out, but no trace of the aircraft or her crew were found. Both Ted and Ken had two children and one of the crew had been married only a couple of weeks previously.

An Air Ministry order issued in early November stated that flight times entered in our flying logs were to be from airborne to waterborne, not buoy to buoy. This meant that times manoeuvring on the water were not included in our operational hours. This was a blow, as we had to spend considerable amounts of time on the water before taking off and after alighting. In addition, the number of operational hours Coastal Command aircrew had to log for a tour was raised from 800 to 1,000. Each RAF command took a different approach to what constituted an operational tour. For example, Bomber Command required personnel to undertake thirty operational sorties to complete their tour. Times logged in Bomber Command were from engines started to engines shut down. Using the time for a raid on Berlin at 7.5 hours as the average for a sortie, completing 30 sorties would amount to 225 hours logged. Coastal Command required 1,000 operational hours, not number of sorties. While not all operational flights were twenty hours, even if every sortie was that long, personnel needed to have undertaken over fifty sorties to complete their tour. As a result, some Coastal Command aircrew spent most of the war completing their operational tour. Every crew member maintained their flying log and these were examined and certified at the end of each month by their CO or flight commander.

In mid-November I was told that two aircraft had to be taken to Greenock. They were Catalina Mark IVs and were suffering from leaking petrol tanks. I was to take one and Paddy Finch the other. My crew was split up to man both aircraft. However, the aircraft I was supposed to take to Greenock was unserviceable, so we all climbed aboard Finch's boat and on 17 November I was at last free of Ireland. Flying over the country for the last time, we saw most of the route to Larne covered in snow. It looked pretty in a way, but desolate.

Having handed over the Catalina, we stayed briefly in Glasgow and then travelled to Oban. The RAF mess at Oban was in the Esplanade Hotel, right on the sea front, but it was full, so Brian Tait, Jock Gilbert, and I were billeted in the Alexandria Hotel, a few hundred yards further along the road. We were back to whiling away time with lectures, drinking sessions, playing poker, cinema, attending dances, and other time-wasting activities. For some reason, we were issued with parachutes and revolvers. One night we had a very pleasant 'do' in the mess with Brian Tait, Brian Crossland, and Daphne, a beautiful, blonde WAAF officer. We went into the ping-pong room and played a foursome between drinks. It was her birthday, which we celebrated with much enthusiasm.

Squadron Leader Campbell rang me in the mess on 29 November and asked me to collect Flying Officers Millem, Potter, Sparks, Harding, and Aiston, and for all of us to report to him at once. On the way to see him we were full of speculation. Were we to go to America to pick up boats? That seemed feasible as Sparks had been before and knew the ropes. Or Gibraltar? That also seemed in the running for both Potter and Sparks had been promised home postings. However, none of us were prepared for what came. We were to fly as passengers in Sunderlands which were going to Australia, but Campbell didn't know if that was where we were going!

We left Oban for London on 1 December with no news about our movements, although I was given leave. I spent several days at Halfridge, where I joined my adorable Peggy. Mrs Bond, Peggy and I went to Henley to do some shopping. How I loved those trips and how I would miss them! Everything about Henley and Halfridge stuck forever in my mind. That was because it was there that I first really fell in love. We did so much together: God, what happiness. We were left alone one afternoon and really made the most of it.

On 7 December I received a letter from Jack Davenport, saying he was back at RAF Leuchars and was to take over the squadron shortly. They were converting to Bristol Beaufighters. He told me he was getting married on 8 January, but I guessed I would be far away by then.

Then I got a bombshell: a telegram from Oban saying: 'Leave extended to 2359 hours 24th December subject to recall. Acknowledge.' As I noted: 'Jesus Christ! That's the Air Force for you! Mad panic to get you away – three days leave before going to the other end of the earth and then a telegram like that! I felt so damned embarrassed. I can't possibly stay at Halfridge all that time that's certain. God only knows what I will do really.'

I did stay at Halfridge and the Bonds went to London for a few days, leaving Peggy and me by ourselves. Initially I stayed in Peggy's flat. However, as luck would have it, I came down with influenza so I moved back to the Bonds' house, where Dr Pooley, the local GP, consigned me to bed. I stayed in bed for five days, by which time the Bonds came back from London. Not long after, I went to London by myself. I caught up with Mike Barry and a lass and spent an evening with them. Peggy came to London the next day. We arranged a room at the Cumberland Hotel as Flight Lieutenant and Mrs Daymond. We went to a dinner and dance at the Berkerley and spent the night at the Cumberland. When Peggy rang Mrs Bond, she was told there was a telegram for me instructing me to report to Pembroke Dock on Monday, 27 December. Mike Barry received the same instructions.

Between getting the reporting instructions and heading for Pembroke Dock, I spent the time in London as the Bonds and Peggy were there. I took the Bonds and Peggy to dinner at the Coq d'Or, bought a wedding present for Jack Davenport, and tried to see as much of Peggy as I could. Then on 26 December, despite me not wanting Peggy to see me off, I relented and asked her to come along to the station. I wrote at the time: 'And so twice in two years came a gigantic farewell and I DON'T LIKE THEM. When, oh when, I wonder shall I see Peggy again.' The dark end of the platform at Paddington – it was there we said goodbye.

Chapter 6

Transit Pembroke Dock, Wales to Redhills Lake, India

(27 December 1943 – 31 January 1944)

I was back at Pembroke Dock on 27 December, where I caught up with Wonk Kennedy, Phil Davenport,[1] and Neville McKeough. I heard that Sparks and his crew had been killed going through the Bay of Biscay as passengers on a Sunderland heading for Gibraltar. We were told we were going to West Africa as passengers on Sunderlands that were replacing the Catalinas of 270 Squadron at Freetown, Sierra Leone. We were to take 270's Catalinas and ferry them somewhere, but we were not told where.

After handing back our parachutes, weighing our kit and putting it aboard the Sunderland, for the second time of my life I said farewell to England from the pier at Pembroke Dock. I wondered where I was going and when would I see Peggy again. As we climbed aboard Sunderland EK592, captained by Flying Officer Peter Brown, a Sunderland was returning from operations having been shot up over the Bay of Biscay.

As we alighted in Gibraltar we scared the living daylights out of the crew of a rowing boat that was where we wanted to set down. We waited in Gibraltar for the remainder of the year. Jock and I began New Year's Eve by visiting some of the cafés for drinks. Shady looking women, musicians, and dancers provided the only entertainment, except for alcohol, for the sex-starved men on the Rock. When the bottles began to fly, Jock and I judged it time to return to the mess and see how the party there was progressing. I found it pretty depressing. Some Wrens[2] had been invited and were outnumbered four or five to one. Jock and I went to bed straight after midnight to the accompaniment of ships' sirens hooting a welcome to 1944.

At first light on New Year's Day, we took off for Port-Étienne,[3] on the West African coast. As we left there was a whacking great convoy coming into Gibraltar from the Atlantic. Port-Étienne, our stop for the night, was French territory on the Spanish border and was pretty desolate. Peter slept aboard the Sunderland with his crew while we all slept ashore in the same Nissen hut.[4] Water was rationed to a gallon per person per day so we were unable to get clean, for the hot salt baths at Gibraltar had not been much help for bathing.

We left for Bathurst[5] in The Gambia about 1 pm and had lunch in flight. As we had not taken on extra rations, it was a pretty scrappy meal. Due to the haze we were unable to see the land most of the way, except when we crossed the coast and flew inland to avoid Dakar. In doing so we ran into the top layer of a swarm of locusts. The swarm stretched for about a mile and a half and they were below us for hundreds of feet. They made a mess of the windscreen. I thought of a

Opposite: Map showing route and stops during Bruce Daymond and his crew's transit from the UK to India. They departed the UK from Pembroke Dock on 29 December 1943 as passengers aboard Sunderland EK592, being delivered to West Africa under the command of Flying Officer Peter Brown. The first leg was to Gibraltar (10 hours 40 minutes), then to Port-Étienne (9 hours 50 minutes), Bathurst (4 hours), and Freetown (3 hours 55 minutes). At Freetown Bruce and his crew took charge of Catalina FP304 and flew it to Lagos (10 hours 35 minutes). In Lagos they took charge of Catalina FP118, which they delivered to Redhills Lake, Madras, India, via Libreville (6 hours), Léopoldville (6 hours), Stanleyville (7 hours 15 minutes), Kisumu (5 hours 35 minutes), Dar-es-Salaam (5 hours 35 minutes), Diego Suarez (7 hours 35 minutes), and then over the Indian Ocean via the Seychelles (6 hours 50 minutes) and Addu Atoll (10 hours 45 minutes) before arriving at Redhills Lake (10 hours 5 minutes) on 31 January 1944. The total flying time was 104 hours and 40 minutes.

great line: 'The locusts were so thick we had to fly through them on instruments!'

Bathurst had a lovely big bay and was a wizard flying boat base. We spent two nights there, filling in the time relaxing, swimming, and catching up with sleep. We were in the air for Freetown, Sierra Leone, by mid-morning. It was a big place, much larger than Bathurst.

Jui, the RAF camp, was home to RNZAF 490 and RAF 270 Catalina squadrons. Once ashore, we found 270 was moving to Lagos and re-equipping with Sunderlands. Peter and his boat were to join 270. 270's Catalinas were being ferried to other squadrons. My crew, as well as Peter and his crew, were to go on to Lagos. Instead of going down in Peter's Sunderland, we were to ferry Catalina 270/D FP304, which had been at Jui for a major inspection. It had been water-tested after its maintenance, so we air-tested it and swung the compass. There was a compass adjuster on the station and he came with us to give Jock a hand.

In my first attempt to take off for Lagos, we began to porpoise and it got out of hand. I stopped and we began again. I got her on the step, but couldn't get the control column forward. I stopped the second attempt quickly because I didn't want to get airborne only to find my controls were ropey. After two aborted attempts to take off, I was really shaken. We checked the aircraft quickly, but could find nothing wrong, so we got off the flare path as Peter was sculling around in his Sunderland waiting to take off. Away he went, and I decided to make a do-or-die effort to get off. This time we were successful, but it took the whole length of the waterway.

We landed at Lagos just before dark, up a narrow channel which had a long jetty sticking out with a couple of ships tied to it. We got a warm welcome at the famous Apapa mess. Squadron Leader Godwin, flight commander of 270 Squadron, told us we were to ferry a Catalina to Ceylon; however, we would not be taking 270/D. I thought that was a shame as she was a fine aircraft with two new engines, however she had only 90 hours to go before her second major inspection so we were assigned 270/S FP118, which had 200 hours less airframe time than 270/D.

We spent the weekend in Lagos sorting out arrangements for our next leg. I spent the Saturday morning with the engineer officer and flight commander and managed to acquire some Catalina handbooks. In the afternoon we took 270/S on an air test. We had to swing the compass and later diced off inland to swing the loop. S was one of those heavy-handed aircraft, which made a lot of work for the pilots. I was thoroughly brassed-off after turning onto twenty-five different courses for the loop swing.

Freddie Aiston arrived late that evening on a Sunderland, bringing news that another Sunderland had been written off in Port-Étienne, though fortunately with no loss of life. That made two out of four Sunderlands destined for 270 Squadron that had bought it in transit.

We took off for Libreville, Gabon, on 10 January accompanied by two corporals as passengers for Kisumu. They were destined for aircrew training in South Africa. Jock Gilbert appropriately remarked, 'I wonder which war they're going to fight in?' It would have been one hell of a time before they became operational, judging by the huge pool of surplus aircrew available.

We arrived at Libreville after six hours' flying, but had difficulty in finding the alighting area. There was a small RAF detachment about 18 km from the town. They were living in tents and Libreville reminded me of my detachment at

Catalina handbook, containing information for pilots and engineers. It consisted of forty-eight pages of text and eight pages of fold-out illustrations of instrument panels, cockpit layout, etc. (Handbook courtesy of Eric Saunders)

Pamanzi. I had a bath out of a small basin of water, standing out in the open. This was followed by a marvelous dinner, including an omelette made of turtles' eggs. It was amazing how meals improved the further one got from civilisation.

The next morning, we intended to be airborne at 7 am, but the electric starter on the starboard engine would not work. We had to go through the dreadful business of hand cranking. The poor crew were really sweating by the time we got the engine started. We flew overland to Chiloango River, and then picked up the railway line which led us into Léopoldville[6] on the famous Congo River. There was a goodly current running on the river, but we landed OK and luckily moored up on the first attempt, thereby earning the praise of the BOAC people, who said we had put up the best show of any Catalina passing through. Apparently, most of them bounced on landing, and because of the river's current they had difficulty mooring up.

Léopoldville, like all African towns, looked wizard from the air, but was the exception that proves the rule, for it was wizard on the ground as well. We were taken out to Sabena, the Belgian airline's guest house. We had a few days in Léopoldville, during which we went shopping and swam in a grand swimming pool. Not having been able to buy any swimming trunks, I had to use a pair of very pansy underpants I had bought.

My lasting impressions of Léopoldville were of lovely big American cars and taxis that ran smoothly about the streets, lovely new buildings, very modern in appearance, some that were completed and some in the course of construction, and fine concrete streets. You couldn't walk along the streets without one of the taxis sliding up to you and being asked, 'Taxi sir?' by the African driver. This was a marked contrast to London a few weeks previously, when it was the devil's own job to get a taxi and one would stand screaming, 'Taxi!' at passing cars.

Freddie Aiston and his crew arrived the day before we left Léopoldville and gave me some bad news. Before I left Pembroke

Dock, I asked Gordon Millem to bring out any mail that had accumulated for me. He was bringing twenty-six letters for me in the Sunderland that pranged at Port-Étienne. No one was hurt, but all my letters were lost.

We were airborne early on 14 January. We flew up the Congo River to Coquilhatville and did a slow circuit of the place before setting course across the huge Congo forest to Stanleyville,[7] Congo. I wouldn't have given much for our chances if we had to force-land in the forest, as it looked impenetrable. The trees were so close together that from the air they looked an unbroken sea of dark green: an inland ocean. Our abode at Stanleyville was a few kilometres out of town. Once again, we were put up at the Sabena guest house. A water shortage prevailed and we could get no water for a shower. So, we went to bed hot and dirty after the day's flying.

There was nothing to keep us in Stanleyville, so we pushed off early the next day. The electric starter on the starboard engine was still unserviceable so the crew had to hand crank the engine each time we flew. This was not the best way to start the day in hot climates. We set course for Irumu, thence across the southern end of Lake Albert to Kampala, and on to Kisumu. Alighting at Kisumu completed a full circle for me. It was pretty tough to come ashore on the same wharf from where I left for England, and Peggy, on 4 April the previous year. It was such events as these that I found hard to take and which released in me a whole flood of longing to be with Peggy.

I spoke about our movements by phone with Rolf Luck in Nairobi. He informed me we were routed from Kisumu to Dar-es-Salaam to Diego Suarez to the Seychelles to Addu Atoll to Redhills Lake, near Madras, India. We had some time to fill in Kisumu as our aircraft had to have a ninety-hour inspection before departing.

The next day I sent cables to the family, to Peggy, and one to Jack Davenport congratulating him on his wedding. Jock went to the slipway to check on progress with maintenance. I was told that Eric Saunders was arriving in an Anson at midday to take me to

Nairobi. Eric arrived and brought old Jimmy Mecklem with him. It was grand to see these two old buggers again. It appeared that most of the old 209 Squadron types would be in Nairobi, so I could catch up with them.

We took off in Anson AX402 and en route to Nairobi we shot up the Ryans' house at Molo. We could plainly see Molly and Tony. We landed at RAF Eastleigh, on the outskirts of Nairobi, and in no time had met Bill Powell, Ray Woolley (ex Q's crew), and old Vincent, our navigator on Q. It was fine to see them all again.

Eric sprang a surprise. He was to be married on 22 January to Katherine 'Mouse' Messer,[8] an English WAAF Section Officer. That evening, Eric, Jimmy Mecklem, and I went to the WAAF mess, where he introduced me to Mouse. I spent five days in Nairobi and together with Squadron Leader Fitzpatrick, Jimmy Mecklem,[9] Ken Murray,[10] and Des Hosking, we took a cottage at the Norfolk Hotel. On my last day in Nairobi I had a big lunch party at the Lobster Pot with all the boys. When we got back to the Norfolk, our cottage was full of Yanks being entertained by Fitzpatrick.[11] Des Hosking organised some nurses for a dance, but he had to bow out because we thought malaria had him in its grip. In any event, it was a pretty mediocre show.

I returned to Kisumu on 20 January on a RAF Communications Flight de Havilland Dragon Rapide. Our Catalina was ready to go down the slip. Cleaning and loading took most of the morning. We took her up on an air test in the afternoon. The air test revealed too many snags to leave the next morning as scheduled. Among the problems were an unserviceable generator, leaking bomb aimer's window, and second pilot's turn and bank indicator offset.

Two days later, we did a final air test and everything was more or less OK. During the take-off, Sergeant Lewis reckoned he saw a hippo about 20 yards on our port side just as we were about to become airborne. It submerged as we passed. It would have been curtains to hit one.

The next day we left Kisumu en route for Dar-es-Salaam. We had two army passengers we were taking to the Seychelles. They were Major Pritchard and a lieutenant, both of the Hong Kong and Singapore Royal Artillery. I saw again mighty Mount Kilimanjaro, snow-capped, rearing through a sea of stratocumulus cloud. We used the monarch for a bearing. I got keen and took a sun sight, which came right through our dead reckoning position. We crossed the coast opposite Zanzibar and then did a coast crawl into Dar-es-Salaam.

The next day, we pushed off at dawn for Diego Suarez, Madagascar. We flew to Ras Mkumbi to set course for Diego and I couldn't help but be reminded of those days in 1942 when we used to do creeping-line-ahead patrols between the Comoros and the mainland, returning to Dar-es-Salaam at dawn. The weather was good all the way. We crossed the coast of Madagascar at almost the same spot I did when coming from Pamanzi in August 1942. The sunken ships still lay in Diego Harbour and one still had to take care to miss them when landing and taking off.

We took off for the Seychelles early on 26 January. We ran into bad weather with a very strong wind blowing on our starboard beam at 25 knots. After some exchanges of messages with Mombasa about the prospects of bad weather, I decided to push on to the Seychelles, where we landed in a heavy swell in the outer harbour and bounced to hell.

We spent a couple of days in the Seychelles. One day we had a damned fine five-course meal, complete with oysters, red wine, and liqueurs with some locals who were friends of Major Pritchard. He drove Jock and me out to North East Point, where we had a marvelous ocean swim. There was a lovely yellow sandy beach and crystal-clear water, but unfortunately the bottom was mostly coral and this made wading pretty tricky. I bought a rather nice tortoiseshell cigarette case for 28 rupees. I also got another local curiosity: a double coconut coco-de-mer, which looked awfully suggestive of the spot that 'tickles and teases'.

We were due to leave for Addu Atoll, in the Maldives, early on 28 January. However, rain was absolutely pelting down and it had been doing so for hours. I had a confab with the meteorology officer and all he could promise was continuous rain for the first half of the trip to Addu Atoll and scattered showers after that. The winds were not helpful, so there may have been a chance of arriving in darkness. I was none too keen on doing night landings in places one didn't know when it could be avoided. And besides, our laundry hadn't come back. We lazed around in the mess for the rest of the day.

We left the Seychelles on 29 January when we had enough light to taxi. There was a long swell running and my first attempt to take off provided some hair-raising porpoises. I closed the throttles and started again. I overcame the swell to some degree by rocking the control wheel back and forward to climb up or go down the side of the swells. We were thrown into the air off one swell at about 55 knots, hitting the next swell, and kept being thrown into the air until we had enough speed to remain airborne. There was nothing I could do to prevent this punishing take-off. I had to hold the stick well back as we crashed down on the water to prevent the nose going in and destroying the boat, and possibly us.

Nothing of note happened on the 1,100-mile ocean crossing to Addu Atoll. Most oceans look alike. The atoll was an awfully small spot of land in an awfully large ocean. Jock did a jolly good bit of navigation. We couldn't pick the atoll up on the radar until we were 30 miles away, although we did receive the medium frequency beacon much further away. We landed in the inner lagoon on crystal clear water. One could see to the bottom (30 feet) nae bother at all.

I had intended to continue our journey the next morning, but by the time we had gotten ashore and had dinner, it was 10 pm local time, and that would have meant only six hours before we had to get up again. That was not good after ten and three-quarter hours' flying from the Seychelles and another ten-hour trip to Madras. The quarters were primitive, but good. We went to bed to the sound of surf on the coral reef and a breeze in the palms. It was my first night on an atoll.

Addu Atoll pier and part of the alighting area, 3 November 1942. A Catalina is moored in the centre of the photograph. It appears to be aground. Clear waters such as these presented major problems to aircrew of flying boats as it was extremely difficult to judge where the surface of the water was and the irregularities on the bottom appeared to be close to the surface. Bruce Daymond and his crew alighted here on 29 January 1944 en route to Redhills Lake, Madras, India. (Bruce Daymond)

Breakfast was late, the transport was late, and the dinghy was bloody late. Consequently, we were late off on 31 January on the last lap of our journey. There would have been one or two people on disciplinary charges had I been remaining there. We flew over a long stretch of ocean until we hit the north-west coast of Ceylon.

Left: Bruce Daymond in a classic 'I flew for the King' pose. Note the bulky flying helmet and microphone hanging below the right earphone. The propeller hub and one propeller blade can be seen behind his head. *Right:* Bruce Daymond at the controls of a Catalina. The large control wheel and the tropical flying 'uniform' of flying helmet, short-sleeved shirt, shorts, and long socks can be seen. There is a man standing behind the cockpit, therefore the aircraft must have been on the water. (Bruce Daymond)

We stooged up the Indian coast about 30 miles out to sea. We turned inland at the Palar River and flew up the railway line, the railway being one of the corridors into Redhills. Even from the air the RAF camp looked primitive, and it was. The huts' walls were of light bamboo latticework. There were no electric lights except in the mess and there were no baths or showers. Instead, there was a small tub in which I could just fit if I tucked my knees up under my chin. I felt quite a sense of satisfaction having brought the boat all that way to Redhills safely. If anyone had told me a few years previously that I would fly a boat from West Africa to India, it would have taken some believing.

Chapter 7

357, 628, and 240 Squadrons, India and repatriation to Australia (1 February 1944 – 16 April 1945)

On arrival at Redhills Lake, I experienced more of the administrative cock-ups I had been exposed to throughout my air force service. Having sent cables to the family, Peggy, and Kodak House, giving them my new address, I met Squadron Leader Hawkins DFC and bar, the acting CO of RAF 357 (Special Duties) Squadron. The squadron had been formed the day we arrived. It was established to supply Allied forces operating behind Japanese lines. The translation of its motto was: 'We bring death to the enemy.' It consisted of A and B flights. A Flight operated land-based Liberators and Hudsons from Digri, Bengal, and B Flight operated Catalinas out of Redhills Lake, 969 miles from the squadron HQ at Digri. Hawkins gave us a warm welcome, but it was to some extent dampened by his news that the squadron had more than enough crews, there was a possibility of us losing the boat we had delivered, there was a possibility the crew would split up, and he did not know whether we had been posted or merely attached to the squadron. This applied to me, Goodfellow, Nicholson, and Warrant Officer Brooks, and presumably it would apply to Aiston when he arrived. A subsequent signal explained that the flying boats and the NCOs were posted to the squadron, but the officers were only posted as supernumeraries.

We began more make-work duties to kill time while we were in limbo. One duty was to go for an hour's clay-pigeon shooting with Warrant Officer Brooks' crew. As Jock succinctly put it: 'To come

10,000 miles to shoot clay pigeons, Christ!' We were welcome at the beautifully appointed Gymkhana Club with its excellent sporting, and bar facilities. I did a lot of letter writing, going to the cinema, censoring mail, shopping, and going to dances.

The crew and I were back in the air in 357/Q FP118 on 4 February taking Squadron Leader Hawkins to Bangalore. We landed at the Hindustan Aircraft Company, where aircraft major inspections were carried out. We flew back, leaving Hawkins there. The whole country from Madras to Bangalore was nothing to write home about.

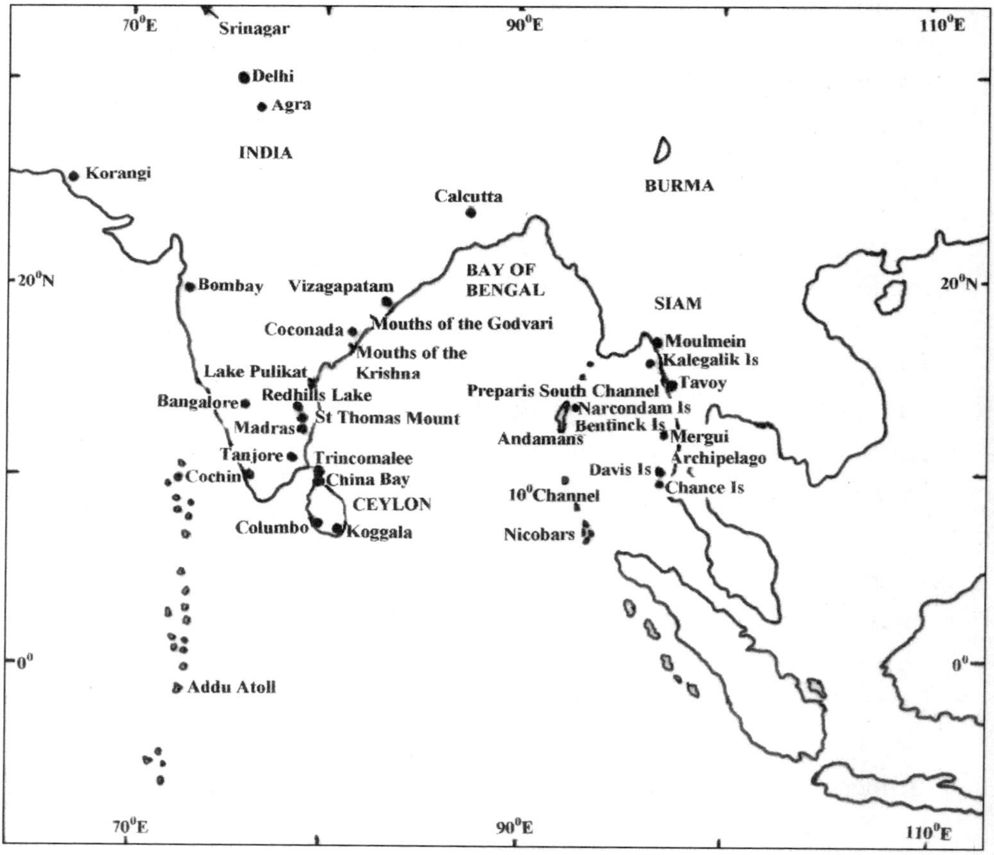

Map of India and the Bay of Bengal showing locations from 1944 and 1945 mentioned in the text.

There were desolate-looking hills and a big river that was completely dry. I did find that strange as there were small lakes dotted everywhere.

Not long after, Sergeants Foxall and Walker of my crew were struck down with diarrhoea, which according to the doctor would lead to dysentery in India unless a person got immediate treatment. He thought that the diarrhoea was not the local kind, but a variety contracted in the Seychelles.

On 11 February, as captain of FP118, I was ordered on patrol immediately. A U-boat had been sighted a couple of hundred miles up the coast and we were to proceed to the RAF advanced base at Cocanada and then carry out our patrol looking for the submarine. However, that meant that after a three-hour flight to Cocanada, we would have to land a heavy boat in rough water. To avoid this, the flight commander rang Group and got the search laid on immediately. There was a bit of a hold up before take-off, for a new order had come in that safety pins had to be put in bomb racks when aircraft were waterborne. This was sensible, as it would have prevented the terrible accident when 209/P was blown up by its depth charges, which were dislodged in Mombasa Harbour in September 1942. Of course, the safely pins had to be removed before becoming airborne. We did a cross-wind take-off and I had to drag the old kite off as we were getting pretty near the moorings. So began my first operation with 357 Squadron. We bogged up the coast, past the Mouths of the Krishna and then across land by the Mouths of the Godavari and on to patrol. Our patrol instructions had been changed two or three times by radio but at last we settled down to a creeping-line-ahead patrol. At dusk, on the first leg, just off Vizagapatam, we came upon a merchant vessel of about 5,000 tons with a heavy list to starboard as if she had been torpedoed. It was accompanied by two escort vessels and two tugs. Away to seaward were splodges on the surface as if depth charges had been dropped recently. We searched all night for the U-boat. I felt good as this was Coastal Command at war. Just as darkness fell, I descended to sea level and reset the altimeter. Who knew what the night might bring? In a U-boat attack at night, one had to be careful not to dive right in. We loaded flares into the chutes and round and round the patrol we went. The moon came up about 10.30 pm and this aided the search. In fact, it was all we had from 3 am onwards because the radar packed up. I saw millions of 'submarines' that night after hours of staring. There was a lot of fractocumulus[1] cloud about and this was the cause of the false U-boat sightings. Dawn broke about 6.45 am and we got half of a circuit of the patrol in before 8 am, when we set course for Cocanada. We landed after eighteen hours in the air. Cocanada lay inside a long, thin peninsula of land. There was a stretch of about 5 miles of muddy brown water. We had been told that it was calm there in the morning, but it turned out to be quite rough. The dinghy ride from the aircraft took about half an hour up a long, canal-like affair to get to the RAF camp.

We took off in Q on time at 8.45 am on 14 February to provide convoy escort to thirteen merchant vessels and two escort vessels. We set course for a position 30 miles astern of the convoy, which was heading southwards. We crossed the Mouths of the Godavari and we had just crossed the coast when we saw the convoy. Jock hadn't even had time to find a three-course wind.[2] The convoy was 20 miles astern of its scheduled position so we arrived in plenty of time. We came on patrol at 10 am and were ordered by the senior naval officer to do a patrol circling the convoy. So, round the convoy we went all day. As the convoy approached the Mouths of the Krishna, our patrol, had we stuck to it, would have taken us over land. A fine place to look for subs! We were due off patrol at 5.30 pm but as the Wellington relief aircraft hadn't arrived, we stayed on until it did half an hour later. We alighted on Redhills Lake just at dusk. At ten and three-quarter hours, it was a gentleman's trip.

The next day, after lunch, I was in the adjutant's office when Squadron Leader Frank Godber, the commander of B Flight, 357 Squadron, walked in. At that stage, he did not know too much about our future special duties. However, he told me as much as he knew about the nature of our proposed duties and it sounded exciting. Shortly after, he went to Calcutta to be briefed on our proposed operations and he then briefed the crews. He told us our special duty operations involved putting agents and stores behind enemy lines, and pulling the agents out when their missions were accomplished. Operations were to be carried out during the full moon period each month, monsoon months excepted. Target areas were along the coast of Burma and Siam[3] and certain offshore islands. Usually, two aircraft would be involved, one to carry out bombing a few miles distant from where the second aircraft was to alight with the agents and stores. We were told it would be a risky and dangerous business. If forced down and captured, we would be regarded as spies and would face torture and execution by the Japanese. Because of the dangers, Godber made it clear that he was seeking only volunteers for the operations. Married men in the four crews were advised to consider their decisions carefully. He assured us there would be no adverse reflection on any man who chose to withdraw. Nor would it count against him in his service career.

Training for special duty operations included take-offs and landings without flare paths, simulating operating conditions across the Bay of Bengal. Accurate navigation was required to pass through the channels north and south of the Andaman and Nicobar Islands. Secrecy was paramount, as radar detection by the Japs would have compromised operations. To avoid Jap radar, low flying at 50–100 feet was obligatory from 200 miles west of the Andamans until 200 miles east. That meant flying at very low altitude for three to four hours at night. Crew training also included assembly of folboats[4] at night in the blister compartment, launching, and loading the agents and stores into them. On landing in enemy territory, and while taxiing, two crew members armed with Sten guns were to exit the blister, move forward on the hull, and clamber against the slipstream on to the main plane, one going out to each wingtip, where they were to lie down, look for enemy opposition, and be ready to repel it should it appear. To save weight for these twenty to twenty-six-hour flights, the aircraft were to be stripped of armaments and any gubbins[5] not essential for operations. Crew members would also be armed with revolvers and machetes. Since my captain's course at Killadeas, my crew and I had been together for ten months. I was proud yet humbled that, when presented with this choice, all eight volunteered. The whole prospect sounded terribly exciting and I hoped I was experienced enough to stay on it.

Flight Sergeant Brown visited Sergeant Walker in hospital and reported he had tuberculosis (TB). The dysentery had evidently so pulled down his health that TB developed. Fortunately, the doctors had got it in the early stages. After a long drought as far as receiving mail was concerned, I had an airmail from Molly Ryan dated 5 February. She told me that Eric Saunders' wedding went off with one hell of a bang.

For several weeks in early March, Hector Monro, Roy Preston, and I went to Tanjore aerodrome to prepare the base for operations. We had Squadron Leader Pimm as our CO, Flight Lieutenant Water as adjutant, and we three were flying control officers. Our accommodation used to be a collector's bungalow. It was a two-storey place with an enclosed roof garden affair without the garden. But by far the most amazing feature was a double-storied covered walk, which ran from the main building to two outlying houses of the bungalow. It looked most impressive by day and most romantic by night.

My job was to prepare the camp to hold 60 officers and 350 men. The rooms had to be furnished with beds, tables, chairs, wash bowls, and baths. I also had to sort out catering arrangements. I had to chase up hurricane lamps, cooking utensils, and a hundred and one things from Trichinopoly, Cochin, and Madras. I was running the officers' mess and cookhouse as well as getting the British other ranks' cookhouse going.

Left: Collector's Bungalow (RAF officers' mess), showing part of the two-decker covered walk, Tanjore, India. *Right:* Pilot Officer Hector Monro at Tanjore, India, March 1944. He returned to Britain in July 1944. He went on to be a Member of the House of Commons for thirty-two years. He was knighted in the early 1970s, long before he retired. Subsequently, Tony Blair's Labour government raised him to the peerage, although Hector was a Conservative. He became Lord Monro of Langholm in 1997. (Bruce Daymond)

On the aerodrome side, Roy Preston and Hector Monro had to supervise the unloading of an ammunition and bomb train. This took a hell of a time due to the lack of facilities. When the 350 bombs were unloaded, they had to be transported to the aerodrome and put in dumps. After a week of rising at 6 am, getting to bed by midnight, and working flat out during the day, we were all pretty much on our knees. So, when the cypher and signals people began to be posted away from the unit and the Yanks didn't arrive as expected a few days after we arrived, we naturally let up the pace a little.

I was annoyed at being at Tanjore for so long without anything happening because I was missing the training for special duties at

Redhills. However, as old Wing Commander Tommy White[6] told me at Bournemouth, 'Everything that happens is for the best.' It was not a bad philosophy, though it was hard to accept at times.

As a telephone had been installed, I moved into the CO's office on 15 March. I was really keen to get out of the dump before I got snowed under with bumph.[7] The flap that sent us to Tanjore did not seem to have come to anything and unless we kept on making a noise, we were easily forgotten in the backwoods by the powers-that-be. In a bid to get out of Tanjore, I asked the CO, while he was on the phone to Group, to ask Wing Commander Beeman, senior air staff officer, to see if Preston, Monro, and I could be recalled. He said he didn't see why we shouldn't and he would ask the air officer commanding.

I received a letter from Jock Gilbert that confirmed a rumour I had had from Kajamalai that a Catalina was missing from Redhills. It turned out it was poor old Freddie Aiston and his crew. They had got caught in a cyclone that hit Madras ten days previously. Poor Freddie never did seem terribly happy about flying. I've never forgotten what old Adjutant Vernon at Killadeas said about him: 'Aiston and crew are going to die, Daymond, they're going to die.' He was on a transit flight carrying agents from Calcutta en route to Ceylon. Not only did we lose Freddie and his crew, we lost a lot of agents as well.

One evening, we were sitting on the verandah of the mess. After a few beers, there was much singing of 'Cats on the Rooftops' and other old favourites. Singing was followed by relating odd flying experiences that had happened to each of us during training. Even then, while we were still in the service and the war was still on, these were happy reminiscences, and with time, they would acquire an even greater nostalgia about them. I agreed then, and after half a century I still did, with T.E. Lawrence's outlook when, out of the service, he wrote, 'My longing to be in the RAF is a homesickness which attacks me at the most casual sight of their name in the papers, or their uniform in the street.'

Finally, we received a signal stating all attached personnel were to return to their units except one administrative officer to be decided by Squadron Leader Pimm. It was decided Roy Preston would remain at Tanjore as his crew had no boat.

On 25 March, Hector Monro and I returned to Redhills. Once there, I received forty letters and three cables, and then at lunchtime, four more letters and one cable, and eight whole lovely and loving letters from Peggy. I wrote at the time:

> God how happy I feel to hear from her. At first I was prepared to think that it was an infatuation that would wear off. Two years have now gone by and we are more deeply bound up in each other than ever. Or is this introspection all very youthful – a stage that everyone goes through? I will admit that Peg is the first person with whom I have really fallen in love. There have been other infatuations and more or less hectic affairs with all the consequences. But never have I been so completely intimate with anyone. Now is it because of this that I feel as I do? I should like to know. A revealing page this – but then what is a diary for?

As mentioned earlier, 357 Squadron consisted of two flights: land-based A Fight and water-based B Flight. The authorities found that having two flights separated by nearly 1,000 miles was not efficient, so the boat flight was hived off to form 628 Squadron, officially set up on 21 March 1944. Its secret role was to carry out special duties operations, but its nominal role was to carry out meteorological reconnaissance and air-sea rescue.

The powers-that-be ordered that all special duties crews had to undertake a jungle training course to learn how to live off the land, in case they were forced down in Burma and had to avoid capture by the Japs. Between 30 March and 6 April, my crew and I, minus Jock Gilbert, who had been sent on some administrative mission by the CO,

Left: The jungle training party, absolutely shagged out. From left to right: Sergeant Foxall, Bruce Daymond, Warrant Officer Trailer, Flight Sergeant Lewis, and Flight Lieutenant Campbell. *Below:* Two wild pigs the party killed. A third was taken by a tiger before it could be collected. The jungle training party from left to right: Flight Sergeant Ward, Flight Sergeant Lewis, Sergeant Foxall, Sergeant Bell, Flight Lieutenant Campbell, Warrant Officer Carrington, Bruce Daymond, Warrant Officer Trailer, and unidentified. (Bruce Daymond)

were sent to a jungle area in southern India. Flight Lieutenant John Campbell, a tour-expired pilot, was also on the jaunt. He was awaiting repatriation to England, but the jungle survival course appealed to him. A warrant officer, appropriately named Trailer, an experienced bushman, was sent with us to impart his know-how, but should we fail to support ourselves by killing our food, he carried reserve iron rations to ensure we didn't starve. Clothed with heavy gear from head to foot – gaiters and boots, a backpack, and armed with a machete – we laboured for eight days through the humid jungle. With a small compass, we endeavoured to go from A to B. At one stage, I recall, to slake our thirst, we peeled the paper wrappings from some malted milk tablets, throwing the wrapping to the ground. To our horror, some fetid days later, we came across these same wrappings. We had obviously committed the novices' error of travelling in a great circle: and this after graduating from a general reconnaissance course!

During this purgatory, we killed and skinned a deer, shot three wild pigs, one of which was taken by a tiger before we could collect it, encountered some elephants, slept on hard ground with a mosquito net face mask, and generally spent an interesting but exhausting week in the heat and humidity emulating 'the great unwashed'. I vividly remember the agony of having to shave off a week's stubble with a far-from-sharp razor blade on our return to civilisation.

I flew with Peter McKeand's crew in FP152 on 12 April to Trincomalee on China Bay, Ceylon. We took Squadron Leader Godber, together with three passengers who were connected with our special duties. As we arrived, the *Queen Elizabeth* and the HMS *Renown* were steaming out with a screen of destroyers. Inside were all kinds of ships, British, French, American, and even one Italian. The huge French battleship *Richelieu* was there, dwarfing everything else.

One morning, I was lying in bed in Trincomalee and heard an aircraft coming in to land. There was a bang and when I ran outside to see what was going on, I saw two separate sheets of flame. A Vought

F4U Corsair, a large, powerful, single-engined fighter, coming in to land, had collided with one taxiing. Both pilots were incinerated. It made a pretty horrible sight in dawn's light to see the dense black smoke rising on the still air. Then the ammunition started to go off. All in all, I didn't have much appetite for breakfast.

Squadron Leader Godber returned from Colombo and we waffled back to Redhills, where new early working hours had been instigated: breakfast was over by 6.45 am, then work until 1.30 pm. And that was the working day over. It was not a bad idea, for the ground crews working on the kites later in the day found conditions devilish hot.

I spent days on odd jobs, spent time in the mess, getting whistled with the blokes, playing tennis, reading, writing letters, sailing, learning to use the Sten gun, doing time in the Link Trainer at St Thomas Mount, acting as flare path officer, being made officer-in-charge of swimming, and with occasional time in aircraft, including take-offs and landings without a flare path. I found them nowhere

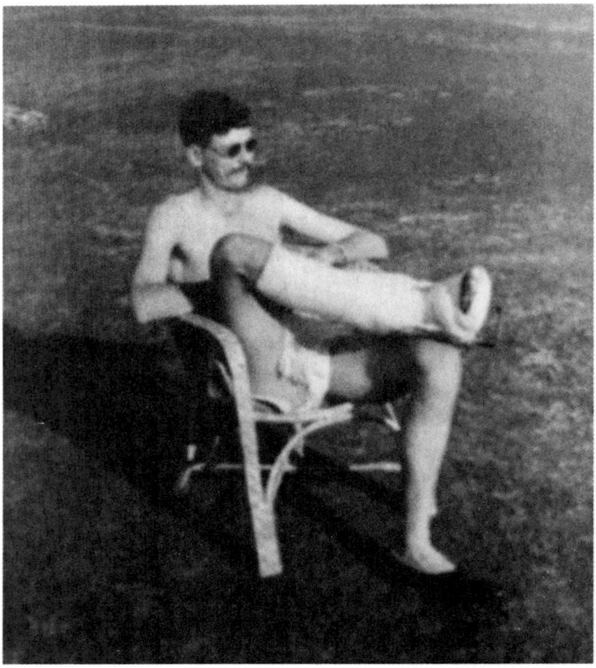

Squadron Leader Godber (6 feet 7 inches tall), CO of 628 Squadron, recovering from a broken ankle, Redhills Lake, Madras, India, 1944. (Bruce Daymond)

as difficult as I thought, although admittedly water conditions were excellent.

One night I had a long talk about the women problem with Ken Riddy DFC. He was expecting to go home and was going to be married soon after. We talked a hell of a lot about marriage, pre-marital relations, the state of being in love, and found that we had practically identical ideas on those things. I had reasoned most of my own ideas out for myself and was rather glad to see that they coincided with those of Ken, who was so obviously such a steady and thoughtful type. I had two wizard letters from Peggy that day and they needed a little thought to reply.

I flew Squadron Leader Godber to Bangalore in FP180 on 8 May to see the air officer commanding as there was another special duty operation coming up and sanction for it was required. There was a bit of a hold-up before take-off as daily inspections weren't finished and

Left to right: Flight Lieutenant Campbell (RAF), Flight Lieutenant Kellock (RAAF), Flying Officer Mitchell (SAAF), and Flight Lieutenant Bruce Daymond, Redhills Lake, Madras, India, April 1944. (Bruce Daymond)

a patch had to be put on one of the blisters. Then I clumsily put my knee through the other blister and this delayed us for another hour. We got to Bangalore just after 10.30 am and Godber went straight over to Group. He was in a hurry to get back so we were airborne again by 1.30 pm.

I took off in FP180 late on 12 May for some fighter affiliation with a couple of Hurricane fighters from St Thomas Mount. It was a grand half hour. I started off at about 4,500 feet and eventually got right down on the deck. We had much more chance of coping with fighters there than upstairs, for up top they could employ the vertical diving attack and there was not much one could do about that. However, by going down on the deck, they could not use this tactic, there being not much room to pull out. The intercom cut out for one critical period and I couldn't hear the instructions coming through from the fire controller. We were 'shot down' beautifully.

Jock and I went on leave in the middle of May and headed for Kashmir. We took a train to Bangalore and from Hindustan aerodrome we caught an American Douglas C47, tail number 118115, captained by Lieutenant Dickman. Our route, Bangalore to Cochin to Bombay to Agra to Delhi, was a rather roundabout one, but we didn't particularly mind as it gave us a chance to see more of India. We spent the night in Bombay and then went on to Agra, where the Yank ground staff were polite, and drove us to their officers' mess, a colossal, single-storied building. At a rough guess I should say it would have seated 300 for dinner at the one time. And, wonder of wonders, there was a table full of women: postal sorters or something, we later found out, but honest to God, white women. Being the only Britishers on the base, we were the only officers in shorts. I wondered why the Yanks stuck to slacks in hot climates.

As we were catching the night plane to Delhi, we tore off after lunch to see the Taj Mahal. The Taj came fully up to expectations. To me, there was a most amazing lack of commercialisation about the place. It was a lovely jewel in the surrounding sunbaked, dry countryside.

The next day we flew to Delhi, took a train to Rawalpindi, and a bus to Srinagar. Approaching Srinagar, we drove through lovely, long avenues of poplar trees. And away in the distance were the rugged, snow-capped Himalayas. We stayed on a houseboat with three bedrooms, a dining room, and a lounge. We explored beautiful Srinagar, then travelled by bus to Tangmarg, and on horseback to Gulmarg. We stayed there for a couple of days and climbed Killen Marg, 14,000 feet above sea level. On 1 June we returned to Srinagar and stayed on a bigger houseboat than our earlier one.

I had met Nora before going up to Gulmarg and, back in Srinagar, I took her to the dance at the Club Annex at Nagin Bagh. It was a lovely moonlight night. We sat in the open on the balcony and spent a very pleasant evening. We returned by shikara, which I believe to be the most effective means of transport for destroying one's willpower and self-control. Kashmir and the romantic moonlight got to both of us.

The 3 June was a write-off. Jock and I went to the Club Annex for a beer at midday. We got involved with Group Captain Stringer and Peggy, his popsy. Nora joined us a short time later and the stage was set. Bash, bash, bash, down they went: some special concoctions made up by the barman. I remember driving the tonga home and bringing the Group Captain and his popsy on board, and then I went out like a light. I came to around 8 pm, but just couldn't face going out as I had promised. Jock deputised for me in spite of the pouring rain.

I went swimming with Nora, and that evening Nora came to dinner. Old George, our cook, put on a wizard meal, the highlight being a very tasty pigeon. After dinner, we set off to see the illumination at Shalimar. The trip down by shikara was fun. We were a bit late and arrived at the entrance to the gardens just in time to see the lights go out. Nothing daunted, we went into the gardens, located the bloke who operated the fountains and lights, and gave him a chip to do his stuff. Only one big fountain was illuminated with coloured lights. Although everyone had gone, we wandered round the whole of Shalimar. Terribly romantic by moonlight and I wasn't the first to fall under its spell. The return trip in the shikara under the moon was a very passionate affair.

The next day, I was bowled over by a hell of a pain in the tummy and was violently ill. I had to put off my dinner date with Nora. Jock reckoned it was a chill on the stomach so I went to bed and had a beer bottle full of hot water. The next morning, I went to Nedous to make my peace with Nora after standing her up the previous evening. She was most frightfully decent about it. Prior to her going over to Nagin for lunch, we did a spot of shopping. Nora and I had a heavy session before saying goodbye.

Jock and I headed back to Redhills, taking eight days for the journey. Despite the lengthy travel, Kashmir was well worth it.

While we were away, on 16 May, Bob Levack, aged 22, and most of his crew were wiped out when FP191 crashed. Apparently, on landing, the nose dug into the water, threw the second pilot forward onto the control-yoke, and they crashed. As a result, we had to wear our Sutton harnesses for take-offs and landings.

In response to the absolutely super letters I got from Peggy, I wrote three to her. There was absolutely no doubt about us. Peace was going to bring forth some domestic strife if we were all still around then.

Just before lunch on 27 June, we brought FP134 up the slip. She was in fair condition. With 240 Squadron she had been C; however, with a change of squadrons, she became 628/U. The next day, the crew began to check over the boat inventory. U had many deficiencies; however, according to Stan Pearson, the engineer officer, she was a good boat with a hull in wizard condition.

While we were on leave, in accordance with squadron tasks, the crews had been doing meteorological flights. These involved taking barometric, temperature, and wind velocity recordings throughout the flight. On 29 June I set off on my first meteorological flight with Jack O'Meara. We took off in 628/R FP180 at dawn. The first 150 to 200 miles of the trip, which was in the form of a triangle out to 90°E, were pretty dirty with heavy rain showers. But after that we ran into some lovely weather. The last 200 miles before landfall contained heavy rain.

After spending a day or so sorting out U, testing equipment, swinging the compasses, and carrying out an air test which showed up some instrument and wireless snags, on 2 July we were on board at dawn for our next meteorological flight. We tried to start the port engine. But could we? Could we hell! Everything pointed to a burnt-out booster coil, and so we reported on coming ashore at 7 am. Because of a failure to take off on an operational trip, bags of bumph work had to be done. Old Stan Pearson's boys could find nothing at all wrong with the engine. Pearson reckoned the engineer had flooded the engine with fuel by heavy priming. That was hard to believe because we couldn't get even one cylinder to fire in the numerous attempts we made to start. When we did a taxi test at 1 pm, everything ran beautifully!

The next day we took U on a meteorological flight over the Bay of Bengal. The weather was grand all the way, with some isolated showers falling from cumulus clouds. Each hour was brightened by coming right down on the deck and taking the barometric pressure. When we were about one and a half hours from base on the return trip, the starboard engine developed a bad oil leak. We were losing a gallon every ten minutes. By the time we reached base, we were down to 30 gallons. With the Catalina, the propellers needed to be feathered and the engine shut down when down to 15 gallons, so with 30 gallons we had plenty to spare. It was these little elements of uncertainty that put the spice into flying.

We were off on another meteorological flight in U on 6 July. A few miles from the coast we ran into shocking weather: rain, lightning, and the ride was bumpy as hell. 'George' was unserviceable so we had to fly manually through this stuff for about one and a half hours. The weather improved and at 90°E was grand. But it went to hell when we turned for home and the whole 600 miles back was through unadulterated filth. We had head winds the whole way and our ground speed was down to 70 knots at one stage. The whole trip was fourteen and a half hours. Then, to end it all, we got soaked going from the operations room to the mess. In the mess we said farewell to Bert Kellock and Jerry Wright, who were leaving early the next day for Bombay and thence to the UK. While it was not home for either of them, as one was an Australian and the other Canadian, England was a hell of a lot better than India.

We were airborne mid-morning in R on 8 July to do battle with a couple of Hurricane fighters. There was no sign of the Hurricanes at the rendezvous so we stooged over to St Thomas Mount to look for them. No joy, so back to Redhills we flew and got on the radio to get the controller to chase them up. Just as we were doing this, they appeared. I let Flight Sergeant Brown play around with them at 3,000 feet. I took over after quarter of an hour and went down low. We had some wizard dicing, with steep diving turns from 100 feet. I felt we coped quite effectively. We landed and I got a gharry[8] over to St Thomas Mount to have a natter with the Hurricane boys. I had advocated this liaison for a long time, for so much more could be got out of the whole exercise if the exercise was discussed between both parties. Both the fighters and ourselves had camera guns, but our gunners couldn't bring their guns to bear because of the violent evasive action. The talk with the fighter boys was most encouraging. They reckoned they got in only three effective shots during the half hour. Two of them were from dead astern, our blind spot, when we completely lost sight of the fighter. If we indulged in weaving, it coped with that type of attack. They were rather shaken by the lack of success and stated definitely that the low-down stuff put them right off. That was our modus operandi.

We were off on another meteorological flight in U on 9 July, taking Flying Officer Ness, the adjutant of 628 Squadron, with us. During the engine run up before take-off, there was a magneto drop of 400 revolutions which we couldn't clear. We tried pitch control, auto-lean, and running up, but all gave no joy. We signalled to the controller that we were mooring up, for I thought it must be a disconnected spark plug lead. Taxiing up to the moorings, I tried one last test and the drop had cleared itself. I was pleased, for I didn't fancy a second operational failure within a week. However, I really had to drag the old bitch off the water. As we were already late, if we had to taxi back for a second go, it would have made us later still. The weather was bad from the word go and with cloud almost down to the deck, it was as bumpy as hell. Old Ness was sick early in the piece. Sergeant Foxall held the blister open for him to do his stuff and collected the backwash. It was foul for Foxall, but very amusing for the rest of us. We battled strong winds at 43 knots all the way home. The whole trip was fourteen hours and thirty-five minutes, with a night take-off and landing.

We took Flight Lieutenant McGregor, the Group defense type, with us on our meteorological flight in U on 12 July. We climbed to 3,000 feet about 150 miles from base to get some meteorological readings. I did three diving steep turns to get back to the deck. Flight Sergeant Carrington, the rigger, an ex-London bus driver, yelled, 'What's he doing, swinging the loop?' The weather was a little better than on our previous trip. We had a tail wind of 35 knots on the way out and reached the turning point at 10 am. We throttled her back on the way home so we made it a fourteen-hour flight.

We had a big party in the mess on 14 July. The place was made to look quite presentable. A green carpet had been brought from the library and covered some of the bare concrete of the ante-room. A couple of the Group Captain's Persian rugs also helped. A bar had been constructed, running the whole width of the mess. On the front was a design of a Catalina skimming over the tops of some cumulus clouds. The whole thing was in three-ply, and with grey, blue, and white paint it looked pretty fine. There were a great number of guests, including the Governor, the Air Officer Commanding, an odd sprinkling of group captains, and quite a few very presentable popsies. As we were off on a meteorological flight early the next day,

Jock and I couldn't lash out. That was a great pity, for it was the sort of party that one really felt like cracking on. Two whiskies saw me through the whole night.

We put in fourteen and a quarter hours on our meteorological flight and the weather was far better than the previous trips. It was sunny most of the way, with no rain except for one isolated squall. Flight Sergeant Brown did the navigating and made a jolly fine job of it.

The next day I spent the first part of the morning writing a letter of condolence to Mrs Walker who, at the time we left the UK, was the three-week bride of Sergeant Ron Walker. He went down with dysentery when we arrived in India. This so pulled down his health that TB came to light. He was sent away to the hills, and then to South Africa, where he died. It was tragic as he was such a solid, healthy-looking chap.

I was going past the Guard Room early on 20 July when Group Captain Brougham came up in his car and said, 'Hey big boy, didn't

Bruce Daymond's days as a flight commander. It was not a pose. He was on the phone when the intelligence officer came in with his camera, Redhills Lake, Madras, India, August 1944. (Bruce Daymond)

I promise to take you flying?' He had done so a week or ten days previously, and as he was just off to do his early morning flip, I went with him. It was my first trip in a Tiger Moth since March/April 1941. How strange it was, and how small the Tiger Moth was after two and a quarter years on Catalinas. He handed the controls over to me just after we were airborne. I did a few steep turns. We then climbed and did a few flick rolls, a couple of loops, a solo roll, and some low flying. It was bloody good fun and such a change after nearly three years of straight and level flying.

The same day, my old friend Rolf Luck arrived to join 240 Squadron, which was also based at Redhills. He had finished his operational tour, but was posted for a second tour more or less out of spite, as far as I could gather. He had turned down a job with BOAC, and Middle East HQ was so annoyed with him that they sent him to India instead of the UK. Of course, he wanted to join us on 628 Squadron as the work was more exciting than any general reconnaissance on 240 Squadron. I hoped he could work it as he was an experienced second-tour type who was just the sort of bloke we wanted.

I received two wizard letters from Peggy. We were both really feeling it this time. I felt so bad that I wrote back immediately and tried to get us sorted out. Would she divorce Ken and marry me when the war was over? I knew that she loved me more, but there was the difficulty of my going back to Australia and being so far away from the centre of this emotional mix-up.

We were unable to complete our meteorological flight in U on 24 July because of bad weather. At the end of the first leg and the beginning of the second, we saw a lot of dirty weather a few miles to starboard. The pressure had dropped considerably and the winds strengthened to 55 knots. As I thought we were near the centre of the depression, I abandoned the scheduled patrol as our track would have taken us right through the bad weather. I sent a signal to base saying that we were returning along our outward track. Winds were strong the whole way. We ticked up fourteen hours and twenty minutes.

Rolf Luck thought he would be able to transfer to 628 Squadron. Ted Hawkins, 240's flight commander, returned from Bangalore, where he had spoken to Group about the change-over. That day, Rolf was flying with another 240 type. This chap was doing a stall landing and he yanked the stick back too soon, the aircraft dropped a wing, smashed the chine and bulkheads, and was a complete write-off. Fortunately, no one was hurt.

Group Captain Brougham saw me as I going to fly in U on 26 July and asked what I was doing. When I told him we were doing fighter affiliation, he decided to come along. We had a hell of a do with two Hurricanes, with most of it at tree-top height. At times we had to lift a wing over lone palm trees. The Old Man thoroughly enjoyed himself and wanted to know when there would be more so he could join us. The next day we did another meteorological flight in U in mainly fine weather and got back early because of favourable winds. We bowled along at 105 knots for most of the trip.

There were bags of panic in the operations room on 2 August. A U-boat had been sighted and there was a hunt to exhaustion in progress. There were five boats out from Redhills, as well as some Liberators from St Thomas Mount. Shortly after we crossed the coast in U, we saw some flame floats being dropped near us. It was from one of the aircraft finding a three-course wind. The weather on our meteorological trip was absolutely perfect.

I did some low flying over the sea by moonlight in U several days later. Two navigators came along to practice drift taking at night to get some practice for the special duty jobs. On the way out, we came across five motor torpedo boats silhouetted in the moon's path. I guessed they were carrying out an anti-submarine hunt. We came back to Redhills and spent an hour or so practicing landings without the flare path.

The weather for the meteorological flight in U on 6 August was pretty fair. The winds were not terribly strong and it was after noon before we turned for home. As luck would have it, the wind sprang up and we had to do the last four and a half hours at 110 knots. As we looked like being late back, I climbed to 5,000 feet to get the benefit of the extra airspeed. I went back to the navigation compartment to look at the navigation, but was only there briefly before the aircraft began to be thrown unmercifully. I tore up to the 'office' and found we were getting into filthy weather. We had to go down to 1,000 feet, so the whole effort to get home faster was a loss. The trip was fourteen hours and twenty minutes.

On 7 August the squadron officers had a night out. We started off in the Connemara for dinner and drinks. The highlight of the evening was the CO blowing up a condom in the lounge, much to the disgust of a lady nearby. She blanched visibly when it burst prematurely. From the Connemara twelve rickshaws went in line astern to the picture house, where we saw *For Whom the Bell Tolls*.

Left: 'Hardly a pretty sight but these are the things we have to put up with. The rigours of an Indian Campaign.' Jack O'Meara removes the towel from Jock Gilbert after Jock's bath, Redhills Lake, Madras, India, 1944. *Right:* Bomb scow coming alongside a Catalina, Redhills Lake. (Bruce Daymond)

No. 628 Squadron officers – a very happy crowd, Redhills Lake, Madras, India, July 1944. Left to right, back row: Flight Lieutenant Jack O'Meara (Goldy-locks), Flying Officer Bert Hawkins (O'Meara's second pilot), Flying Officer Bert Beach, Pilot Officer Tom Straker DFM, Flight Lieutenant Peter McKeand DFC (flight commander), Flying Officer Morgan, Flying Officer Don Evans (McKeand's navigator), Flight Lieutenant Stan Pearson (the engineer officer, who used to be engineer officer with 209 Squadron with Bruce Daymond in Kenya), and Pilot Officer Gibson (intelligence officer). Middle row: Squadron Leader Godber (the commanding officer, with the cast on his leg), and Flight Lieutenant Jock Gilbert (Bruce Daymond's navigator). Front row: Flight Lieutenant Ness (the adjutant), Bruce Daymond (flight lieutenant), and Pilot Officer George Speer (gunnery officer). (Bruce Daymond)

We had another meteorological flight in U on 11 August and we were lucky enough to have almost perfect weather. After about four hours out, I decided that I would have a go at the navigation, so I took over from Jock Gilbert. It was the first time I used the air-plot system, but it was easy to pick up and I thought it gave greater accuracy than the old track crawling method I was taught at general reconnaissance school. We hit Madras on the nose, much to my surprise, but the estimated time of arrival was a good bit out. I navigated for ten hours altogether. The longest navigation trip I had done before was about three hours.

Our thirteenth meteorological trip in U, on 14 August, started off the same way as the others. But before the day was out, we were to have the scare of our lives. We went out on a northerly track. The winds dropped to 3 knots, 2 knots, and at one time Jock was unable to get any wind at all. We turned for home and ran into rain and low cloud. Turbulence began to increase and became so violent that I took 'George' out. Then the party began. We were a veritable leaf in the storm. We were tossed all over the sky and I couldn't control our headlong rush toward the sea. We hurtled down from 1,000 feet at 2,000 feet per minute despite the fact that I had the control wheel hard back in my stomach and full throttle applied. I caught one glimpse of the angriest-looking sea I had ever seen. As we were rushing towards it, I prayed to God to help us, for there was nothing more I could do. Flight Sergeant Lewis told me later that he and the crew had readied the dinghy in the blister compartment during our plunge seawards. Flight Sergeant Haskins was in the second pilot's seat at the time. He couldn't understand what I was telling him when I asked for a reciprocal heading to be set on the compass. I dared not take my hands off the control column, so hard was she fighting. I yelled for Jock to come and set the reciprocal heading. The intercom had water in it and I was screaming to make myself heard. Jock set the reciprocal heading and we turned about. By then, we were down to 290 feet and were holding our altitude. He said afterwards that my face was yellow with fear. It was the closest dice with death I had ever had. We decided not to tempt Providence again that day and, after an exchange of signals with base, set course for Cocanada. We went like hell, for I feared the cyclone would move south-west and cut us off. We got in by 6.45 pm. Flying Officer Mitchell was in charge at Cocanada and he made us comfortable and lent us clothes, etc. We needed a good, stiff drink, and again he obliged. As we gulped our drinks, Jock's and my glances met and we smiled knowingly, realising how damned lucky we were to be there at all. I felt thoroughly teased out, but decided with the others to go to the film *Now Voyager*, starring Bette Davis, which I had long wanted to see. During the show, Jock remarked that it was one of the amazing things about the air force that a couple of hours before, we were dicing with death, and then on the same day we were looking at a film in perfect safety!

The next day Group would not allow us to do a transit flight back to Redhills. We had to go off on another meteorological flight. Redhills rang to give us the latest weather gen, telling us that Jack O'Meara ran into some sticky stuff the day before. They could only promise us foul weather, a belt of which had moved up to just off Cocanada. They also gave us the news that 240/J had been shot up by flak[9] from an Allied ship while doing Leigh Light exercises. Some of the crew were wounded and the crew were circling and waiting for dawn before landing.

Our take-off was 6.20 am. That was later than usual as it was not as far out to our extreme point from Cocanada as from Redhills. We went off at first light without the flare path. The weather right from the first was pretty bloody so we were flying in heavy rain most of the day. Out at the extreme point, we had to shorten the scheduled patrol, as we had to be back at Redhills by 7 pm. We came in at 6.45 pm. I was put out to find that no mail had arrived for me during the three days away.

We headed out on another meteorological flight in 628/V JX347 with a promise of all sorts of bad weather: cyclones not excluded. Apart from one tiny patch of filth which we skirted in ten minutes, we had perfect weather all the way. Flight Sergeant Brown did the navigating and put up a good show, though his estimated time of arrival was twenty minutes out. Our social commitments meant we were in a bit of a hurry to get back as Squadron Leader Godber had promised to take Jock and me to the Adyar Club for supper. We landed at 6.10 pm after a twelve-and-a-half-hour trip. Squadron Leader Hawkins came with us to the Adyar as both he and Squadron Leader Godber were members. It was such a pleasure to eat good food again as that in the mess was pretty bloody.

We did a long meteorological flight in U on 23 August. As Jack O'Meara had a beautifully sunny trip the day before, with hardly a cloud in the sky, we were expecting something similar, but didn't get it. On the 634-mile leg home, I took a couple of sun shots which put us 30 miles behind our dead reckoning position. An hour later I took another couple which put us 45 miles behind. We decided to use them and altered dead reckoning accordingly to see how it would work out. As our landfall proved, the sights must have been pretty well bang-on. The only reason that I can give for our estimated time being so far behind dead reckoning was that the wind in the storms that we passed through must have got up to a high velocity and no allowance was made for this. The calculation error from log analysis was small and air speed indicators were OK, as proved on good weather days. Next trip, if we encountered any storms, we planned to time the period we were in storm and test out this theory.

The weather on our meteorological flight in U on 26 August was grand. We saw the sun the whole time and were able to get in a lot of astro. The sun sights kept putting us behind dead reckoning. We altered on this and a further couple of sights confirmed our action. Three or four hours later, we were again 20 miles behind dead reckoning. We left it for a while and, when we were able to get a fix with Madras radio, we altered dead reckoning. Our landfall again confirmed our action. Our theory about increased wind velocity in storms putting the dead reckoning out appeared to have gone for a Burton, for the weather had been perfect all day. Jock's drift sightings were OK. They were checked on two instruments and his calculation error was small. So that only left the air speed indicator and pilot error. We sat on the airspeed carefully, so I thought it was the instrument over-reading.

The normally unruffled routine of our meteorological flight take-off in U was disturbed on 29 August. One of the flares was out and adrift somewhere on the lake, and the flare path had been laid in a cockeyed direction. This was bad because I had to stay on the water long after the last flare. When we finally got airborne and I was able to see clearly how the flare path was laid, I was shaken more than somewhat to see how close to land the last flare was. There wasn't as much sun as on the last trip. In fact, at the furthest easterly point, monsoon conditions were starting to build up. However, we were able to get a number of sights and further check the air speed indicator. On the trip, we used a position error of +3 knots instead of the time-honoured +7 knots for Catalinas. And this worked out very well. Why there should have been this sudden change over the last three trips, I was at a loss to say.

After I completed all the monthly returns on 1 September, we climbed aboard U and set course for China Bay, Ceylon, for my first special duty operation. Peter McKeand came with us as captain. The trip down was made in grand weather. Trincomalee Harbour was crammed full of ships: a King George V class battleship; two Queen Elizabeth class battleships, HMS *Warspite* and HMS *Valiant*; a Revenge class battlecruiser, HMS *Renown*; a couple of aircraft carriers; and the French battleship *Richelieu*.

Up at the permanent mess, perched in a delightful location on the top of a hill, we met two American naval officers who were our contacts for the special duty operations. After lunch, they took us out to their camp, which was about 12 miles up the coast. There we discussed the operation in all its aspects and met two of the three agents we were to deliver onto Davis or Chance islands over the Bay of Bengal. They were both American army second lieutenants. The third was a Malay agent. There was little information available about the two islands.

The next morning, we got off to an early start with the Yanks. We drove back to China Bay. The drive just after dawn was really lovely and most stimulating. The countryside was wet with dew and looked very fresh. This was such a change from India, which looked permanently shagged out. The Malay agent was unserviceable with a bleeding gum from a tooth extraction so we carried out the practice with the two Yanks. We took off and flew about 15 miles south-west to Kantale Tank, a smallish lake. We landed there and then spent the morning practicing anchoring, taking soundings, off-loading, panic take-offs, and worked out, we hoped, a drill for any eventuality that might arise.

Jack O'Meara and his crew arrived about 2 pm. He said that it had looked at one stage as if they wouldn't join us, for on the air test after the major inspection their oil temperatures and pressures were all over the place. The oil filters were absolutely choked with carbon: the starboard one had collapsed.

With the station intelligence officer and Brian Gibson, our intelligence officer, I went to naval HQ on 3 September to see if we couldn't unearth more information about Davis or Chance islands. The chart the navy gave us was a small-scale Admiralty one. They then produced one a little bigger, but not sufficiently so to be of much use. We went aboard HMS *Adamant*, the submarine depot ship, and saw the submarine intelligence people. They had just received a report on the target, but it did not provide any further information. While we were doing this, Jack was practicing with the Yanks.

The next day we gave U an air test and combined a practice off-loading with it. We had three extra Americans on board who did nothing but take photographs with the most super-looking cine cameras.

We were told the plans had all suddenly been changed. The directors of the operation wanted a daylight reconnaissance done. This sounded a bit hazardous, especially as it meant going past the Andaman and Nicobar islands in broad daylight.

At the time, because of the need for secrecy, I was not allowed to keep any accounts of the special duty flights I conducted. In 1992, I went to the UK Public Record Office, Kew, believing that the security on these operations had been lifted after thirty years. Not so! The fifty-year embargo still applied: that is, no information was available until the end of 1994. When Bob Lewis, one of my former engineers, visited Australia in 1993, he and I sat down with charts, logbooks, and diaries and produced our recollections of the clandestine operations.

In 1944, the Japanese were sending supplies from Singapore to Rangoon by 100-foot wooden Tavoy schooners. To avoid detection, particularly by rocket-carrying Bristol Beaufighters, the schooners sailed hugging the coast by night and anchored under cover by day. Unfortunately, the Beaufighters were operating at extreme range, leaving them little time to search for their prey and less time for attack. To make better use of this limited time, agents were positioned as coast watchers along the Mergui Archipelago to provide reports on the movements of Japanese shipping.

The American Office of Strategic Services (OSS) wanted to become involved in these clandestine operations, but both the French and Dutch had rejected American involvement on nationalist grounds. However, Colin Gubbins of the British Special Operation Executive (SOE) and Bill Donovan of the OSS had a good working relationship and SOE agreed that the Americans could undertake Operation Balmoral to see how they could perform. The Americans were also making a training film for the OSS, first at Kantale Tank, and they wished to add a segment taken on Operation Balmoral. The operation on 6/7 September was to be carried out from Trincomalee by Flight Lieutenant Peter McKeand and crew in U, with Flight Lieutenant Jack O'Meara and crew in 628/R carrying out diversionary bombing. I was Peter McKeand's second pilot.

The objective was to land the two American lieutenants on Davis Island; failing that, the secondary drop was to be on Chance Island, off the southern end of the Burma coast. Other agents had been sending back reports on the movements of the Tavoy schooners and the landing of these two was to provide back-up for this coast watching. In addition, we were to carry Major General Cylos William Dunsmore, an American officer, who was filming the training film.

Security on all special duty operations was critical and only those who needed to know had any information on them. This tight security was to prevent the operations being compromised and the agents captured and executed. However, as our flight progressed, we began to think that security had been blown. We took off from the outer harbour at Trincomalee after a run of two minutes and twelve seconds, out of wind, and with many bounces. We flew eastward across the Bay of Bengal, but on going through the Ten Degree Channel between the Andaman and Nicobar Islands, we ran into a Japanese convoy. To avoid giving away our destination, we turned westward as if heading to India. When out of sight of the convoy we resumed course. When we arrived at Davis Island, we came low around a headland to see a transport in the bay and a beach crowded with Japanese, running everywhere. I don't know who got the greatest surprise, the Japs or us. Dunsmore, busy filming from the open port blister, got such a shock he dropped the camera over the side, much to the amusement of our crew.

We high-tailed it out of the area, heading north to put the Japs off our scent and not reveal that our next target was Chance Island. On approaching Chance, the alighting area looked terrifying. The water was crystal clear, making it difficult to judge where the surface was, and the coral reefs appeared to be right on the surface. The Chance group consisted of two islands and we landed in a strait between them about midday. We switched off engines and anchored. It was an eerie feeling, being a sitting duck in enemy territory.

The two Americans launched a dinghy, got into it, and then loaded it with stores handed to them from the aircraft. The Americans were carrying two lightweight carbines, and on getting into the dinghy one of them accidentally discharged four rounds. Flight Sergeant Lewis was afraid one of the rounds might have gone through our aircraft's tail, with the possibility of damaging one of the control cables. A check revealed no damage. However, the noise of the discharges was a great way of indicating our presence and our vulnerable situation.

The agents went ashore on the southern island to check the layout and its suitability for their purposes. The only sign of habitation on the island was a fisherman's hut. At one stage we heard the sound of a diesel engine and a patrol boat went by to the north of us. We remained absolutely quiet as sound carries over water. Fortunately, we were undetected, probably because our black camouflage merged into the island behind us.

Flight Lieutenant O'Meara in 628/R finished his diversionary bombing attack and passed over us. Seeing we were safely on the water, they headed for home. We sat like shags on a rock for about two hours with no word from the agents. Our instructions were to wait until they reported all OK, in case we had to take them off. Finally, they sent us a wireless message signifying they would remain on the island. There appeared to be no-one on the island and they planned to use the hut as a base. We were more than happy to leave after such a long time sitting on the water. We were concerned about having to pass the Andaman Islands in daylight and the presence of Jap fighters less than 12 miles from our low-level track through the Ten Degree Channel.

Before heading back to Madras, I went on board *Adamant* to give the Naval Intelligence people the information we gathered on the flight. The naval authorities opened the harbour boom gates so our three boats, U, V, and R, took off in the open sea, got into formation over China Bay, and flew in formation for the three-hour trip back to Madras. We changed stations on the trip to enable photographs to be taken. Flying conditions were pretty bumpy as soon as we crossed the coast. We flew over Redhills Lake in formation and, according to the blokes below, it looked pretty good. We did a strictly verboten formation landing. We heard later that the ground staff had gotten a good kick out of the performance.

The next few days were spent cooling our heels, including attending a party at the 240 Squadron mess to say farewell to Flying Officer Mitchell. It was the best party for some time, marred by one of the mess waiters saying that he was in charge of the furniture when we lifted 'our' table out to the lawn. The next day there were a few repercussions over Mitchell's party. The Group Captain had old Des Stephen on the mat, wanting to know where the table was. The president of the mess committee told someone to go to 628 Squadron and collect the table. Everything was smoothed over when it was discovered in Mitch's room, whither we had borne it. The table was a hell of a lot worse for wear because the party-goers had danced on it. It was a jolly good thing that no-one had access to a saw at the party, else Mitch would have had his piece of table, being a shareholder. The Group Captain would really have gone to town if that had happened.

We conducted another meteorological flight in U on 15 September. I was beginning to find these flights pretty binding as they were merely knocking up boring flying hours with no operational action. The weather was pretty good all the way. The winds were light, but from all points of the compass. The sea was so calm that we saw lots of marine life. It was strange to see floating trees in the middle of the Bay of Bengal. Visibility was superb and on the return trip, we saw the coastline from 65 miles away.

While I was at Group HQ on 22 September, getting orders for our forthcoming special duty operations on behalf of the CO, Group received a shattering signal from Air Command South East Asia. From 1 October 628 Squadron was to be disbanded. Two of her boats were to go to 240 Squadron, and the rest to 357 Squadron, our special duty partners. We had known for some time this was in the wind, but never thought it would come so soon, especially because of all the work in the offing. The CO was pretty shattered when I told him of the date of the disbanding. He hadn't heard anything about it. He said it looked like some of the directing powers were working on the side of the Japanese. I felt very sorry for him, for the whole establishment of the squadron was his and he had worked so hard to make it work. The squadron had existed for little over six months.

I received three air letters from Peggy. Her mother had died a few days before she wrote to me. Her mother's death was very sad. I was as much mixed up in her make-up as she was in mine and no matter how hard she tried, I did not think she could alter that. With Ken about to return home she was doing her best to put aside our love, but she was fighting a losing battle. Her letters said as much. I wrote at the time: 'For God's sake, Peggy do something positive.'

We were off on another meteorological flight in U on 24 September. The bad weather in the bay had moved slightly south and so south went the 'cyclone chasers'. The trip was slightly shorter, so take-off wasn't till 6 am. I let Flight Sergeant Brown act as captain for this trip, even doing the full-load night take-off. Squadron Leader Jock Shaw came with us, though Lord knows what for, because he spent most of the trip on the bunk. I took quite a few shots with the marine sextant and my results were good. The flight was the bare twelve hours forty minutes.

The next day we held a squadron parade, during which the CO told us officially of our being disbanded. When that transpired I had several options. If I counted my second pilot's operational times, I was officially operations tour-expired and the crew, although they only had 500 operational hours, could return to the UK with me. That, of course, was their preference. Or I could go to 240 Squadron and do the remaining 200 hours to the 700 mark there. It would probably have taken an age, especially as general reconnaissance work was so scarce and 191 Squadron was moving to Redhills. That would halve any work available. There was some talk of the 628 Squadron crews that went to 240 being allowed to do any special duty work that might come in, but I felt this was no more than talk. They would have to take their turn with the rest of the squadron crews. Personally, I had a horror of going to 240 with its colossal training programme.

In the meantime, U was completing her maintenance, including fixing leaks in her hull. She had to have some rivets replaced and various other problems dealt with before she was ready for operations.

I did some landings without flare path with Rolf Luck in V. The aircraft was pretty heavy and there was a slight cross-wind, which made for good practice. I got bags of confidence about conducting full stall landings at night. Normally, on calm waters, the aircraft was flown under control onto the water. However, in open water with large swells, the technique was different. The aircraft was stalled on the top of the swell so it landed on the downward slope. To flying boat people, it was known as a Gibraltar or Gib landing, as boats often had to land off Gibraltar in the open sea. It required fine judgement, as by stalling the pilot lost flying speed and therefore control, so the aircraft had to be positioned correctly in order not to crash into the oncoming swell.

Captain Leslie Thom arrived with two British other ranks on 29 September for Operation Barnowl I on 1/2 October. We spent a strenuous day getting loads of packages ready and getting them on board U. We also loaded rations, repaired the two dinghies Captain Thom had brought, tended to a number of other little odd jobs, and refuelled with 1,610 gallons. The operation's objective was to land two British other ranks to reinforce the intelligence-gathering capacity along the Mergui Archipelago. We were to carry Captain Thom, his two merry men, and some supplies in U. Jack O'Meara in R was to carry additional supplies. I briefed both crews. Take-off was at 11.50 am. Despite the heavy fuel load, the take-off run was only eighty-two seconds, which rather amazed me, as I was expecting something nearer the two minutes twelve seconds we took at China Bay. R took off after us and formed up with us, and away we went. Weather to 87°E was OK, but after that it got steadily worse. The usual squalls associated with the South-West Monsoon were developing. We pressed on to 92°30'E until last light, when we were about to go through the Preparis South Channel, to the north of the Andaman Islands, flying very close to the water to avoid detection by radar. In order to decrease the chances of us being detected visually, dampeners had been fitted over the engine exhausts to minimise the flames coming from them. As an aid to help formation flying at night, a small blue light had been fitted to the top of the main plane. Jack O'Meara in R had to fly in particularly close formation in driving rain to keep us in view. As we were low to dodge radar, there was land ahead, and the weather showed absolutely no sign of improving, we exchanged signals by Aldis Lamp and decided to pack it in. During our return trip we had been unable to take any astro fixes because of poor weather and we hit the coast north of Lake Pulicat, but thought we were south and altered accordingly. The result was that we went

This photograph of Jack O'Meara's Catalina, 628/R, RAF serial FP180, was taken from Bruce Daymond's 628/U, RAF serial FP134, near the Andaman Islands, Bay of Bengal, on 4 October during the outward leg of special duties operation Barnowl I to put coast watchers ashore on Bentinck Island. A large hole was torn in her hull during the attempt to alight. The landing was aborted and Jack successfully returned the boat to Redhills Lake, where he landed near the slipway so the engineers were able to haul her ashore before she sank. Due to the extensive damage to her hull she was struck off charge on 5 October 1944. Note that for special duties operations, she had been stripped of her radar, armaments, and any other equipment to save weight and carry more fuel. (Bruce Daymond)

tooling up the coast almost to the Mouths of the Krishna. This navigation error added a considerable amount to our time in the air. We eventually landed at 6 am after eighteen hours and five minutes. We were completely shagged out.

On 4/5 October we completed Barnowl I to Bentinck Island with Jack in R. We took off in U at 10.45 am and made landfall on Narcondam Island at last light as planned. We put the agents ashore on Bentinck Island and returned to base. The flight took twenty-eight hours, of which twelve were by day and sixteen by night, much of the time at low levels. Unfortunately, 'George' went unserviceable early in the flight and the second pilot and I flew manually for twenty-five hours, which was thoroughly exhausting.

The trip was not uneventful for poor old Jack O'Meara. While coming in to land at Bentinck Island, the aircraft hit a log, which ripped a great hole in the hull. He felt the aircraft bounce as if thrown

Catalina Mark IB 628/U, RAF serial FP134, Redhills Lake, Madras, India, 1944. She was declared unserviceable on 19 October 1944 and was struck off charge on 26 October. It was the first flying boat that Bruce Daymond flew as an aircraft captain from Lough Erne, Northern Ireland. He had the aircraft's control wheel in his study for the rest of his life. (Bruce Daymond)

in the air by the ocean swell and he did not realise it was holed. He could not understand why he didn't carry out a stall landing off the bounce, as training in the previous months had taught him to do. Instead, he opened the throttles to go around again for another landing attempt. Flight Sergeant Eddleton rushed into the cockpit and told Jack there was a gaping hole in the hull under the navigator's compartment. The hole was big enough to climb through. Had he stalled the aircraft off the bounce, it would have meant the loss of the boat, crew, stores, and equipment.

Jack and his crew provided cover for us, and then set course for home, 1,200 miles away. Once near base he was able to break radio silence and let them know the condition of his hull and request help from the Marine Section to beach the aircraft. Flight Sergeant Eddleton closed the watertight doors between the cockpit and navigator's compartment, and the latter and the blister compartment. He also blew up the rubber dinghy for added flotation. Jack carried out a skilful stall landing as close to the slipway as he could manage, which allowed the Marine Section types to get mooring lines around the boat and haul it up the slipway before it sank. Because of the extent of the damage to her hull, R was struck off charge that day.

As a result of this operation, Jack received a Mention in Despatches. He was without an aircraft and was posted as CO of a transit camp at Mackays Gardens for personnel from 628 Squadron awaiting posting or repatriation. From there, he went as a test pilot to Hindustan Aircraft Company at Bangalore for two months, before being repatriated to Australia.

The next day I stayed in bed until just on lunchtime, but even so felt pretty shagged out. With the long hours in the air, my eyes had taken a hell of a pasting. Leslie Thom produced a bottle of Murree beer which he, Jock, and I despatched right smartly. Leslie took the officers of the two aircraft, plus a couple of others, to dinner at the Connemara. It was a nice gesture by way of thanks for what we thought was a successful operation.

As Peter was out on a meteorology flight on 8 September, I was acting flight commander as well as CO. From various signals that came in, it seemed that the CO had little joy in stopping the squadron's disbanding while he was in Kandy. He and the Group Captain arrived back in V during the afternoon and confirmed the bad news. The authorities planned for McKeand, Luck, and Brooks with their crews to be posted to 240 Squadron to do special duties work. I was to be attached temporarily to help them out, after which I was to be repatriated to UK. That was the plan and it suited me fine. Wing Commander Wood, CO of 240 Squadron, could turn nasty and make me continue to tick up my 1,000 hours. To guard against that, I decided to go with Rolf Luck on the next day's meteorological flight in FP215 to get another thirteen hours up, for I felt there would be little flying for us on 240 Squadron, particularly as we would not have a boat because U was being put into storage. I went on the meteorological flight and I used the time to get some practice with the marine sextant. It was a wizard little machine. I used it both on Jupiter and the sun. I was getting position lines right through dead reckoning. I ticked up another 12 hours 50 minutes, which gave me a grand total of 1,411 hours.

Over the next few days, we moved to the 240 Squadron quarters and mess. We moved out of the tents back to the main camp. It was strange how we didn't like the idea of going into the tents in June, and in October we didn't like leaving them and coming back to the tatty huts in which we had to share rooms. One good feature about our moving back was that we enjoyed more decent food. It was the best that I had eaten in the air force. It was a strange contrast, for at the 628 Squadron mess just a few hundred yards up the hill, I had never eaten worse food in the service.

U came up the slip for a minor inspection before the next bout of special duties. When the engineering officer, bearing in mind what had happened to R's hull on the last job, saw U's hull he wasn't prepared to pass the aircraft as serviceable. The stringers just forward of the main step were slightly bent, probably due to many stall landings. He felt that another heavy landing might burst her hull. So U was officially struck off charge on 26 October 1944. She was the first boat I flew as a captain from Lough Erne. As she was being scrapped and cannibalised for parts, I asked if I could have the captain's control wheel. I was given it. I took it back to Australia and kept it in my study as a souvenir of my flying boat days.

In lieu of U, we were assigned 240/F. She was VA723 and had a Leigh Light. She was in pretty fair condition both inside and out. The only snag was that she had no fitting for the astigmatic drift sight, to which Jock had become attached. We hoped there was sufficient time for the engineers to put one in. In order for her to be used for the long-range special duty flights, she had to be lightened by stripping off the

Catalina Mark IIA 240/F, RAF serial VA723, moored at Redhills Lake, Madras, India, 1944. Canvas covers can be seen on the engines, the cockpit, and front turret. (Bruce Daymond)

radar, the Leigh Light, and any other gubbins not deemed essential, including her armaments.

One day, Jock and I went to the Gym Club for a swim and then on to Mackays Gardens for dinner with Jack O'Meara and co. It was a pretty good service hostel. It was mixed, too, which made it even more attractive. Jock and I were intending to see *The Life and Death of Colonel Blimp* but Jock had been unable to get seats so we all hived off to the Connemara and drank Scotch. There was a dinner dance on. It did me absolutely no good, in fact harm, to see lots of pretty girls. A lounge full of women-hungry men was a pretty depressing sight. We went on to the Gym Club as the dance there was a much mateyer affair. I danced with Nella Swan, a Rumanian, who had a wicked line. I drank far too much. At the next table there was one of the loveliest girls I had seen for a very long time: blond, fairly slim, lovely teeth, and, drat the term, so refined-looking. The sort Mother wouldn't mind you bringing home.

Once the maintenance people had stripped F of all non-essential gear and checked her out, we lined up the drift instruments, swung the compass, and went down the slip. We did a quick air test flight and found 'George' unserviceable. I wanted it repaired quickly as I did not want to have to repeat an earlier performance of a twenty-five-hour flight with no automatic pilot.

The Barnowl II party arrived on 24 October. We went on board to do the inventory check, and then ashore to make up deficiencies. Captain Paddy Cheltam MC, whom we had met several nights earlier and whom I promised in a drunken moment to take flying, pitched up for a flip. Fortunately, we were doing a consumption test flight down to Point Calimere. Interestingly, Madras was lit up like a fairy land and looked super when we returned about 10 pm. The next day we were on board and airborne at 9 am to do a rehearsal for Barnowl II. It was a poor morning for the practice as it was raining like hell. Everyone got wet through, but the rehearsal was a success. That night there was a cyclone and four aircraft were sunk, one was blown aground, and billets were blown down; however, 240/F was OK.

Special Operation Barnowl II was conducted on 27/28 October. We were airborne in F at 9.20 am, in company with Rolf Luck and his crew in 240/K. We carried Captain Bobby Nichols of the Kachin Levies and four Burmese agents to reinforce those on the island. We arrived at our destination, landed, and put the agents ashore successfully. At some earlier stage we flashed a message to K by Aldis Lamp saying, 'Do not land.' That was the last contact we had with K. She did not return. The weather deteriorated during our return journey and we presumed that Rolf and his crew were victims of the cyclone we passed through. We returned to base after a flight of twenty-five hours. Such was the callousness of war that I accepted the loss of Rolf Luck without any undue sorrow.

Left: Left to right: Rolf Luck, Jack O'Meara, and John Sebre, Redhills Lake, Madras, India, 1944. *Right:* Rolf Luck, who, together with his crew, disappeared with no trace in the Bay of Bengal on special duties operation Barnowl II in 240/K on the night of 27/28 October 1944. (Bruce Daymond)

In lieu of Rolf Luck and his crew, we conducted Operation Biff I in F on 29/30 October. We were supposed to take off at 12.25 pm but an oil leak developed while taxiing. As a result, after the leak was attended to, we were airborne an hour late. We made up time by our first landfall at Preparis Island. Our orders were to land two agents on Kalegauk Island, near Moulmein on the Burmese coast. They were to contact two Chinese agents and give them two kitbags of Burmese counterfeit money. The Americans in Calcutta had produced this money and had over-printed 'Japanese Occupied Government' on it. During the first part of our journey, we saw a number of aircraft searching for any signs of Rolf Luck and his crew. Like so many Coastal Command losses, no trace was ever found.

We flew past Preparis Island at zero feet and continued to the target, passing low over what looked like an Arab dhow. This got a hell of a blow from the wash of our propellers as we passed by. We landed in bright moonlight and, despite there being a number of stakes marking fish traps in the area, we alighted with no problem. We put the agents ashore. They made no contact with the Chinese agents and they returned to the aircraft with the counterfeit money. After a flight of twenty-three hours, we arrived back at base. When added to the twenty-five hours taken for Barnowl II, we had been airborne for forty-eight hours of the previous ninety-six.

Operation Biff II was ordered for 31 October/1 November because of the failure of Biff I and the high priority for delivery of the counterfeit money. We normally flew these special operational flights with two second pilots, and on this operation Wing Commander Wood came as the relief pilot. When he proposed to come, I was told to leave Warrant Officer Cyril Brown, my second pilot, behind. I refused as he had already been prevented from returning to the UK to do his captain's course because of these special duty flights and if he had been left behind, he would have missed out both ways, which seemed unfair to me. However, we had to leave someone behind, so Flight Sergeant Bell, our second engineer, was left out. The crew on this operation consisted of: me (captain), Wing Commander Wood and Warrant Officer Brown (second pilots), Flight Lieutenant Gilbert (navigator), Flight Sergeant Lewis (engineer), Flight Sergeants Haskins and Foxall (wireless operators/air gunners), and Warrant Officer Carrington (rigger/air gunner).

The flight out in F was uneventful and we landed between Kalegauk Island and the mainland on what was a lovely, bright moonlit night. Bobby Anderson was the conducting officer. He and one of his men went ashore to deliver the money. On shore, they called out the code word 'Victory' as they walked up and down the beach and made quick sorties into the jungle. They made no contact with the Chinese agents they had come to meet.

As they returned to the aircraft, a large cumulonimbus cloud came up and obscured the moon. This made it impossible for them to locate the aircraft as it merged into the dark background of Kalegauk Island. There was a strong tide running and it took the dinghy south towards the fishing stakes and the agents' position became rather precarious. As luck would have it, Jock Gilbert was in the navigation compartment, preparing his charts for the return journey, and he inadvertently knocked one of the charts against the blackout curtain on the compartment window. This dislodged the press-stud on one corner of the curtain. The resulting flash of light was a godsend to the agents, who then knew where to head while battling the fast-running tide. It was a very relieved pair who climbed back through the blister, both considerably agitated after their ordeal. So, once again, the task of distributing the counterfeit money failed. We set course for base, arriving after a total time of twenty-four hours and twenty minutes. When we finally got to bed we had been in the air for about 72 hours out of an elapsed time of 144 hours. The 144 hours included briefings, debriefings, preparations of the aircraft, and other activities connected with the operations.

That night Wing Commander Wood took us to the Madras Club for a swim, collecting Mrs Bunny Fairbairn, his popsy, on the way.

Bunny was a nice, pretty woman with lovely, big blue eyes. If it hadn't meant cutting my throat, I wouldn't have minded having a lash, though it would have been a bit hard to compete with a wing commander who had transport. Jock and I went back to the club for drinks and the Wing Commander collected yet another popsy, one Grace (name not recorded), and we all hived off and ate Chinese food. It was a pleasant evening's diversion.

With the loss of Rolf and his crew, the special duty crews were understaffed during a period of heavy operational activities. To help us cope, the medical officer gave us Phenobarb to help us sleep at the end of each trip and Benzedrine to pep us up for the next trip. As a result, we were sleeping off the effects of three long special duties operations in six days when the agents on Bentinck Island sent an immediate signal saying there had been a lot of Japanese air reconnaissance of the island and an enemy submarine had put into the bay. All the indications pointed to a Japanese search party being put ashore to capture them. They would try to avoid capture until a Catalina was sent to rescue them. We were told by HQ that as the agents held vital information, we were to get them off the island 'at all costs'.

On 3 November, we were airborne from Redhills in F at 10.20 am. John Chapman, an Australian from Collaroy, came with us as second navigator. Captain Bobby Anderson and one of his men accompanied us to assist with the extraction. Before reaching the Ten Degree Channel, navigators Jock Gilbert and John Chapman, and Cyril Brown, the second pilot, all took simultaneous star/planet shots so that we had a series of three star fixes with which to plot our position accurately for navigating the channel. We passed through the channel very low over the water without detection.

On reaching 90°E, the weather turned bad and we had to contend with cumulonimbus cloud. When we were about 200 miles from the channel and about the same distance from the Andaman Islands, I found that the intermittent moonlight reflecting off the waves as we rushed over the sea had an almost hypnotic effect on me. I had to fight off the effects of this mesmerising phenomenon as there was little room for error flying a 15-ton aircraft at 100 knots only 50 feet above the waves. This effect was a result of fatigue and the strain of the week's heavy operational load.

We arrived over Bentinck Island in full moonlight with ideal conditions for landing. We received a signal from a torch on the ground giving us the all clear to land. While we were on the downwind leg, Sergeant Lewis, who was in the bow turret to keep an eye out for coral, came on the intercom to say that there was a Jap submarine lying in the bay, broadside on, and directly in our landing path. The Japs may have realised that a rescue attempt could be mounted and left earlier in the afternoon, possibly to lull the agents into a false sense of security. Unbeknown to the agents, the submarine returned later. I told the crew that we were going to land as our orders were to get the agents out at all costs and there was no way we were going to leave the poor buggers down there.

We came in low over the submarine, alighted, and then taxied at high speed on the step heading down-moon in a shower of spray. We surged to a stop and, with Bob Lewis in the bow taking lead-line soundings for depth, we taxied to a spot out of sight of the submarine and just off a beach. We had to stop the engines and drop the anchor as the agents would have found it almost impossible to get their rubber dinghies alongside against the slipstream, and the whirling propellers would have made an extra hazard. The eight agents, including Captain Nichols, in their two dinghies were full of good cheer and extremely happy to be rescued. They were blissfully unaware of the return of the submarine. One of the men was in a bad way with malaria, and two others were also sick. The aircrew briefed them in low voices about the situation and the need for stealth and speed, and pulled them into the aircraft through the blister. The dinghies were slashed with a knife and cast adrift. Bob Lewis cut the anchor line to save time, leaving behind the beautiful aluminium

'The song of the Wasp.' One of the Pratt & Whitney Twin Wasp engines as seen from a Catalina cockpit. The Twin Wasp was thoroughly reliable and crews had enormous faith in them. The propeller tips were close to the cockpit and the noise from them was one of the reasons most Catalina pilots were deaf later in their lives. (Bruce Daymond)

anchor. The ever-reliable Twin Wasp motors started instantly. At this stage, the moon was behind the cloud and we were camouflaged by the land behind us. We took off downwind, passed low over the sub, and dodged behind a cliff to avoid any fire from the Japs.

The Japs were well aware of our presence. Knowing there were fighters based only minutes away at Mergui and Tenasserim, which may have been alerted by the submarine, we headed south-west for some time before altering course directly for Redhills. Flight Sergeant Earl Haskins picked up a lot of Japanese radio traffic, which we were worried may have been a call to arms, but fortunately we saw no enemy aircraft.

The bunk and blister compartments were crowded with the agents. At dawn all of them shook hands with the aircrew in appreciation of their rescue as they had been in danger of capture, which was a particularly unpleasant prospect at the hands of the Japs. We found out that the agents had put out ground signals when one of our reconnaissance aircraft appeared, but Jap aircraft that were clearing the area for the arrival of the submarine chased it off.

At the debriefing, Bob Lewis was shown a book of silhouettes of Jap submarines by an intelligence officer and asked if he could recognise the one with which we had had a close encounter. He was unable to do this as it had been lying down moon to us. The intelligence officer then said to Bob, 'And tell me again exactly what it was that Bruce said.' Bob told him I had said, 'We can't leave those poor buggers down there.' And the intelligence officer replied, 'Well I'm going to put him up for an award.' Five of the crew were decorated at the conclusion of the September to November special duty operations.

Between 27 October and the conclusion of this rescue, F had flown four special duty operations with a total of ninety-five hours and eleven minutes of air time: that is, it was airborne for four days out of eight. This performance must surely have ranked among the longest and most intensive bouts of continuous operational flying by any one crew during the Second World War.

This rescue prompted Air Marshal A.G.R. Garrod, Deputy Air Commander-in-Chief, South East Asia, to write to the CO of 240 Squadron on 10 November 1944, citing Ref. Air/6193:

> I have read with interest the report of Sortie No. 7 dated 4th November 1944 by your Squadron, reference 240S/1531/Int. I would like you to congratulate the Captain, F/Lt. B.C. Daymond and the crew of Catalina F of your Squadron for their excellent work on this occasion.

So passed eight days that I would never forget. Airborne for ninety-five hours and eleven minutes. I could have made it 100 hours for the sake of the round figure, but because of the case of malaria we had on board, we had to come back in a hurry. Everyone at base was jubilant and we received hearty congratulations from those few people who knew the goings-on of special duty work. The Group Captain was particularly nice.

Bobby Anderson gave a dinner party for the crew in the Connemara. The Group Captain, also Group Captain Clayton (ex-240 Squadron

CO), Wing Commander Wood, Squadron Leader Godber, Chapman, Flight Lieutenant Warren, the engineer officer, and the medical officer, as well as a few others, made up the party. Loads of Scotch got things well under way, and by a later stage in the evening blokes were spearing off and asking women from adjoining parties to dance. A bloody fine night and a very fitting ending to a fine week's flying.

I saw the president of the officers' mess committee on 8 November and asked his permission to bring the eight NCOs of my crew to the mess for a drink. They appreciated this way of saying thanks to them for their sterling efforts during the operations. After dinner we went to the sergeants' mess and the do developed into a piss-up. Sergeant Bailey, the instrument repairer, gave some wizard impersonations of station characters, including Jock and me.

The crew of 628/U. Left to right top: Bruce Daymond, Flight Sergeant Jock Bell (wireless operator), Warrant Officer Brown (second pilot), and Flight Lieutenant Jock Gilbert (navigator in pith helmet). Flight Sergeant Ward (engineer in forage cap on the blister). Flight Sergeant Bob Lewis (engineer), Flight Sergeant Haskins (wireless operator/mechanic), Flight Sergeant Foxall (wireless operator), and Warrant Officer Carrington (rigger), Redhills Lake, Madras, India, September–October 1944. Note the handhold on the trailing edge of the main plane, above the head of Flight Lieutenant Gilbert. (Bruce Daymond)

Bruce Daymond's crew after 100 operational hours, October–November 1944. Back row: Flight Sergeant Bell (aged 25), Warrant Officer Carrington (24), Flight Sergeant Lewis (20), Flight Sergeant Foxall (23), Flight Sergeant Ward (22), and Flight Sergeant Haskins (21). Front row: Warrant Officer Brown (24), Flight Lieutenant Bruce Daymond (25), and Flight Lieutenant Gilbert (32). (Bruce Daymond)

Jock and I then went on leave to Ceylon. We spent a couple of days at the Grand Oriental Hotel in Colombo, organising accommodation in the hills, sight-seeing, shopping, and calling in to see people friends had suggested we look up. We looked in at the Galle Face Hotel just to say we'd been there. It was one of the most famous hotels in the East. It commanded a good outlook across a large expanse of lawn which stretched down to the sea shore.

We caught a train for the hills and got a room at Nuwara Eliya. It was lovely to feel cool. We rang the Bandarawela Hotel and found that they could accommodate us a few days later. We had decided to go there because Nuwara Eliya was deadly quiet, and there were no popsies. We spent a pleasant couple of days in Nuwara Eliya, doing little but relaxing. Then we went to Bandarawela, where we got a nice room in the Bandarawela Hotel, although it had no toilet or hot running water. It was a far cheerier place than Nuwara Eliya, which was an absolute morgue.

We spent our time in Bandarawela sleeping in, having breakfast in bed, reading, writing letters, playing tennis, walking around the district taking in the lovely views, playing liar dice, partying, and sight-seeing. Stan Pearson had put us in contact with Wren Section Officer Joan Melaney, who was in charge of the Wrens' rest camp at Diyatalawa, near Bandarawela. She was very helpful to us, inviting us on several occasions to the rest camp's wardroom, and introducing us to some Wrens. On one occasion, Joan asked us to lunch and

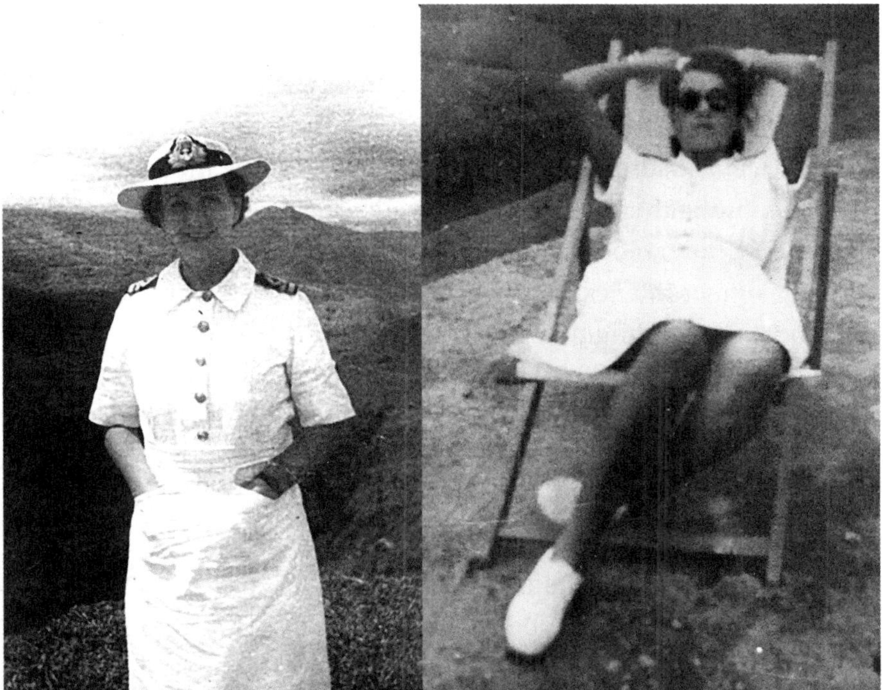

Left: Women's Royal Naval Service Officer Joan Melaney. *Right:* Naval Nursing Sister Muriel Haigh, Bandarawela, Ceylon, November 1944. (Bruce Daymond)

Muriel Haigh, a naval nursing sister from Yorkshire, joined us. She had a wizard pair of legs and they had such a lovely tan I could not take my eyes off them.

Joan and her major friend arranged a party for 23 November. That night we got into the bar early and rolled the liar dice. It wasn't long before we had a big liar dice school, including Major General Kent, who had arrived a day or so earlier, a full colonel, two lieutenant colonels, and other odds and sods. The old general lost the first round and had to stand us all drinks. 'Ho, ho, ho! A full house, eh. By Jove, it's there. Ho, ho ho!' The Scotch lasted well and we were still at it when Joan, her major, and Muriel Haigh arrived. Muriel danced as lightly as a feather and pitched a pretty nifty bit of woo. Everybody was bright. It was one of the best nights for a while.

One evening we were sitting down to dinner with Ted Garside of 230 Squadron when I was handed a telegram. It was from Wing Commander Wood and was addressed to Flight Lieutenant B.C. Daymond, Hotel, B'wela, and read: '4 November congratulations from all the squadron on your immediate award of the DFC.' It was unbelievable and a red-letter day. I also received a telegram from Squadron Leader Godber. 'Hearty congratulations from the old firm.'

After dinner the next day, we had a party in General Kent's room and one of the highlights was to see the Old Man a few sheets to the wind, singing 'Alouette' with all its actions. It is not often that you have a general, who used to be General Officer Commanding Orkney and Shetlands, sitting at your feet asking you to tell him the words of: 'Someday I'm going to go, far away from Sullom Voe.' It was another jolly fine night.

Jock and I were out walking when Joan Melaney drove past and said she would pick us up at midday and take us for a picnic to Ella Rock, which was about 8 miles from B'wela. She miraculously produced three bottles of beer, which we drank, sitting out on the grass. The view wasn't all it might have been as there were some heavy rain clouds hanging over the pass. We went to the wardroom for afternoon tea.

Everyone rather conveniently left Muriel and me alone. We got down to some really healthy woo, the best bout for a very long time. She was very attractively dressed, the first time I had seen her out of uniform. She had on a brown coat and skirt with a beige sweater and, what with those lovely brown legs, she looked pretty smooth altogether.

We left for Colombo on 27 November, where Jock and I spent a couple of days catching up with old friends and colleagues, including from my days in Qantas accounts. Then, on 1 December Jock and I flew in a Transport Command Dakota, KG585, captained by Pilot Officer Bracken, to Madras and then by truck to Redhills. There was a goodly collection of mail waiting for me. One from Air Chief Marshal Sir Richard Peirse, Allied Air Commander-in-Chief, South East Asia, was addressed to: F/Lt. B.C. Daymond (Aus. 403323), No. 628 Squadron, Royal Air Force. It was dated 22 November 1944 and stated: 'My warmest congratulations on the award of your Distinguished Flying Cross.' Another was from Air Commodore Noel Desoer, the Air Officer Commanding 225 Group: 'F/Lt. B.C. Daymond, D.F.C., R.A.F. Station, Redhills Lake, Madras, 24 November 1944, Dear Daymond, I should like to congratulate you very much on your well earned award of the Distinguished Flying Cross.' There were also two lovely letters from Peggy who, despite Ken's return, was feeling our parting as much as I was.

I received a letter from Wing Commander Wood on 10 December. In it, he asked me for my views on who in my crew should be recommended for 'gongs'. He had already recommended Brown for a DFC and wanted to give another gong and a Mention in Despatches. I discussed this with Joe King and was surprised to learn that Jock had not been put up by Wood. I recommended that Jock be nominated. Joe told me that I was up for an immediate Distinguished Service Order (DSO) and made me promise that I would not mention the fact. This was bloody shattering news. I didn't hold out much hope of cracking it, for both Squadron Leader Hawkins and Squadron Leader Godber were put up for DSOs and neither of those came off.

I was finally in the air again, on a thirteen-hour meteorological flight in FP304, on 16 December. We were in the air at dawn and the weather was grand all day. We went up to 11,500 feet on the way home. We were above a sea of stratocumulus with thin, wispy cirrus in a blue sky above us. The next meteorological trip would put me on less than 100 hours to go for my 1,000 operational hours.

Several days later, I had another meteorological flight in F. I was keen to tick up every hour that was going, as getting 1,000 hours up was the only way to get out of India. On that trip I clocked off the first of my last 100 hours. The weather off the coast was pretty foul. Coming back, we had an exercise to try and cheat radar. We came in at 50 feet from 200 miles out. However, as we were about 10 miles off the coast, the weather got so bad that it was too dangerous to stay so low and arrive undetected at the lake. We climbed to 500 feet, and discovered that was the first time radar picked us up.

Just after Christmas, Group Captain Laws, the new Group commander, gave me some circuits and bumps in his Tiger Moth. My first take-off was frightening as it was almost cross-runway. And one of my landings nearly wrote us off. But I got the feel of it towards the end and set down one or two fairly smooth jobs. He said that after another session I could take it away and play. That evening was a case of vice versa for I gave him some dual in Catalina 240/D JX307 just before dusk and then went on to do some landings without flare path. Just as we were finishing, he tried one of these moonlight landings and did a wizard job, and so he should, as he was a very experienced Sunderland pilot and had flown a lot of modern landplanes. The next day I flew the Tiger Moth with the Group Captain and coped much better. We went up to 3,000 feet and did a loop, which I was told later looked OK from the ground.

On 8 January I did a bout of dicing with my crew. I was on this heavy-load landing racket in aircraft 240/B Z2146, an old warrior with over 2,600 hours on her airframe. She had 1,200 gallons on board but was no trouble to set down. The dicing was supposed to be for two hours, but I gave Flying Officer Bradford three quarters on an hour dual out of that. We were down for some local again in the afternoon, but it turned out to be some special duty nonsense: refuelling from one aircraft to another on the water by means of a line between the two and rubber dinghies loaded with 4-gallon tins. While it sounds a pretty Heath Robinson affair, it worked extremely well. On the way out in the dinghy, Wing Commander Wood told me that he had a signal in from Air Command South East Asia offering me a squadron leader's post on completion of my tour, as RAF liaison officer with Force 136, a special duties Group. He asked me to think it over. The pros were: promotion, rank, and pay of a squadron leader, which was considerable in India, and a very interesting job. The cons were: remaining in India, and possibly being made to do another tour in India on completion of 'the rest'. If they guaranteed me that it would be for six months only, and that on its completion I would definitely be sent home, I thought I would accept. It would have done me good from a service point of view. However, if it meant nine to twelve months and then probably having to go on flying again here in India, I was not so keen. The family wanted me back and I had been away nearly four years.

The Yanks wanted to do some trial parachute jumps from a Catalina, so on 10 January Wing Commander Wood and I took them up in FP225, and Peter McKeand followed in another Catalina to take photographs. They fitted a wooden platform in the blister, level with the rim. The jumpers sat on this platform and jumped from it. They tied a static line from the parachute to the gun mount and this, when they left the aircraft, pulled away the cover and opened the main chute immediately. They did one dead drop using a dummy and four live drops, all of which were successful.

We did more parachute dropping the next day, this time from 1,500 feet instead of 2,200 as the day before. We did five live drops. Then we did some local flying with Bradford in D. On landing, I had barely enough strength to crawl into bed before dinner. The doctor came and took my temperature: it was 104°+ F and there were some

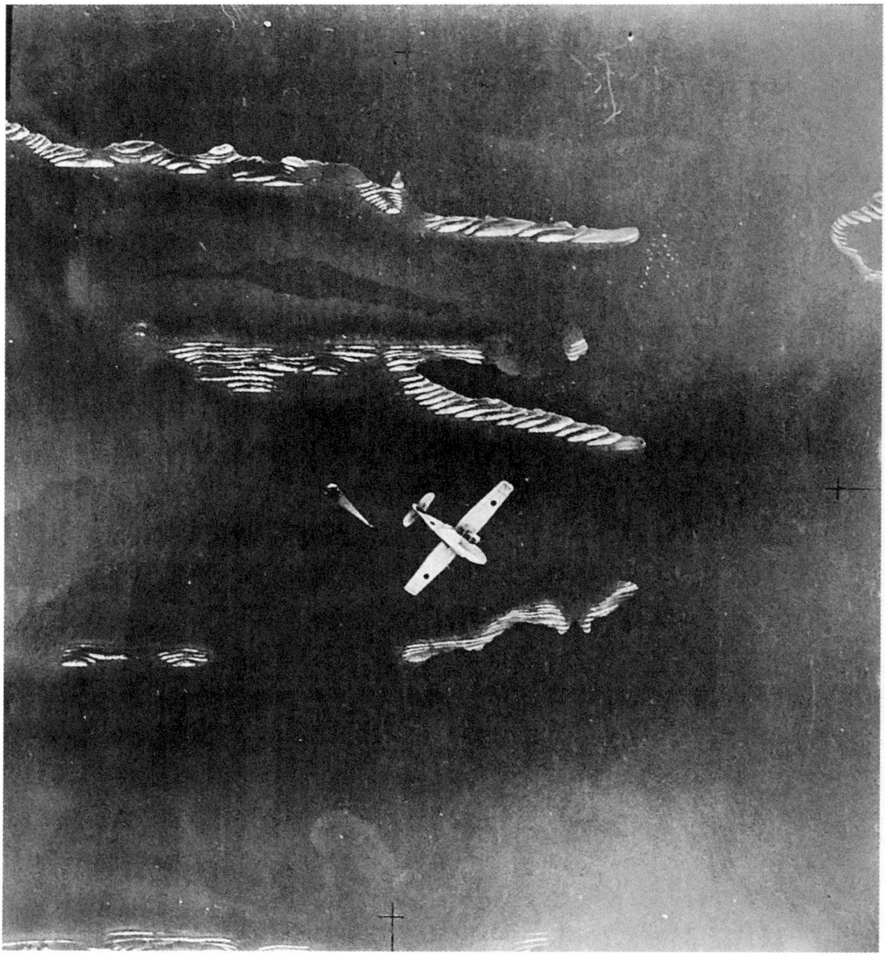

Parachute dropping from Bruce Daymond's Catalina FP225 over Lake Pulicat, India, 9 January 1945. Note the roundels on the underside of the main plane and the open tunnel hatch in the underside of the rear of the aircraft (it appears as a black spot on the rear underside). (Bruce Daymond)

funny noises in my chest, so 8 pm saw me once again in hospital, having sulfanilamide pumped into me. The doctor feared pneumonia. I was confined to hospital for the next few days, then on 15 January he ordered me away on ten days' sick leave. He told me I had no physical reserves left at all.

I travelled by train from Madras to Kodaikanal Road, then by bus to Kodai, a hill station. I had no difficulty getting into the club chambers with a suite of rooms. After unpacking, I went to the club and met Rosemary Wilson, a captain in the Royal Army Medical Corp at Avadi, who was staying at the Carlton Hotel. We got talking and arranged to spend the afternoon rowing on the lake. That evening Rosemary went to a dance and afterwards, having met Peter Walker from 240 Squadron, we all went over to his place, played gramophone records, and drank Gordon's gin. I took Rosemary home and didn't get to bed till 2.30 am. It was a good start to my sick leave.

The next morning, I collected Rosemary from the hotel and we went for a walk to some waterfalls about a mile from town. The wind was blowing strongly, although the sun was brilliant. We got back about 11 am and found Jack O'Meara had arrived. Rosemary, Jack, and I spent the next few days sight-seeing, walking, picnicking, reading, spine bashing, and going out to dinner with other residents. On 21 January we saw Rosemary off, having arranged to go to the races in Madras with her when we got back. This we did subsequently when Doc Clinton-Thomas, Jack O'Meara, George Drummond, Rosemary, and I met for lunch in the Connemara and then went to the races. We returned to town with Wing Commander Phillips, CO of 191 Squadron, had a bath at the Madras Club, and knocked back a lot of Scotch in a very short time. I took Rosemary to dinner at the Connemara and then drove her back to Avadi in the ambulance, which the doc rather courageously lent me.

After I returned to Redhills, Wing Commander Hugh Verity DSO and bar, DFC, the number one special duty king, turned up. Before dinner one day, I had a long talk with him about the special duty job I had been offered. Verity and I received an invitation from the sergeants' mess for both of us to go over for a drink. Walking back after the do, I was sufficiently alcoholically courageous to shoot off my mouth about the state of affairs regarding the CO and flight commanders in 240 Squadron. As a result, I expected that I would be posted.

On 30 January there were bags of special duty activities for the boys. It made me more envious than I can say, to see them all getting ready for a job and to know that I was finished, and would not go on another. I wondered if all people felt like this at the end of a tour?

On 5 February, Jock, Bob Lewis, now a pilot officer, Bradford, and I caught the train to Mettupalayam for our leave at Kotagiri. Our accommodation, Glen Carse, was very nice. It was more like a private home than a boarding house and was nicely furnished. The food was excellent: roast beef, grilled chops, strawberries, and cream were the highlights. Miss Loveday Shepheard, the lady in charge, was nice, though a bit gushy.

One of life's most pleasant gifts was the joy of being in bed under a load of blankets when it was cold outside. Our first night in town

Left: Pilot Officer Bob Lewis, Bruce Daymond's engineer, shortly after he was commissioned. He stayed in the RAF after the war and became a pilot and a flight lieutenant. *Right:* Flight Lieutenant Jock Gilbert, Bruce Daymond's navigator. Both photos were taken in Kotagiri, India, February 1945. (Bruce Daymond)

was the one night in the month when they held a late dance. It was really a British other ranks dance, but as there were so few people at Kotagiri at that time of year, officers were allowed. We went along, well-fortified with Scotch, and added to the stock there. I had met Helga, a Swedish lass, at the club earlier and she was at the dance. I had a good night, ending it with a fair bit of woo with Helga in her bungalow. As a result, I didn't get to bed till 4.30 am.

The next day, I left the others shortly after dinner and went down to Helga's bungalow. She met me on arrival in a pair of pyjamas! We started to learn a card game called Bezique, but it degenerated into a solid necking do in front of the fire. Walking home in the early hours, I discovered my wallet missing. It gave me an anxious half an hour or so, but I eventually located it at Helga's, or at least she had found it for me. She was just getting up when I arrived and she appeared in a sunsuit. She really had a smashing body.

The next morning, Jock, Brad, Helga, and Nora set out for a walk to Catherine Falls. It was supposed to be 14 miles all told, downhill all the way. Bob and I decided they could go without us so we spent a very lazy day: beer and a game of liar dice at the club, two hours' solid zizz after lunch, and we listened to Beethoven's 5th Symphony in the twilight, and then welcomed back the hikers. I took Helga back to her bungalow: they didn't call the Swedish healthy for nothing. Mercy!

It was a red-letter day on 15 February. First of all, I answered Jack Davenport's letter in which he asked me to be godfather to his infant, which was to be born in June. I was a bit of a gash about this, but was delighted to accept the job. And then, at teatime, I received a telegram from Group Captain Laws, Station Commander, Redhills: 'Hearty congratulations to you and F/Lt Gilbert from station commander on your recent award stop good show.' This was all a bit vague, for I'd heard nothing of any awards. There had been a bit of buzz round the club the previous evening that a bar to the DFC had come through for me, and a DFC for Jock. We guessed that that was what it must have been. We all went to the club, had a game of billiards, and were sitting about when Steve Beeson came in bearing a telegram from Wing Commander Wood: 'Air marshal commanding 222 group has signalled hearty congratulations to you on award distinguished service order stop good show bruce and congratulations from all much drinking required on your return stop.'

We were introduced to Brigadier Spain, who lived in the district. On 19 February, a whole party of us set out to visit his tea plantation and factory. Mrs Spain put on a super morning tea and then took us through their tea factory. She walked us around part of the estate, with lovely views of the surrounding valleys. We had a picnic lunch and walked 3 or 4 miles down the mountain to take part in a Hindu festival during which fire walkers demonstrated their skills. When we arrived, there were logs burning in the pit, but the logs had been removed before the fire walkers strode through. A layer of ashes and coals remained but it was hot, for water thrown on the fire resulted in steam fairly whizzing up. To the clanging of tins and beating of drums, the fire walkers did three circuits around the temple before striding quickly through the fire pit, which was about 20–25 feet long. Talking to Brigadier Spain in the club about it that night, he said that he once tried it in a pair of socks. These were scorched but his feet weren't burnt. He thinks that as all the natives have been without shoes all their lives, the soles of their feet must be almost like leather. A mild session at the club was followed by a wizard session of liar dice back at our accommodation.

We left for Mettupalayam on 27 February in a furnace of a train, and on to Madras. We were back at Redhills the next day by 5.30 pm. I collected loads of mail and congratulations from all the blokes. Jock and I turned on a joint party in the mess and it developed into a wild do, beer over everybody, singing, it was one hell of a celebration.

The official recommendation for my DSO read:

> Flight Lieutenant B C Daymond, together with his crew, joined the Squadron on October 1st 1944, for the purpose

of carrying out Special Duties Operations for which he and his crew had volunteered. During the month of October, F/Lt Daymond carried out four special duty flights of 25 hours, 22 hours, 22½ hours, and 22½ hours duration making a total of 92 hours flying. These flights were carried out during a period of eight days: almost half of this period was spent on operational flying. From the Service aspect, all of these flights were successfully completed. They involved an extremely high degree of flying skill, perseverance and initiative. Out of the total time of 92 hours flying, approximately 33 hours were spent by moonlight over enemy-controlled waters or in the near vicinity of enemy occupied territory.

The last flight involved an operation which merits particular mention, being successfully carried out under the very bows of a comparatively heavily-armed enemy naval vessel. For 20 minutes the aircraft was a vulnerable target and it was only due to the resources and skill of F/Lt Daymond that the aircraft was not subject to destruction by enemy action. Moreover the weather conditions for the greater part of the trip were extremely bad and it is of the highest credit to F/Lt Daymond that he appreciated the importance of the task and carried it through to a successful conclusion in the face of adverse conditions, created by both weather and the presence of hostile forces which would have formed adequate reasons enough for any Captain of Aircraft failing to complete the mission. The resource, skill and daring shown by this officer on this and the other three flights is of an extremely high order. His endurance, perseverance and enthusiasm for operational flying shown during this period could not be surpassed. His disappointment, on the receipt of the news that a flight of over 27 hours following rapidly after

> his last flight had been cancelled, was very evident. He has set a magnificent example to all other crews on this Squadron and the competence, keenness and resolution of his crew, speak highly of his powers of leadership.

In my mail was a letter from Wing Commander Verity. The Australian authorities would not wear a month's leave for me at home, so I was to be repatriated. I was sorry to lose the job, but getting it at the cost of not seeing the family for another two years was too high a price to pay.

Both Jock and I were given 'Exceptional' ratings in our logbooks. Neither of us had seen such a rating before. We saw the flight commander and discovered we really were operations-expired. We handed in our flying clothing and did practically as we liked.

Wing Commander Wood provided Jock and me with an excuse for a jaunt to Bombay on 12 March. He was being flown there for repatriation. As we were not doing much, Wing Commander Robinson gave us a few days off. Steve Beeson and his crew flew Wood, Jock, and me to Trombay in JX278. The trip across India was deadly dull. What a shagged-out looking waste of a country it was. Trombay was up at the north end of Bombay Harbour, about 14 miles by road from the city. Jock and I cooled our heels in Bombay for several days, then flew back to Redhills with Warrant Officer Raynor of 191 Squadron in JX352. There was a pleasant Wren officer on board. I flew for a time and it was a shock to see a woman sitting in the second pilot's seat. It was the first time I had been in an RAF aircraft with one of 'em! She stayed in the seat from take-off to landing. I came back to quite a load of mail. I found out from a family letter that I had been gazetted a squadron leader from 1 January.

On 26 March I said farewell to Redhills. Steve Beeson flew Group Captain Brougham and me to Trombay in JX278. I did both the take-off and landing. The water at Trombay was very rough and we bounced like a bastard. That was the last flight I did with the

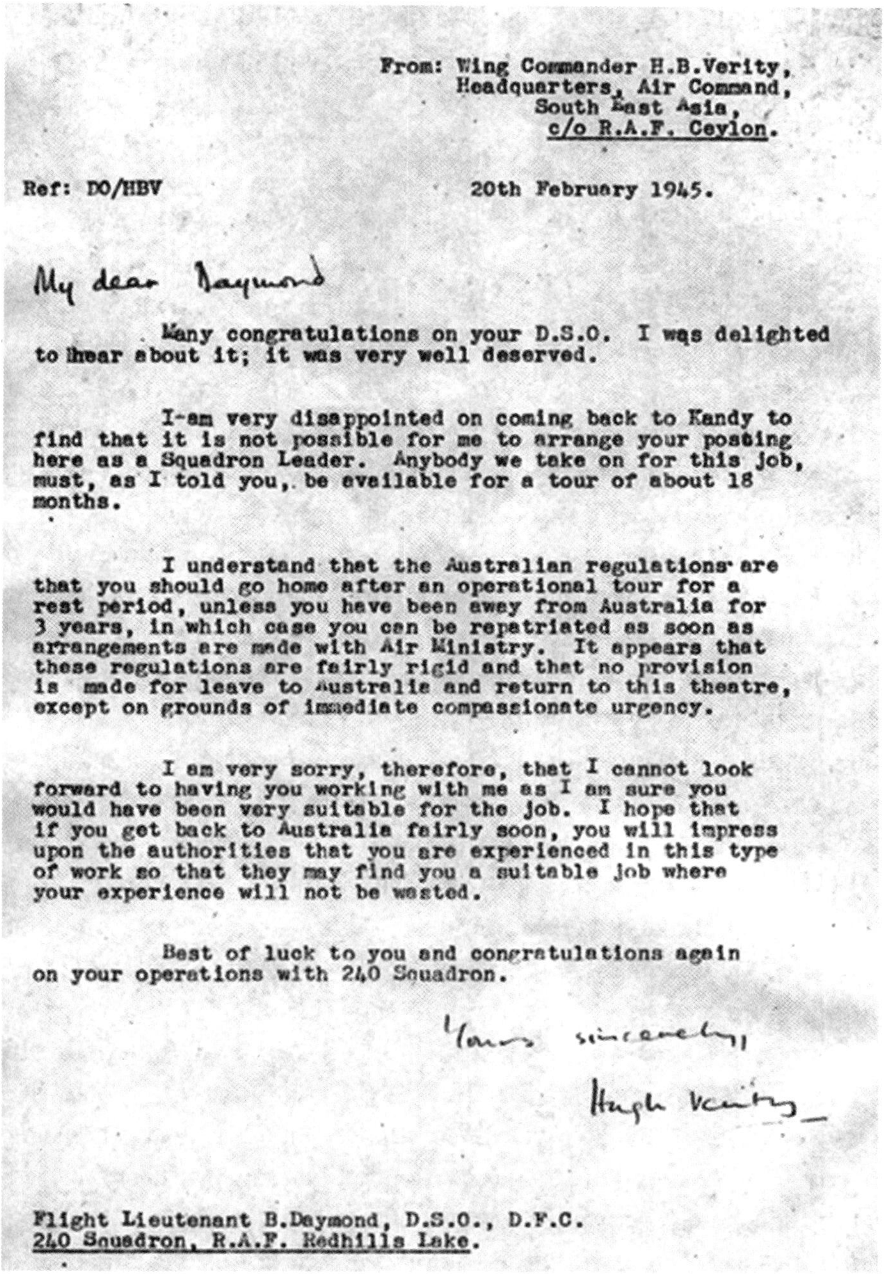

From: Wing Commander H.B.Verity,
Headquarters, Air Command,
South East Asia,
c/o R.A.F. Ceylon.

Ref: DO/HBV

20th February 1945.

My dear Daymond

Many congratulations on your D.S.O. I was delighted to hear about it; it was very well deserved.

I am very disappointed on coming back to Kandy to find that it is not possible for me to arrange your posting here as a Squadron Leader. Anybody we take on for this job, must, as I told you, be available for a tour of about 18 months.

I understand that the Australian regulations are that you should go home after an operational tour for a rest period, unless you have been away from Australia for 3 years, in which case you can be repatriated as soon as arrangements are made with Air Ministry. It appears that these regulations are fairly rigid and that no provision is made for leave to Australia and return to this theatre, except on grounds of immediate compassionate urgency.

I am very sorry, therefore, that I cannot look forward to having you working with me as I am sure you would have been very suitable for the job. I hope that if you get back to Australia fairly soon, you will impress upon the authorities that you are experienced in this type of work so that they may find you a suitable job where your experience will not be wasted.

Best of luck to you and congratulations again on your operations with 240 Squadron.

Yours sincerely,

Hugh Verity

Flight Lieutenant B.Daymond, D.S.O., D.F.C.
240 Squadron, R.A.F. Redhills Lake.

Letter from Wing Commander Verity DSO & Bar, DFC, explaining why Bruce Daymond could not remain with special duties operations.

Bruce Daymond at the controls in January 1945. Note the Mae West, the hard seat behind his back, the Perspex cockpit hatches, and the port engine. The round handle to open the pilot's sliding window is by his left shoulder. (Bruce Daymond)

RAF. We got a transport straight to the embarkation depot at Worli. Jack O'Meara arrived and was installed with me in Kooka Court. My promotion to squadron leader had come through officially.

Jack and I celebrated our last night in India suitably in the mess on 30 March, with John Chapman and Sammy Sims as willing co-bibulators. The next day, Jack and I were at the docks by 7.30 am and joined by Wing Commander Stewart, ex-225 Group senior medical officer, who was going home to New Zealand. Our ship, *Admiral Benson*, was a specially constructed troop transport. In our cabin we had eighteen officers with three-decker bunks. There was no lounge, no chairs on the decks: just some narrow wooden seats. Meals were cafeteria-style with a tray stamped into various compartments, into which one collected the whole meal. There were a lot of women on board. They were American nurses, Red Cross people, missionaries, and women who had married American servicemen.

The trip home was uneventful. On 14 April we sailed up the Brisbane River and docked at Hamilton. I rang the family, the first time I had heard their voices since September 1941, when they rang me at Charlottetown, Canada. We loaded baggage on the transport, had an early lunch, and were driven to the troop train. We had breakfast at Gloucester, lunch at Gosford, and got into Sydney about 3 pm. It was not at all the way I'd hoped to arrive. I had wanted to sail into Sydney Harbour. However, I was home at last.

Epilogue

I joined the RAAF as an Aircraftman II on 6 January 1941, aged 21. My full-time service was terminated on 21 May 1946. I transferred to the RAAF Reserve as a Squadron Leader the following day. As I presciently had thought a number of times during the war, I found it difficult to return to civilian life. After a few months, I sensed an opportunity to be an Australian trade representative in Kenya, then a colony of the UK. Despite going to Kenya, this came to nothing, but with Bill Dewar, an ex-RCAF pilot, I drove a war surplus jeep from Nairobi to Cape Town, South Africa, and back on an 8,000+ mile adventure.

In early 1948, while on my jeep odyssey in Africa, I received news of Ken Pammenter's death from black water fever, a severe complication of malaria he contracted during service in Burma. I wondered about Peggy Pammenter, my lovely flame of 1942/43 Nettlebed and Henley days. Our love affair was a truly enduring memory. My parents told me that I was not to go to the UK to see her. She died in Canada in 1992.

On returning to Australia in mid-1948, I joined B. Daymond & Coy, Manufacturing Tailors, the family company in Chippendale, Sydney. I hated the business, which had been a successful one since it was founded by my father during the First World War. It had become less successful as the demand for men's suits dropped. When my father died in 1965, I took steps to sell or close the company. I then became a stockbroker and worked with several firms until I retired at the end of 1989, aged 70.

My first operational patrol in a Catalina was with RAF 209 Squadron on 14/15 June 1942, when I flew as second pilot to

Flying Officer Eric Saunders at the start of our transit to Mombasa. My last flight in a Catalina was on 27 December 1948, with Squadron Leader Eric Saunders in RAAF 11 Squadron A24-92 on an eighty-minute circuit over the fleet at the start of the fourth Sydney to Hobart Yacht Race.

According to my flying log book, during my 4 years and 5.5 months in the RAAF, I flew 1,740 hours and 50 minutes, most of that time in Catalinas. Reflecting on my wartime experience, four and a half years is a sizeable slice of anyone's life. Despite the many tragedies it contained, I would not have missed it for the world. Fortunate enough through God's grace to have survived the war unscathed, I look back on those years as being the most momentous period of my life. It provided the excitement and danger of wartime flying, it allowed me to travel the world, it gave me many fond memories of people and places, and above all it rewarded me with the treasure of some wonderful friendships which endured for the rest of my life.

Bruce Daymond wearing his service medals: Distinguished Service Order, Distinguished Flying Cross, 1939–45 Star, Atlantic Star, Africa Star, Burma Star, Defence Medal, War Medal 1939–45, and Australian Service Medal 1939–45.

Endnotes

Chapter 1

1. Early in the war, navigators were classified as observers, with an O in a half wing above the left pocket of the uniform. Later this was changed to an N. The term navigator is used throughout this book.
2. A detailed account of the politics, conduct, success, and the impact on graduates of the Empire Air Training Scheme is provided in John McCarthy's excellent book *A Last Call of Empire: Australian Aircrew, Britain and the Empire Air Training Scheme*, published in 1988 by the Australian War Memorial.
3. Imperial measurements are used throughout. Conversion factors are: 1 inch = 0.025 metres, 1 foot = 0.305 metres, 1 mile = 1.609 kilometres, 1 knot = 1.852 kilometres per hour, 1 imperial gallon = 4.546 litres, and 1 pound = 0.454 kilograms.
4. Sergeant Jack Thompson was killed on 15 February 1943, aged 21, on operations with RAF 14 Squadron, flying Marauders, in the Middle East.
5. No. 1 Course, No. 5 EFTS, Narromine, commenced on 24 May 1940. It closed with the graduation of No. 48 Course on 15 June 1944. During that period, it was attended by 3,734 students, of which 2,580 graduated as pilots.
6. Service and civilian aircraft have an individual serial number displayed on the fuselage or tail. Serial numbers on RAF aircraft consisted of one or two letters and a number (e.g., R4886 and AH543). During the Second World War, each RAF squadron had an identifying code consisting of two letters. For example, the code for 209 Squadron was WQ. In addition, a letter identified

each aircraft in the squadron. For example, RAF serial Z2142, squadron code WQ-Q, was referred to as 209/Q, or Q. Later in the war, the squadron code was deleted. Aircraft being transferred to different squadrons retained their RAF serial number, but their individual letter was changed. Pilots noted the serial number in their log books when recording their flights.

7. Circuits and bumps is a training manoeuvre during which pilots practice take-off and landing repeatedly without a stop after each landing.
8. In a side-slip the aircraft is moving sideways as well as forward relative to the oncoming wind. It is used to counteract the effects of a cross-wind during landing so the aircraft's nose aligns with the runway.
9. Flight Lieutenant Hervey Longmuir survived the war.
10. Flying guided by a radio beam.
11. Pilot Officer Gordon Lee was killed on 4 April 1943, aged 22, on operations with RAAF 460 Squadron, flying Lancasters.
12. Shot up or shooting up refers to a low-flying simulated attack on a house, base, transport, or group of people, and in modern parlance is called beat up or beating up.
13. Wing Commander Jack Davenport AC, DSO, DFC & bar, GM, MID survived the war and became a captain of industry. He was the subject of a biography, *Jack Davenport: Beaufighter Pilot* by Kristen Alexander, published by Allen & Unwin in 2009.
14. Sergeant Rae Frost was killed on 10 April 1942, aged 25, on operations with RAF 12 Squadron (flying Wellingtons) over Germany.
15. Flying Officer Ray Hornby survived the war.

Chapter 2

1. No. 7 RCAF Service Flying Training School was set up under the British Commonwealth Air Training Plan in December 1940 and closed on 17 November 1944.

2. Flight Lieutenant John Weatherlake MID survived the war.
3. Flight Lieutenant Tom Blackley survived the war.
4. Flight Lieutenant James Thomson survived the war.
5. Flying Officer James Kearns survived the war.
6. Flight Sergeant John Martin was killed on 15 October 1942, aged 31, with RAF 12 Squadron (flying Wellingtons) over Belgium.
7. Flight Lieutenant Charles Lark was shot down over Holland, became a POW, and survived the war.
8. Flight Lieutenant Robert McGuinness survived the war.
9. Sergeant Ian Dunn was killed on 3 July 1943, aged 27, with RAF 11 Squadron over Belgium, flying Blenheims.
10. Flying dual involves flying an aircraft with dual controls where an experienced pilot is present to provide instruction and safety oversight to a student or inexperienced pilot.
11. Sergeant Gordon Gatenby survived the war. He wrote an autobiography, *Gordon's Story*, which he self-published in 1998.
12. No. 31 General Reconnaissance School was an RAF establishment training navigators for ocean patrolling. The school had been moved from the UK because there was no base from which to train safely, as all were in reach of German aircraft.
13. Coastal Command was the RAF maid-of-all-work and contained a wide variety of aircraft: land-based fighters, bombers, Spitfires for reconnaissance work, and flying boats. While it primarily cooperated with the Royal Navy, it assisted Bomber and Fighter Commands by assessing target damage. From the outbreak of war, it had expanded to twice and probably three times its pre-war size. The functions of Coastal Command were general reconnaissance, escort duties, convoy protection, and anti-submarine patrols.
14. An Aldis Lamp was a signalling device, communicating by flashes of light using Morse code.
15. Dead reckoning is the process of navigating from a known position, a fix, using course flown, ground speed, and elapsed time interval to determine the current position. The fix could

be determined visually or by astro-navigation. The drift sight enabled vital wind direction and velocity to be determined.

16. The Dalton Computer was a device used for navigation calculations. On one side was a circular slide rule used for mathematical calculations, and the reverse side enabled graphical calculations.
17. Swinging the compass is a procedure to determine and correct the compass deviation caused by magnetic interference from the aircraft in which the compass is mounted.
18. Flying Officer Rodney Archer DFC was killed off Norway on 17 May 1942, aged 23, with RAF 42 Squadron, flying Beauforts.
19. Flight Lieutenant Ernest Hallet DFC survived the war.
20. Flight Sergeant John Doepel was killed off Jervis Bay, New South Wales, aged 25 with RAAF No. 6 Operational Training Unit, flying Beauforts.
21. Flight Lieutenant Vernon Dyason survived the war.
22. Catapult Armed Merchantmen (CAMs) were freighters armed with a Hurricane fighter on a ramp. The fighter could be launched from the ramp by a catapult stretched from the foremast to the bow. In the event of the convoy being attacked by aircraft, the Hurricane was launched to defend the convoy and when its fuel was exhausted, it landed on the sea by the host freighter for the pilot to be rescued.
23. On 2 September 1940, the UK and US governments signed an agreement in which the US agreed to supply fifty destroyers to the Royal Navy in exchange for access to British naval and air bases throughout the British Empire.
24. U-boat or *Untersee-boot* was a German submarine.

Chapter 3

1. Flying Officer Vincent Mansell was killed in June 1942, aged 25, with RAF 149 Squadron, flying Stirlings.
2. Flying Officer Ian Ross was killed on 29 November 1942, aged 22, with RAF 225 Squadron in North Africa, flying fighters.

3. Sergeant Bruce Sharkey was killed on 12 July 1942, aged 30, with RAAF 460 Squadron over the Frisian Islands, Netherlands, flying Lancasters.
4. Flight Sergeant David Bloomfield was killed on 28 March 1942, aged 25, with 457 Squadron over the North Sea, flying Spitfires.
5. Flight Lieutenant Bruce Buls was killed on 21 January 1943, aged 25, with RAAF 461 Squadron over the North Atlantic, flying Sunderlands.
6. Flying Officer Clifford O'Riordan was killed on 30 July 1943, aged 34, with RAAF 460 Squadron over Hamburg, flying Lancasters.

Chapter 4

1. Main plane is the technical term for an aircraft's wing.
2. Feathering propellers involves stopping the rotation by turning the blade's knife edge to the front to prevent them from turning in the airflow or windmilling. A windmilling propeller also creates considerable drag, that adversely effects aircraft performance.
3. There was a definite class division between officers and other ranks in the RAF. Most aircrew were either officers or sergeants. While they flew together as a crew, on the ground the officers and other ranks did not socialise. When filling in their flying logs, pilots noted the names of officers on each flight, but the other ranks were lumped as crew and not named individually. This discrimination can be seen in Bruce's account. For example, initially he refers to Sergeant Lewis in his account, but later, when Lewis was commissioned, Bruce refers to him as Bob Lewis and went on leave with him.
4. The automatic pilot was referred to as George.
5. Flight Lieutenant Stewart Brundell survived the war. At 31 when he enlisted, he was one of the oldest students Bruce met at ITS.

6. The Leigh Light was a powerful carbon arc searchlight of 22 million candelas, with a diameter of 610 millimetres and weight of 390 kilograms, used to light up submarines on the surface at night while the aircraft was attacking.
7. Stomach pains and diarrhoea.
8. Kisumu was the location of the RAF's major flying boat maintenance base for East Africa. It was operational from October 1942 to May 1943.
9. Now Tanzania.
10. Flight Lieutenant Kenneth Neill was killed on 13 July 1943, aged 26, with RAAF 458 Squadron over Sardinia, Italy, flying Wellingtons.
11. *The Sketch* was a British illustrated weekly magazine.
12. A creeping-line-ahead patrol involved low-level flight, crossing at right angles to the expected track of what was being searched for or escorted, flying out for a set distance, turning through 90°, flying for a set distance, turning back to fly at right angles to the expected track and following this procedure for as long as fuel allowed.
13. Smooth water with no ripples posed problems for flying boats as it was difficult to break the water's friction. This meant long take-offs on full power, with the risk of overheating the engines. If a launch was available, this was sent along the flare path to create ripples, allowing the aircraft to overcome the water's friction sooner.
14. Asdic (named after the Anti-Submarine Detection Investigation Committee) was a sonar system for submarine detection. The surface ship sent out a pulse of sound and if the pulse hit a submarine, it bounced back to the surface ship. The timing of the return pulse gave an indication of the submarine's depth.
15. Mae West was the nickname of the RAF-issue inflatable life jacket. It was named after Mae West, the American actress due to its busty shape when inflated.

16. A drogue is a conical or funnel-shaped device with open ends. It was towed behind the boat when taxiing to reduce speed or improve stability.
17. The *Scottish Chief* was torpedoed by *U-177* on 19 November 1942 with the loss of 26 lives. There were 12 survivors. *U-177* was itself sunk by a US Navy Liberator on 6 February 1944 in the Atlantic Ocean, west of Ascension Island. Fifty of the U-boat's crew were killed and 15 survived.
18. The *Llandaff Castle* was torpedoed by *U-177* on 30 November 1942 with the loss of two lives.
19. Z2142 209/Q was operated by 209 Squadron from Mombasa until July 1944, when a Board of Survey report on her condition noted that Z2142 'is claimed to be the oldest Boat in the Service and we wonder if it will not be written off this time'. Because Mark I Catalinas were seriously obsolescent, mostly due to their early model radar and the increasing supply of Mark IVs, Mark Is were not considered for any upgrade and she was struck off charge on 28 September 1944 (David Legg, The Catalina Society via correspondence).

Chapter 5

1. Flight Lieutenant Douglas Dolphin RCAF was killed when his Sunderland crashed at Castle Archdale on 18 November 1943. He was 23.
2. Air Chief Marshal Sir John Barraclough KCB, CBE, DFC, AFC survived the war and remained in the RAF until his retirement in 1976. He kept in contact with his 209 Squadron colleagues long after the war. He was responsible for the commissioning of a memorial to all those who served with RAF Coastal Command and successor formations. The memorial was unveiled by Queen Elizabeth II in Westminster Abbey on 16 March 2004. On Barraclough's invitation, Bruce Daymond attended the service

in Westminster Abbey, as did Denis Saunders, in lieu of Eric, his father, who died in 2003.

3. Q codes are a standardised set of three letters used for concise radio communications between pilots and air traffic controllers. QGH approaches were controlled descents through cloud using instruments or a radio beam.
4. Wimpey was the nickname for the Wellington bomber.
5. Gen is slang for genuine or reliable information.
6. A synchroscope is used to indicate the degree to which generators or power networks are synchronised with each other.
7. Ronald Roberts (service no. 400292), Kenneth Blackham (400269), and Eric Saunders (400334) were students together at No. 8 EFTS Narrandera, No. 7 SFTS Macleod, Canada, and No. 31 School of General Reconnaissance, PEI, Canada. They were posted together to RAF 209 Squadron on 4 December 1941. Pilot Officer Blackham was killed in a flying training accident on 22 February 1942 aged 22, Flight Lieutenant Roberts was killed in a flying accident on 20 August 1943 aged 27, and Wing Commander Eric Saunders MBE survived the war and remained in the RAAF until 1967.
8. Wing Commander Robert Holmes MID survived the war.
9. Taxiing on the step involved a high-speed taxy with the flying boat aquaplaning high in the water on the step, which was the aft part of the hull.
10. Flight Lieutenant Lloyd Butler DFC (RNZAF) survived the war.

Chapter 6

1. Squadron Leaders Philip Davenport and Neville McKeough both survived the war.
2. Women's Royal Naval Service.
3. Port-Étienne is now Nouadhibou, Mauritania.

4. The Nissen hut was a prefabricated structure made from cylindrical corrugated iron and widely used for military barracks.
5. Bathurst is now Banjul, The Gambia.
6. Léopoldville is now Kinshasa.
7. Stanleyville is now Kisangani.
8. Eric and Mouse Saunders remained married until Eric's death in August 2003.
9. RAAF Squadron Leader Jim Mecklem survived the war.
10. RAF Squadron Leader Ken Murray DFC survived the war. On the day before the European war finished, he and his crew, flying a Catalina out of Sullom Voe in the Shetlands, destroyed the last German U-boat of the war (*U-320*). The crew scuttled their submarine and there was no loss of life. Sometime after the war, Ken and his wife were invited by Herr Emmerich, the former U-boat captain, to join him and his crew for a reunion. The Murrays attended the reunion and were treated royally.
11. Air Commodore David Fitzpatrick CB, OBE, AFC & Bar survived the war and retired from the RAF in 1974.

Chapter 7

1. Fractocumulus clouds are small, puffy, irregular-shaped clouds formed below cumulus clouds that cast irregular, potentially confusing shadows on the water.
2. Three-course wind was a technique for determining wind direction by taking readings from three different aircraft headings using the drift sight.
3. Now Myanmar and Thailand.
4. Folboats were folding kayaks.
5. Gubbins were miscellaneous items.
6. Wing Commander White was one of the first trained Australian military pilots in the First World War. He was captured by the Turks in 1916 and wrote a book about his experiences as a POW,

Guests of the Unspeakable – The Odyssey of an Australian Airman – Being a Record of Captivity and Escape in Turkey, published by Angus & Robertson, Sydney, in 1932. After the Second World War he became a Member of the Australian House of Representatives.

7. Bumph was unimportant, bureaucratic, or uninteresting written material.
8. A horse-drawn taxi.
9. Flak is short for the German *Flugabwehrkanone*, meaning aircraft defence cannon, or anti-aircraft fire.

Appendix

Personal details, grading on completion of the course, and service fate of the men who commenced their elementary flying training in No. 10 Course at No. 5 Elementary Flying Training School, Narromine, New South Wales, with Bruce Daymond in early 1941.

Surname	Given Names	Service No.	Birthday	Age	Enlistment Date	Course Grade (%)	History (5 EFTS Unit Records: WW2 Roll: War Memorial Roll of Honour)
Ada	Alan Fletcher	403297	16 May 1913	28	6 Jan. 1941	81.66	Died 6 May 1942 (sergeant, 58 Sqn RAF), flying in combat over the Bay of Biscay in a Whitley bomber
Asboe	Arnold Kenneth	404889	31 Oct. 1920	20	6 Dec. 1940	75.44	Discharged 6 July 1945 (flight lieutenant)
Baker	Allenby Leslie	403159	18 Nov. 1918	22	9 Dec. 1940	84.66	Died 4 Jan. 1942 (pilot officer, 452 Sqn RAAF), in an accident in a Spitfire fighter in the UK

Surname	Given Names	Service No.	Birthday	Age	Enlistment Date	Course Grade (%)	History (5 EFTS Unit Records: WW2 Roll: War Memorial Roll of Honour)
Baxter	Russell Vincent	403461	16 Jan. 1918	21	6 Jan. 1941	86.44	Discharged 9 Jan. 1946 (flight lieutenant)
Blackley	Thomas	404901	4 Mar. 1917	23	6 Dec. 1940	85.33	Discharged 26 Nov. 1945 (flight lieutenant)
Brittingham	Raymond Arthur	403160	16 Apr. 1914	27	9 Dec. 1940	79.33	Died 27 Jan. 1943 (pilot officer, 460 Sqn RAAF), flying in combat over Germany in a Lancaster bomber
Campbell	Arthur Peter Eglinton	403315	10 Aug. 1914	27	6 Jan. 1941	87.11	Discharged 21 Dec. 1945 (flying officer)
Clark	William James	403318	6 May 1917	24	6 Jan. 1941	80.22	Died 26 Apr. 1943 (flight lieutenant, 11 Sqn RAAF), in an accident in a Catalina flying boat in the Solomon Islands
Colquhoun-Thomson	Ian Douglas	403177	2 Jul. 1917	24	11 Dec. 1940	81.33	Died 26 Aug. 1942 (pilot officer, 92 Sqn RAF), in an accident in a Spitfire fighter in the Middle East
Daymond	Bruce Cunynghame	403323	28 Jul. 1919	22	6 Jan. 1941	86.88	Discharged 21 May 1946 (squadron leader, DSO, DFC)
Davenport	Jack Napier	403403	9 Jun. 1920	21	6 Jan. 1941	81.11	Discharged 3 May 1946 (wing commander, DSO, DFC & bar, GM)

Day	Frederick Allan (Tom)	403125	12 Jul. 1920	21	9 Dec. 1940	62.88	Discharged 13 Sep. 1945 (flight lieutenant)
Deignan	Lloyd Charles	404808	7 Dec. 1916	25	8 Nov. 1940	59.88	Discharged 4 Mar. 1946 (flight lieutenant, DFC)
Dimmock	Harold Edgar	404819	2 May 1912	29	6 Dec. 1940	67.33	Died 3 Jun. 1942 (flight sergeant, 12 Sqn RAF), flying in combat over Belgium in a Lancaster bomber
Doudy	Colin Thompson	403127	10 Sep. 1917	24	9 Dec. 1940	73.55	Discharged 24 May 1946 (squadron leader, DFC)
Dunn	Ian Clarke	404927	11 Dec. 1914	27	6 Dec. 1940	78.00	Died 3 July 1942 (flight sergeant, 11 Sqn RAF), flying in combat over Holland in a Blenheim fighter
Frost	Rae Rees	403047	8 Nov. 1916	25	9 Dec. 1940	79.66	Died 10 Apr. 1942 (sergeant, 12 Sqn RAF), flying in combat over Germany in a Lancaster bomber
Gordon	Robert George	404865	14 Apr. 1919	22	6 Dec. 1940	79.44	Died 29 Apr. 1942 (flight sergeant, 12 Sqn RAF), flying in combat over Germany in a Lancaster bomber
Hannan	John Newman	403137	13 Jan. 1918	23	9 Dec. 1940	80.00	Discharged 25 Oct. 1945 (flight lieutenant, DFC)
Holden	Robert George Kenyon	403092	27 Mar. 1912	28	9 Dec. 1940	75.66	Died 31 May 1942 (flight sergeant, 12 Sqn RAF), flying in combat over Germany in a Lancaster bomber

Surname	Given Names	Service No.	Birthday	Age	Enlistment Date	Course Grade (%)	History (5 EFTS Unit Records: WW2 Roll: War Memorial Roll of Honour)
Hornby	William Thorpe	404919	16 Jul. 1910	31	6 Dec. 1940	77.88	Discharged 4 Dec. 1945 (flying officer)
Kearns	James Patrick	402867	25 Jul. 1917	24	11 Nov. 1940	69.44	Discharged 14 Mar. 1946 (flying officer)
Lark	Charles Roland	403409	21 Jun. 1918	22	6 Jan. 1941	86.88	POW (shot down over Holland in a Wellington bomber); discharged 22 Sep. 1944 (flight lieutenant)
Lee	John Gordon	403363	14 Apr. 1921	20	6 Jan. 1941	62.00	Died 4 Apr. 1943 (pilot officer, 460 Sqn RAAF), flying in combat over Germany in a Lancaster bomber
Littlejohn	Gordon Brefny	401070	15 Jul. 1917	24	8 Dec. 1940	70.00	Died 7 Sep. 1942 (flight sergeant, 12 Sqn RAF), flying in combat over Germany in a Lancaster bomber
Marre	Rex Joseph	403355	22 Mar. 1918	22	6 Jan. 1941	82.11	Died 15 Mar. 1942 (sergeant, 3 Sqn RAF), in an accident in a Hurricane fighter in the UK
Martin	John Edward Freese	403060	24 May 1911	30	9 Dec. 1940	60.22	Died 15 Oct. 1942 (flight sergeant, 12 Sqn RAF), flying in combat over Belgium in a Lancaster bomber
May	Kenneth Bayley	404938	17 Jul. 1920	21	3 Jan. 1941	81.66	Discharged 20 Oct. 1945 (flight lieutenant)

McGuinness	Robert Joseph	403361	4 Oct. 1918	23	6 Jan. 1941	73.11	Discharged 7 Nov. 1945 (flight lieutenant)
McKeough	Neville Neil	403465	10 Apr. 1920	21	6 Jan. 1941	85.66	Discharged 26 Sep. 1946 (squadron leader)
McLeod	Finlay Donald	403431	18 Jun. 1918	22	6 Jan. 1941	83.55	Died 26 Mar. 1942 (sergeant, 12 Sqn RAF), flying in combat over Holland in a Lancaster bomber
Meldrum	George James	403446	10 Nov. 1918	22	6 Jan. 1941	83.77	Discharged 11 Dec. 1945 (flight lieutenant)
Morse	Ian Sutherland	403358	5 Mar. 1922	18	6 Jan. 1941	82.11	Discharged 26 Feb. 1946 (flight lieutenant)
Murphy	Roger Bede	403143	9 Sep. 1914	27	9 Dec. 1940	82.00	Died 3 Jan. 1942 (sergeant, 23 Operational Training Unit RAF), in an accident in a Wellington bomber
North	Roger Landsborough	404828	30 Jan. 1922	19	6 Dec. 1940	73.88	Discharged 2 Apr. 1946 (flight lieutenant)
Short	Lionel Edward	403382	21 Nov. 1911	30	6 Jan. 1941	90.33	Discharged 25 Jun. 1946 (flight lieutenant, DFC)
Tait	Colin Kenneth	403157	23 Aug. 1912	29	9 Dec. 1940	75.55	Died 8 Jun. 1942 (flying officer, 602 Sqn), flying in combat off the French coast in a Spitfire fighter
Taylor	Andrew Bayne	403080	28 Nov. 1920	21	9 Dec. 1940	81.44	Discharged 2 Jan. 1946 (flight lieutenant, DFC)

Surname	Given Names	Service No.	Birthday	Age	Enlistment Date	Course Grade (%)	History (5 EFTS Unit Records: WW2 Roll: War Memorial Roll of Honour)
Thomson	James	403374	1 Jun. 1921	20	6 Jan. 1941	79.55	Discharged 17 Oct. 1945 (flight lieutenant)
Thompson	Jack Irvine	403437	23 Apr. 1922	19	6 Jan. 1941	78.55	Died 15 Feb. 1943 (flight sergeant, 14 Sqn RAF), flying in combat in the Middle East in a Marauder bomber
Utz	Eric Arthur George	403438	18 Jun. 1913	28	6 Jan. 1941	87.55	Died 31 Mar. 1944 (squadron leader, 460 Sqn RAAF, DFC & bar), flying in combat over Germany in a Lancaster bomber
Waddell	Alan Albert	408133	15 Nov. 1917	24	6 Jan. 1941	82.22	Died 31 May 1942 (flying officer, 12 Sqn RAF), flying in combat over Germany in a Lancaster bomber
Watson	Alan Berton	404843	23 Apr. 1920	21	6 Dec. 1940	73.44	Died 25 Feb. 1942 (sergeant, 253 Sqn RAF) in an accident in a Hurricane fighter in the UK
Watson	Ian Horace Sydney	400895	21 Sep. 1915	26	10 Nov. 1940	73.88	Discharged 15 Jan. 1946 (warrant officer)
Watts	Norman Edward	404917	24 Mar. 1919	21	6 Dec. 1940	76.77	Discharged 11 Sep. 1945 (flight lieutenant)
Wheeler	William Anthony	404841	31 Jan. 1911	29	6 Dec. 1940	78.55	Discharged 6 Feb. 1946 (flight lieutenant, DFC)

Wheeldon	William James	404840	13 Dec. 1920	21	6 Dec. 1940	72.11	Discharged 20 Sep. 1945 (flight lieutenant)
Whittick	Alexander Frederick	404844	2 Jan. 1920	20	6 Dec. 1940	77.77	Died 3 July 1942 (sergeant, 460 Sqn RAAF), flying in combat over Holland in a Lancaster bomber
Wright	Maurice Cecil Depratt	404845	17 Feb. 1916	24	6 Dec. 1940	68.55	Discharged 1 Mar. 1945 (flight lieutenant)
Yates	Alan Scholes	403392	22 Sep. 1922	19	6 Jan. 1941	82.66	Discharged 3 Mar. 1948 (flight lieutenant)
Transferred to No. 11 Course Due to Illness							
Longmuir	Ralph Graeme	403362	30 Nov. 1921	20	6 Jan. 1941		Discharged 19 Dec. 1945 (flight lieutenant)
Stormonth	Owen Curruthers	404921	11 Aug. 1915	26	6 Dec. 1940		Discharged 11 Jan. 1945 (warrant officer)
Flying Training Discontinued: Posted to 2 ITS							
Benn	John Walker	404881	13 Jul. 1910	31	6 Dec. 1940		Died 12 Aug. 1942 (sergeant, 207 Sqn RAF), flying in combat over Germany in a Lancaster bomber
Byrne	Kieran John	403120	14 Dec. 1916	25	9 Dec. 1940		Discharged 17 Feb. 1942 (leading aircraftman)
Donn-Patterson	James	403132	10 Mar. 1916	24	9 Dec. 1940		Died 31 Mar. 1942 (sergeant, 23 Operational Training Unit RAF), flying in combat over Holland in a Wellington bomber

Surname	Given Names	Service No.	Birthday	Age	Enlistment Date	Course Grade (%)	History (5 EFTS Unit Records: WW2 Roll: War Memorial Roll of Honour)
Gillman	William James	404825	24 Jul. 1915	26	6 Dec. 1940		Discharged 6 Sep. 1945 (flight lieutenant)
Longmuir	Hervey Rae	403353	30 Aug. 1911	30	6 Jan. 1941		Discharged 5 Sep. 1945 (flight lieutenant)
MacDonald	Neil Gard	403145	13 Jan. 1914	26	9 Dec. 1940		Discharged 15 Mar. 1946 (flying officer, DFM)
Mackenzie	Evan Seaforth	403146	8 Sep. 1918	23	9 Dec. 1940		Died 13 May 1943 (flying officer, 156 Sqn RAF), flying in combat over Germany in a Lancaster bomber
Rogers	John Matthew	404886	25 Jul. 1912	29	6 Dec. 1940		Discharged 7 Mar. 1946 (flying officer)
Discharged Unsuited For Air Crew Training							
Withford	William Raymond	404907	6 Nov. 1912	29	6 Dec. 1940		Discharged 11 Apr. 1941 (leading aircraftman)
Awaiting Result of Medical Board							
Zions	Albert	402901	29 Feb. 1916	24	11 Nov. 1940		From No. 9 Course; discharged 14 Jul. 1941 (leading aircraftman)
Undergoing Detention and Recommended For Discharge							
Persse	Desmond de Burgh	404721	31 Aug. 1918	23	8 Nov. 1940		Detention, then to 2 Initial Training School; discharged 9 Jul. 1941 (leading aircraftman)

Signature on Photograph Not on Unit Records For No. 10 Course							
Baldwin	Jack St Ledger	404879	14 Jun. 1914	27	6 Dec. 1940		Died 30 Jun. 1942 (flight sergeant, 459 Sqn RAAF), in an accident in a Hudson bomber in the Middle East
Lawson	Lloyd George	401223	19 Jul. 1916	25	4 Jan. 1941		Discharged 28 Feb. 1946 (flight lieutenant, DFM)
Patterson	Charles Forbes	401048	24 Nov. 1917	24	8 Dec. 1940		Died 27 Jun. 1942 (flight sergeant, 100 Sqn RAAF), flying in combat in New Guinea in a Beaufort bomber
Pearson	James Christopher	404941	31 Dec. 1914	27	3 Jan. 1941		Died 10 Sep. 1942 (flight sergeant, 460 Sqn RAAF), flying in combat off the UK coast in a Lancaster bomber
Rankin	Norman Frederick	403002	4 Sep. 1921	20	11 Nov. 1940		Discharged 4 Oct. 1945 (flight lieutenant)

Bibliography

Alexander, Kristen (2009) *Jack Davenport: Beaufighter Leader*. Allen & Unwin, Crows Nest, New South Wales, Australia.

Banks, Arthur (1997) *Wings of the Dawning: The Battle for the Indian Ocean 1939–1945*. Harold Martin & Redman Ltd, Worcestshire, England.

Creed, Roscoe (1985) *PBY: The Catalina Flying Boat*. Naval Institute Press, Annapolis, Maryland, USA.

Deller, Alan (2004) *The Kid Glove Pilot: A Personal Account of Flying Sunderlands in World War Two*. Colourpoint Book, Newtownards, UK.

Hendrie, Andrew (1988) *Flying Cats: The Catalina Aircraft in World War II*. Airlife Publishing Ltd, Shrewsbury, England.

Leach, Joe (1999) *RAAF Flying Boats at War: The Way It Was*. Australian Military Publications, Loftus, Australia.

McCarthy, John (1988) *A Last Call of Empire: Australian Aircrew, Britain and the Empire Air Training Scheme*. Australian War Memorial, Canberra, Australian Capital Territory.

McCusker, Breege (1993) *Castle Archdale and Fermanagh in World War II*. Necarne Press, Irvinestown, Northern Ireland.

O'Loughlin, Joe (2005) *Voices of the Donegal Corridor*. Nonsuch Publishing Ltd, Dublin, Ireland.

Probert, Henry (1996) *The Forgotten Air Force: The Royal Air Force in the War Against Japan 1941–1945*. Brassey's, London and Washington.

Saunders, Eric (1941) *Eric Saunders 4COTU Oct-Nov 1941 Student Notes*. https://www.researchgate.net/publication/400176011_Eric_

Saunders_4COTU_Oct-Nov_1941_Student_notes#full TextFileContent

Scarborough, W.E. (1983) *PBY Catalina in Action: Aircraft Number 62*. Squadron/Signal Publications, Carrollton, Texas, USA.

Scarborough, William (1995) *Walk Around Number 5: PBY Catalina.* Squadron/Signal Publications, Carrollton, Texas, USA.

Southall, Ivan (1956) *They Shall not Pass Unseen.* Angus & Robertson Ltd, Sydney, Australia.

Southall, Ivan (1974) *Fly West.* Angus & Robertson Ltd, London, England.

Index